OLD ARTS AND
NEW THEOLOGY

To

MY PARENTS

OLD ARTS AND NEW THEOLOGY

The Beginnings of Theology as an Academic Discipline

BY

G. R. EVANS

CLARENDON PRESS · OXFORD

1980

Oxford University Press, Walton Street, Oxford OX2 6DP

OXFORD LONDON GLASGOW
NEW YORK TORONTO MELBOURNE WELLINGTON
KUALA LUMPUR SINGAPORE JAKARTA HONG KONG TOKYO
DELHI BOMBAY CALCUTTA MADRAS KARACHI
NAIROBI DAR ES SALAAM CAPE TOWN

Published in the United States by
Oxford University Press, New York

British Library Cataloguing in Publication Data
Evans, Gillian Rosemary
    1. Theology, Doctrinal — History — Middle
Ages, 600-1500
    I. Title
    201'.1   BT26   79-42788
    ISBN 0-19-826653-7

Set by Hope Services, Abingdon
and Printed in Great Britain by
Billing & Sons Ltd.,
Guildford, London, & Worcester

Preface

Bernard of Chartres described himself and his twelfth-century contemporaries as dwarfs standing on the shoulders of giants. He wanted, it seems, to acknowledge a debt to the giants of old, who had lifted him up so that he could see further than they. But the most striking justice of the image lies in Bernard's comparison of the relative stature of his dwarfs and giants. The erosive process which causes only a few exceptional individuals in a generation to be remembered, had left only the giants of the ancient world standing, together with a few whose work had been preserved by historical chance. If Bernard compared their achievements with the work of the ordinary scholars of his own day, it is not surprising that he saw a difference. Many of his fellows were indeed small men, who could have seen scarcely any distance at all without the help of the ancient writers.

The twelfth century had its great men. But many twelfth-century scholars were most at home with close, detailed work. The texture of their thought is that of a *pointilliste* painting, or a piece of *petit-point* embroidery. The resulting picture may be very large, but it is made up of closely packed, tiny elements. With notable exceptions — most outstanding of all, perhaps, Peter Abelard and Alan of Lille — the scholars to be found in twelfth-century schools were quiet, conscientious men of limited vision. They were, nevertheless, capable of strong enthusiasm for their work, energetic in debate, with a lightness of touch and often a dry wit which makes their work immensely attractive.

These patient souls were exactly what was needed. The classical tradition they inherited was no longer a living tradition. What remained of it had to be recovered painstakingly from books, and patient assiduity was the first requirement of the scholarship of the day.

This is a bleak scene; when we look at it more closely we shall find many signs of life and an atmosphere of cheerful bustle. But it is important not to lose sight of the spareness and leanness of the twelfth-century scholarly heritage, if we are to understand the magnitude of what was achieved by the earnest endeavour of these men. As we examine the ideas they discussed it will often be clear that they were thinking in very simple terms about matters which had been handled with more sophistication by ancient thinkers. But they had only the slenderest of clues and sometimes none at all. On some subjects they were forced to think for themselves almost from first principles. The clarity and good sense of much of what they have to say is impressive in any case, but it is very much more impressive if we remember the circumstances in which they worked.

They need no allowance made for them at all in certain areas. In their work on the theory of language and upon methods of argument they did indeed see further than the giants of old. And they set up a syllabus of instruction within their schools which helped to make the schools for the first time 'academic' in a recognizably modern sense. These things have no exact parallel in the ancient world. If the beginning of the twelfth century saw a few solitary figures standing on a great plain, torn and faded map in hand, setting out to reach a heavenly city glimpsed in the distance, the end of the century saw the plain populous and busy, the map mended with considerable skill, and a main road being built towards the city.

The developments of the twelfth century owe a great deal to the work of a comparatively small number of scholars of the tenth and eleventh centuries. These were the real pioneers. When Gerbert of Aurillac and his pupil Abbo of Fleury, Otloh of St. Emmeram, Lanfranc of Bec and Berenger of Tours, Roscelin of Compiègne and Anselm of Canterbury, and numberless masters whose names are now lost, began to rediscover the possibilities of dialectic and grammar and arithmetic, they were forced to work in greater intellectual isolation than the twelfth-century scholar need endure unless he chose to cut himself off from the work of the schools. Even for these thinkers, the isolation was not complete. Recent work has brought to light a great deal of activity in the study of the liberal arts in the eleventh century. But what was new in the twelfth century was a proliferation of schools and masters, a multiplication of resources, the creation of a new and far more supportive academic ambience, in which the less exceptional scholar could make a useful contribution to the work of reconstruction, and help forward the endless work of scholarship which began, in a modern sense, in the twelfth century.

These changes were not, for the most part, the work of great men. Anselm of Canterbury, who lived into the first decade of the twelfth century, had little direct influence upon the work of the next few generations. But they show what can be done by lesser men by a steady aggregation of small changes. This is of the essence of the academic tradition, which, from time to time, nurtures major figures, but which is designed to pass on the sum of human knowledge un-diminished and unimpaired from generation to generation, even if those who are available to transmit it are scholars of only mediocre ability. The scholarly world can wait a long time for an Aquinas, a Newton, or a Russell.

John Henry Newman saw a university as a place where the passing on of knowledge from one generation to the next could be carried on 'safe from the excesses and vagaries of individuals, embodied in institutions which have stood the trial and received the sanction of ages, and administered by men who have no need to be anonymous, as being supported by their consistency with their predecessors and with each other'. He puts in a nutshell the elements of what a university had become by the end of the Middle Ages — guardian of soundness and guarantor of continuity in periods of change. On the whole, the universities have succeeded in remaining so ever since. But in the twelfth century the institutions were still in the making, there could be no continuity with a past in which there was no exact precedent for the work of the schools. The scholars of the day were still striving for the very security and authoritativeness of academic orthodoxy which Newman prizes so highly, and it was because of their innate caution that the earliest universities were places of consolidation as well as of innovation, of teaching almost more than of original work. For Newman, a tender glow suffused the learning of the Middle Ages. He imagines Bede, 'the light of the whole western world; as happy ... in his scholars round him, as in his celebrity and influence in the length and breadth of Christendom'. The work of the Anglo-Saxon and Carolingian scholars he sees as 'the foundation of the school of Paris, from which, in the course of centuries, sprang the famous University, the glory of the Middle Ages'. This is historical romanticism, but it is something more than sentiment. Newman saw clearly enough the essentially medieval quality of the idea of a university which had persisted into the nineteenth century, and which is still with us.

When a potter makes a vessel he hollows the lump of clay from the inside at the same time as he models its external shape; and the clay itself dictates the kind of vessel he can make from it. Several studies in recent years have examined the exterior features of the work of medieval schools and universities: the modifications which were made to the syllabus as it developed to meet the needs of a growing civil service and an expanding legal profession; the process by which the schools grew into institutions. In many respects the academic disciplines of the earliest universities were modelled by the society in which they took shape. But these are not the matters with which we are concerned here. The question at issue is not that of the origins of the universities, but of the origins of the academic disciplines which, in due course, came to be studied in them.

An academic discipline must be fashioned from within if it is to endure beyond the period when a need was first felt for it, and if it is to attract students who have grown up in different societies. A number of modern academic disciplines — history and geography, for example, or modern languages — have shown that they have the stuff in them to stand up to the test of changing academic circumstances. Others, like sociology and psychology, are only beginning to prove their staying power. Twelfth-century scholars did not at first attempt to establish new disciplines. They inherited the seven ancient disciplines of the liberal arts, which had amply demonstrated their value and interest in remarkably varied conditions of study. Medieval scholars built upon an old hard core of material when they composed new commentaries and fresh textbooks. As they elucidated each subject and gave it a place in their own syllabus they were dependent

upon a long tradition, which went some way towards determining what kind of study it was, its scope and the methods
appropriate to it. The disciplines themselves imposed imperatives of their own upon the efforts of the scholars who studied
them.

All this activity was a preparation for a higher study whose
students, ironically enough, were always few: that of
theology. This was the most important new discipline of the
medieval schools. Not all universities taught it, but it held a
position of such unchallenged eminence that its needs
influenced the development of the other academic disciplines
throughout the Middle Ages. But like all new disciplines it
had to develop methods of its own by borrowing from
established disciplines, and until it began to model itself upon
the liberal arts in the twelfth century it lacked the attributes
which would justify its being called 'academic'. Of the other
two higher studies of the medieval universities, law and
medicine, law also found its feet as an academic discipline in
the twelfth century, but it was theology whose concerns
proved to be so close to those of the liberal arts that they had
many fundamental philosophical problems in common. It is
in the interaction between theology and the liberal arts, the
fine balance of continuity and innovation, that we can see
the new discipline being forged and the old disciplines being
refined.

The special quality of the work of twelfth-century schools
lies in its accessibility to the general reader. A technical
matter rarely requires anything more than a brief explanation
of the underlying principles to make it understandable. The
life and interest of the process by which the academic
disciplines were formed lies in the actual problems which
were raised by the juxtaposition of old and new disciplines. I
have tried in this study to look at examples of the kinds of
topic which exicted twelfth-century scholars. Some of these
issues are no longer contentious; some seem unimportant
now. But many of them are questions which still require
answers and among them are to be found the perennial
questions of philosophy and theology.

I should like to acknowledge an enduring and ever-growing
debt to those who have helped me with advice and criticism,

especially to the Revd Professor Henry Chadwick, Dr. D. P. Henry, the late Dr. R. W. Hunt, and Sir Richard Southern.

Contents

Abbreviations   xiii

INTRODUCTION   1

I. THE ACADEMIC AMBIENCE
1. The Schools   8
2. The Old Disciplines   15
3. The New Discipline   27
4. Method   46

II. THE STUDY OF THE BIBLE AND THE LIBERAL ARTS
1. The Middle Way   57
2. Conflict   79

III. SPECULATIVE THEOLOGY AND THE LIBERAL ARTS
1. The Tower of Speculation   91
2. The Problem of Knowledge   100
3. The Arts of Language   107
4. Scientific Theology and the Mathematical Arts   119

IV. A MISSIONARY THEOLOGY
1. The Academic Challenge   137
2. Theological Method against the Unbelievers   151

V. THE WORK OF CREATION AND THE WORK OF RESTORATION
1. Philosophers, Heretics, and the Work of Creation   167
2. Philosophers, Heretics, and the Work of Restoration   192

VI. THE MEASURE WITHIN   215

CONCLUSION   222

Appendix: Some of the Scholars Mentioned in the Text   228

Index   231

Abbreviations

Abelard, *Comm. Rom.*   Peter Abelard, *Commentary on Romans*, ed. M. Buytaert, *CCCM* XI (Turnholt, 1969).

Abelard, *Dialectica*   *Petrus Abaelardus Dialectica*, ed. L. M. de Rijk (Assen, 1956).

AHDLMA   *Archives de l'histoire doctrinale et littéraire du moyen âge.*

Anselmi Opera Omnia   *Anselmi Opera Omnia*, ed. F. S. Schmitt (Rome/Edinburgh, 1938-68), 6 vols.

Cahiers   *Cahiers de l'institut du moyen âge grec et latin* (Copenhagen).

CCCM   *Corpus Christianorum Continuatio Medievalis.*

CCSL   *Corpus Christianorum Series Latina.*

Clarenbald of Arras   *Clarenbaldus of Arras: Life and Works*, ed. N. M. Haring (Toronto, 1965).

Gilbert of Poitiers   Gilbert of Poitiers, *Commentaries on Boethius*, ed. N. M. Haring (Toronto, 1966).

Rupert of Deutz   Rupert of Deutz, *De SAncta Trinitate et Operibus Eius*, ed. H. Haacke, in *CCCM* xxi-xxiv.

Historia Pontificalis   John of Salisbury, *Historia Pontificalis*, ed. M. Chibnall (Oxford/Edinburgh, 1956).

LM   *Logica Modernorum*, ed. L. M. de Rijk (Assen, 1967), 2 vols.

MARS   *Mediaeval and Renaissance Studies.*

MGH, Quellen   *Monumenta Germaniae Historica, Quellen.*

PL   J. P. Migne, ed., *Patrologia Latina.*

SSLov.   *Spicilegium Sacrum Lovaniense.*

Textes inédits   *Textes inédits d'Alan de Lille*, ed. M. T. d'Alverny (Paris, 1965).

Theologia Christiana   Peter Abelard, *Theologia Christiana*, ed. M. Buytaert, *CCCM* XII (Turnholt, 1969).

Theological Tractates   Boethius, *Theological Tractates*, ed. F. Steward and E. K. Rand (London 1918).

Thierry of Chartres   *Commentaries on Boethius by Thierry of Chartres and his School*, ed. N. M. Haring (Toronto, 1971).

Ysagoge in Theologiam   *Écrits Théologiques de l'école d'Abelard*, ed. A. Landgraf, 14 (1934).

Introduction

John Stuart Mill saw his own day as 'an age in which education, and its improvement, are the subject of more, if not of profounder study than at any former period'.[1] The same might be said of our own time. In the course of the twentieth century a great deal of new thinking has gone into revising methods of teaching and into reviewing the traditional content of the syllabus, at every level. Education is important and interesting to us because it concerns a great many people directly for long periods of their lives, and because it provides a means of entry to professional careers. When it holds as influential a position in society as that, its organization becomes a matter of interest to governments and administrators, as well as to scholars. For the first time since the end of the Roman world these conditions were coming into existence in the twelfth century. If public interest in education was far from universal, it was certainly substantial. Educational aims and methods became something of a talking-point for the increasing numbers of men of affairs who spent a few years in the schools, as well as for those who spent their working lives as scholars.

When the ancient world gave way to the medieval two major adjustments had to be made. Firstly, the breakdown of the international society of the Roman Empire meant the disappearance of the freemasonry of culture, in which Augustine was able to move from north Africa to Italy to teach rhetoric in the fourth century. Bede spent the whole of his life in seventh- and eighth-century Northumbria getting his learning for himself out of books, in a solitude of intellectual endeavour which must not be exaggerated,[2] but which, in comparison with the richness of the resources available to Augustine, was stark enough. In practical terms, this meant that there were likely to be fewer like-minded scholars within reach, and fewer books to read, despite the salvaging work of Benedict Biscop, who brought the core of a great library back

[1] John Stuart Mill, *Autobiography*, I. ed. J. Stillinger (Oxford).
[2] Cf. R. W. Southern, *Medieval Humanism* (Oxford, 1970), p. 1.

from Italy to the edge of the Empire and provided for Bede the material he needed.[3] Bede and others after him studied the books they had and wrote about them, often without the support of informed and interested colleagues, simply because they believed the work to be valuable. Sometimes the pupils gathered in a monastic or cathedral school supplied an audience and a readership. Remigius at Auxerre,[4] Gerbert of Aurillac at Rheims,[5] Notker at St. Gall,[6] enjoyed such support and interest that a few of their pupils went on to do original work of their own. But it was comparatively rare for a man of their stature to meet his equal. Single figures from the ninth, tenth, or eleventh centuries are often remembered for their very singularity. They received the admiration of those who wanted to learn from them, but rarely either challenge or judicious appraisal from fellow-scholars and friends. The challenge Berengar posed for Lanfranc, or Roscelin for Anselm,[7] was something new in the eleventh century.

For many centuries there were few of those opportunities for casual encounter and general conversation about the things of the mind which an academic community affords at its best, and which promote new ideas in unpredictable ways. These relaxed pleasures were to be had among cultured people in the late-Roman world, but their absence lent an intense seriousness to the work of the scholars of the early medieval centuries. If learning was enjoyable, that was a bonus, but it could not, in the circumstances, often be something to be shared with one's friends in one's leisure moments. The con-

---

[3] M. L. W. Laistner, *The Intellectual Heritage of the Early Middle Ages* (1957), pp. 117–49, for a study of 'The Library of the Venerable Bede'.

[4] On the school of Auxerre, see R. Quadri, 'Aimone di Auxerre alla luce dei *Collectanea* di Heiric di Auxerre', *Italia Medievalia e Umanistica*, vi (1963), 1–48, and *I 'Collectanea' di Heiric di Auxerre, Spicilegium Friburgensium*, xi (1966).

[5] Testimonies to Gerbert of Aurillac are collected in N. Bubnov, *Gerberti Opera Mathematica* (Berlin, 1899).

[6] See L. M. de Rijk, 'On the Curriculum of the Arts of the Trivium at St. Gall from c.850–c.1000', *Vivarium*, I (1963), 35–86.

[7] On Lanfranc and Berengar, See R. W. Southern, 'Lanfranc of Bec and Berengar of Tours', *Studies in Mediaeval History Presented to F. M. Powicke*, ed. R. W. Hunt (Oxford, 1948), 27–48; J. de Montclos, *Lanfranc et Berengar, SSLov.* (Louvain, 1971); M. T. Gibson, *Lanfranc of Bec* (Oxford, 1978). On Anselm and Roscelin, see R. W. Southern, *St. Anselm and his Biographer* (Cambridge, 1963).

ditions of the time encouraged scholars to give their energies to cultivating the qualities which make a man learned (*doctus*) perhaps at the expense of those which make him cultured (*cultus*).

The second major adjustment involved the adaptation of classical education principles and existing courses of study to fit the needs of a Christian society. The marriage of secular and Christian in learning is always an uneasy one because the underlying conflict of purpose leaves substantial differences to be reconciled. Augustine made an attempt to tackle the problem systematically in his *De Doctrina Christiana,* but the emphasis of his work was upon the particular difficulties Christians met in late Roman society: on the one hand, the difficulty of winning respect among educated pagans for the literary and philosophical excellence of the Bible, and on the other hand, the difficulty of persuading simple men that they could understand the Bible without the benefit of higher education. These were not the requirements of Christian scholars in the twelfth century. What was needed now was a further systematic reappraisal of the relation between secular and Christian learning in the light of the revival of interest in the liberal arts which began in the tenth century and became increasingly widespread during the eleventh century. It posed a serious problem for Christian scholarship when the arts began to be applied to the study of the Bible.

This involved a conscious as well as a systematic review of educational practices, not so bold as to make it strictly comparable with that of our own day, but sufficiently marked to make it a striking new development in the Middle Ages. Revolution in education can take place only where new ideas gain some sort of currency. For the first time in the medieval world there existed in the twelfth century a large enough community of teaching masters, and an environment in which they and their pupils could meet freely, for it to be possible to speak of a general revision of educational methods and purposes.

The most noticeable development of our time has been to place the pupil at the centre of the process of education, so that methods and purposes and even content are determined with reference to his needs and even his wishes. The pupil plays a part in directing his own work and it is expected that he will set a pace which is appropriate to his own abilities. This pupil-centredness is rather different from that which inspired the plan on which Rousseau's 'Émile' was to be educated, and the scheme of teaching which John Stuart Mill's father used. The difference is that which lies between the question 'What does the child want to learn?' and the older tradition of asking what it is — morally or intellectually — good for the child to learn. The purpose of education has always until recently been envisaged in terms of a *utilitas* (profitableness) of the latter kind.

But medieval teachers did not envisage what it was good for a young man to learn in quite the same way as their counterparts in the ancient world or in the Renaissance saw the matter. 'Studies serve for delight, for ornament, and for ability', says Francis Bacon. 'Their chief use for delight is in privateness and retiring; for ornament, is in discourse; and for ability is in the judgement and disposition of business.'[8] The first, he suggests, makes a man more agreeable to himself; the second makes him more pleasing to others; the third makes him of practical use to the community. Bacon's account of the profitableness of education to its possessor, to his fellow-men and to the community might, with some changes, serve as the basis for a modern definition of the purpose of education. But with no changes at all it would have seemed perfectly sound to Cicero or Quintilian. Quintilian taught that the perfect orator should be a good and honourable man in whom a cultured mind and gifts of eloquence are united with the moral virtues; he should be able to take a full part, too, in 'public and private business' as a citizen.[9] Bacon suggests that learning is good for a man in another way, too. He says that learning is like bodily exercise. It can be used to make good a man's natural deficiencies. 'There is no stone or impediment in the wit, but may be wrought out by fit studies: like as diseases of the body may have appropriate exercises . . . every defect of the mind may have a special receipt.'[10] The parallel between the training of the mind and the training of

---

[8] Francis Bacon, *Essay I: Of Studies* (London, 1912).
[9] Quintilian, *Institutio Oratoria,* I Pr.9-10.
[10] Bacon, op. cit.

the body has, again, an air of the Greek and Roman world.
The educated man of the sixteenth or seventeenth century
would have felt comparatively at home in the *agora* or the
forum. But is difficult to envisage the majority of the scholars
of the twelfth century in such company. Only the urbane
John of Salisbury and perhaps Peter of Blois, Alan of Lille,
and a few others suggest themselves as men who had a natural
affinity with an educational ideal which made a man *cultus*
rather than *doctus*.

Even in them the ease and grace, the lightness of touch,
the half-serious, half-mocking wit they try to emulate sits un-
easily. They draw on a wealth of knowledge so as to make
striking comparisons, but there is a laboriousness about the
process which is rarely present in the work of Renaissance
writers when they attempt similar devices. Shakespeare's
aristocrats and kings are good conversationalists, in whom
education has produced Bacon's 'ornament' of 'discourse'.
Plato's *Symposium* or Macrobius' *Saturnalia* preserves in a
literary form something of the quality of the table-talk of the
ancient world. No doubt among the men of the twelfth century there were excellent after-dinner speakers, men whose
talk sparkled. But Alan of Lille does not encourage his readers
to cultivate their minds merely so that they will be pleasant
places, and so that they will be able to extend the pleasure to
others in conversation. In the Preface to his manual on the
Art of Preaching he emphasizes the negative qualities of fine
discourse because it serves no serious purpose for the Christian
orator. He says that a preacher should avoid 'scurrilous words
and silliness and the pleasing sounds of rhyme and rhythm,
which are better fitted to please the ear than to edify the
mind.'[11] Medieval education was never general education in a
sense that Cicero or Bacon would have recognized. It was in-
tensive, penetrating, sometimes sententious, always exact and
specific.

But is was not dull to contemporaries. Students gathered in
the schools in increasing numbers, even before experience
proved that to show off one's talents in the schools might be a
way to preferment.[12] It must be remembered that Quintilian's

[11] *PL* 210.112.
[12] On masters in government, see *Mediaeval Humanism*, pp. 175-6.

system of education and that to which Bacon's educated man was submitted were equally remorseless in the demands they made of the beginner. The cultured men of the ancient and Renaissance worlds won their urbanity and elegance of mind only out of many hours of tedious rote learning and painstaking exercises in translation and composition. Quintilian's boy got his general culture by following the traditional academic disciplines. He learned the branches of grammar and rhetoric as well as the elements of philosophy. There is a solidity about the knowledge Bacon's contemporaries display which should disabuse us of the notion that if a man was required only to be cultured, and did not aspire to be learned, he needed no more than a smattering of the arts and sciences. The academic disciplines at their most prosaic and forbidding underlay all the charm of social discourse in Renaissance times, just as they underlay the work of the serious scholar in the Middle Ages. The often tedious work involved in mastering them proved to be no discouragement, even in the later Middle Ages, when the sheer weight of material to be thoroughly mastered must have made the task more oppressive.

When every allowance has been made for practical considerations and more worldly motives, we are left with the evidence that these apparently forbidding disciplines were attractive. The first students of the twelfth century liked what they found and others followed them.

When we look at them closely, it is not difficult to understand their attractiveness. It lies in part in the questions with which they are concerned, which possess an interest quite independent of the context in which they were studied because they are questions which are asked in every age. But it lies, too, in the absolute demands which the discipline itself imposes on the student. Bacon observes that a man's mind and behaviour are formed in different ways by different studies. 'Histories make men wise; poets witty; the mathematics subtile; natural philosphy deep; moral grave; logic and rhetoric able to contend.'[13] He implicitly assumes that these different effects are brought about by intrinsic differences in the demands these studies make upon the mind. It is

---

[13] Bacon, op. cit.

in the nature of rhetoric and logic to be concerned (though not in the same ways) with methods of argument; the study of mathematics makes a man better able to understand abstractions because that is the special concern of mathematics; natural philosophy, or natural science, looks into the causes, physical and metaphysical, of the natural world, and it encourages its students to look not at surface appearances but at underlying causes. Just as an athlete in training enjoys the sensation of developing power in his muscles as he performs certain exercises with specific purposes, so the twelfth-century scholar exulted in the growing power of the muscles of his mind as he practised different disciplines. John of Salisbury describes in the *Metalogicon* how the dialecticians he calls the 'Cornificians' have allowed their enthusiasm for the sport to go to their heads, so that they argue ceaselessly about everything under the sun. The founding of the academic disciplines was, of course, far more than a sport, and the new discipline of theology was always treated with high seriousness. But the hard labour out of which the disciplines were formed in the twelfth century was clearly a pleasurable labour, and the pleasure still communicates itself strongly to the modern reader.

I   The Academic Ambience

1. The Schools

At the end of the eleventh century three kinds of 'school' existed in northern Europe. The first and most common of these was the monastic school. This was, as a rule, an internal school, which served the needs of an individual community and taught the boys and young men of the house at least the elements of what a monk needed to know: how to read Latin competently and to sustain his part in the liturgical round. Such a school was unlikely to achieve much eminence unless it happened to have a master of exceptional ability. The schools at Fécamp and at Holy Trinity, Rouen, had brief periods of importance. For a short time under Lanfranc the school at Bec was famous, and it attracted pupils from the best families, not all of whom intended to become monks.[1] When Lanfranc was replaced by St. Anselm the character of the school changed; it produced 'seeming-philosophers' according to one monastic chronicler,[2] and there can be no doubt that the training which was to be had there was excellent. But the school ceased to take pupils from outside. When Anselm himself went away, the school lost its distinction. Such schools had only the doubtful continuity of belonging to the same house generation after generation. There was no steady development of a syllabus of study, no examination leading to the award of a degree.

Secondly, there were the cathedral schools, like the one at Laon or the school of Notre Dame at Paris or that at Chartres.[3] Their chief *raison d'être* lay in the need of the dioceses for

---

[1] *Vita Herluini*, ed. J. Armitage Robinson, *Gilbert Crispin, Abbot of Westminster* (Cambridge, 1911), p. 97.

[2] Orderic Vitalis, *Historia Ecclesiastica*, ed. M. Chibnall (Oxford, 1969), II.296, ii.246.

[3] The claim of Chartres to be a school has recently become a somewhat contentious issue. See R. W. Southern, *Mediaeval Humanism*, pp. 61–85; and N. M. Häring, 'Chartres and Paris revisited', *Essays in Honour of A. C. Pegis* (Toronto, 1974), 268–329. See, too, *Mediaeval Humanism*, p. 163 on the beginning of the cathedral schools in England.

competent administrators. Here again, much depended upon good fortune in obtaining a first-rate master who could attract pupils and raise the standing of the school to the level of his own reputation. Where a fine master gave a good portion of his working life to a cathedral school, as another Anselm and his brother Ralph did at Laon, a cathedral school could achieve a considerable standing for a time. But its reputation was likely to dwindle rapidly when it lost the master who had made it noteworthy.

So great was the attraction a good master possessed that it was possible for a famous teacher to set up a school on his own account, as Peter Abelard did more than once. These schools of the third type were often ephemeral. They were sheltered by no institution and they were dependent for their continued existence not only on the excellence of their master, but also upon the sometimes short-lived fashionableness of his opinions. Students who came to hear a famous master out of curiosity might leave him as easily as they came.

In Italy a fourth type of school had survived the end of the Roman Empire, to provide a grounding in the liberal arts; it is not easy to establish the continuity of the urban schools, or to be sure what level of teaching they provided, but Lanfranc and Bruno of Asti, who became Bishop of Segni, got their elementary education and probably a good deal more in such schools. At Pavia, the story goes, Lanfranc so distinguished himself at rhetoric that he could outwit his elders in forensic oratory; Orderic Vitalis relates the tale in Book IV of his *Historia Ecclesiastica*. But these schools fall a little outside our ambit. They were at no time centres of theological study during the twelfth century, and they played only an incidental part in the process by which the liberal arts and theology became the academic disciplines of the new universities of northern Europe.

It was in theory perfectly possible for a scholar to move from one milieu to another in the eleventh and early twelfth century. Abelard did so whenever he felt that circumstances justified it — when he wanted to turn from dialectic to theology he went to Laon; when he found himself unwelcome there because he was taking away the pupils of Anselm of

Laon, he went elsewhere. Several masters who are known to have been associated with Chartres at one time or another are to be found in other places, too, especially at Paris. No institution was yet in a position to lay down the requirement that its students should follow a specific course of study under its shelter in order to obtain the licence to teach which was the qualification the degree eventually gave. Indeed, it is out of place to speak of schools as institutions at all as yet. They were simply meetings of masters and pupils. Everyone was free to go where he liked in search of the best masters.

Wherever he went he would find the same subjects being taught from the same textbooks, except where a particular subject was not available because there was no one to teach it, or because there was no copy of the textbook in question to hand. In practice that meant that grammar (which embraced a number of studies from Priscian and Donatus to reading the classical poets) was available everywhere, dialectic very commonly, rhetoric or arithmetic less often, rarely geometry or music or astronomy. But the common coin of all the schools was the study of the liberal arts. The frequency with which a particular art was taught reflects very closely the commonness of the textbooks which were needed for its study. The limited supplies of, for example, Boethius' *Arithmetica,* restricted opportunities for the study of arithmetic. More could be made of course, but unless a demand had been created by the study of existing copies, or unless a particular master had a special interest in the subject, it was unlikely to occur to anyone to multiply copies. The demand came, but more slowly for some arts than for others.

Twelfth-century liberal studies were given unity and coherence by their dependence on certain texts, but not by the existence of great libraries. There is nothing in twelfth-century schools to compare with the library of Hellenistic Alexandria. The best libraries were kept in monasteries, but even these could do little to meet the demand for textbooks of the arts. The bulk of their holdings consisted as a rule of Biblical, liturgical, and patristic texts, with perhaps a few of the classical poets.[4] The new corporate and institutional

[4] For a collection of contemporary library catalogues, see G. Becker, *Catalogi Bibliothecarum Antiqui* (Bonn, 1885).

character which began to creep into the schools as the century went on cannot be put down to the existence of collections of books as a resource for reference brought together in one place.

Instead the process seems to have involved a change to a more corporate pattern of teaching. It is not difficult to see how the pupils who came to hear one master lecture might draw other masters after them, masters who came in the hope of attracting some of his pupils to themselves. Slowly an aggregation of masters in certain schools made it less likely that the departure or death of one of them would bring an end to the school's period of prosperity. In this way a school came to amount to something more than a meeting of master and pupils; it became a meeting-*place*. Long before it became impossible for a man to set up his own school at will (as it did in the thirteenth century) it became unusual for him to do so. John of Salisbury's description of the masters he heard in a dozen years in the schools makes his *Metalogicon* particularly informative about the nature and direction of this change.

It is no coincidence that the forming of theology as an academic discipline went hand in hand with the slow development of the twelfth-century schools into the first universities. Scholars like the early twelfth-century Benedictine, Rupert of Deutz, working independently as monastic writers, were capable of producing comprehensive and learned Scriptural commentaries. Neither largeness of scale nor depth of scholarship was the prerogative of the new schools. But only schools in which comparatively large numbers of students and scholars met could force the pace of development by creating a sizeable demand for working textbooks and summaries, and by encouraging the gathering together of results in an orderly fashion.

At the same time, meetings led to discussion, and new questions were continually being raised (sometimes by misunderstanding: Gilbert of Poitiers said that he knew he had many pupils who had heard him lecture but who had misunderstood what he had said, and who put about false accounts of his teaching as a result).[5] In all these ways the

[5] *Historia Pontificalis*, p. 22.

subject-matter of study and was expanded and the problem of organization grew steadily more complex. Both the phenomenon and the problem it caused were remarked on by Aquinas as he surveyed the proliferating monographs and textbooks of his own day and saw the need for a single work which would reduce them all to order.[6] The public atmosphere of the twelfth-century schools and the early universities had the effect of a catalyst upon the development of the new categories of thought which took shape in them. Gilbert of Poitiers, John of Salisbury says, claimed with pride that he had spoken openly before the world and said nothing in secret (*in scholis et in ecclesiis palam mundo, et se in occulto dicebat nichil esse locutum*).[7] In particular he had spoken *in scholis,* in the new academic forum, where ideas were made public in a way which had never before been possible in medieval times. But it is also true that the existence of a public forum acted as a check on what Newman describes (in the *Preface* to his *Discourses on the Scope and Nature of University Education*) as 'irresponsible' writing and teaching, 'off-hand', 'ambitious', 'changeable', and obedient only to the popularity of the moment.

These conditions were not present in monastic schools if only because they were smaller and because exchanges between them were so much more limited. Otloh of St. Emmeram describes his own experience as an able pupil in such a school in the eleventh century, where he himself set the pace and where he received little stimulus from his fellow-pupils.[8] The strongest formative influence on a young man's mind in such circumstances was likely to come from an older monk, as it did in the case of another eleventh-century monastic scholar, Guibert of Nogent. He praises Anselm of Bec for the care he took in giving him guidance on his visits to the monastery at Fly.[9] There was, despite the practical difficulties involved, a good deal of intercourse between monastic scholars, who sent one another copies of their works and prompted one another to write new books. But

[6] *Summa Theologica,* Prologue.
[7] *Historia Pontificalis,* p. 22.
[8] *PL* 146.56, *Liber De Tentationibus Suis.*
[9] Guibert of Nogent, *De Vita Sua,* ed. G. Bourgin (Paris, 1907), I.17.

these exchanges were mainly of a friendly character and they seem to have lacked, for the most part, that abrasiveness and challenge which the universities eventually provided.

Exceptionally, something of the kind was to be found in the cathedral schools of the late eleventh and early twelfth century. A Roscelin of Compiègne or a Peter Abelard could create an atmosphere of debate among the shifting population of masters and students to be found at Laon or at Chartres or at Paris. But their irritant effect is a rather different matter from the steady pressure exerted by the sheer numbers of students and masters who were assembled in these and other schools by the end of the twelfth century. It was the existence of a growing public and the need to find a means of organizing teaching on a large scale which provided the stimulus to which Aquinas responded in trying to provide a comprehensive textbook, a *Summa Theologica,* for use by students of theology as an academic discipline.

This is not the place to enter into the question of the process of development by which the schools of the twelfth century became the universities of the thirteenth, or to attempt an estimate of the numbers of students and masters who worked in them. That would bring us into another area of enquiry altogether.[10] But in a number of twelfth-century schools what R. W. Southern calls 'a consistent tradition of academic teaching' was maintained, 'where there were many students, a plentiful supply of lodgings and food, a permanent body of masters, and a general environment favourable to scholastic growth'.[11] A quantitative as well as a qualitative change was taking place which eventually gave these schools an institutional character and which made them environments we may describe without undue qualification, as 'academic' in a recognizably modern sense. In them, courses were run and degrees awarded. The whole process required organization, if the disciplines involved were to be reduced to order and made subject to systematic instruction and examination. This was not merely the result of expansion and development

[10] On the question of the meaning of *schola* and the process by which the schools became institutions, see *Mediaeval Humanism* and Pegis, op. cit.

[11] R. W. Southern 'Master Vacarius', *Mediaeval Learning and Literature: Essays Presented to Richard William Hunt* (Oxford, 1976), p. 269.

in the framework of the schools themselves. It was also a response to the pressures created when a large number of questions were asked by masters and scholars.

This working together of practical and administrative change and the pressures of an inward intellectual dissatisfaction among teachers and pupils helped to generate the air of constructive intellectual excitement which animates the most characteristic writings of the twelfth century. A new vision of the potential complexity and variety of intellectual exercise was abroad. The greatly extended opportunities for scholarly intercourse kept enthusiasm high. If we can speak of the new academic disciplines as 'academic' because of the schools which produced them, we may call them 'disciplines' because of the passionate commitment and the hard clear thinking which went into their reduction to a system of study.

To suggest that it was the achievement of the scholars of the early and middle twelfth century to bring to light the principles which were to direct the academic study of theology and the arts for several generations at least, seems on the face of it a large claim to make for the work of a comparatively few thinkers, who were not in most cases outstanding figures in the history of thought in their own right. What they did amounted in itself to no more than a readjustment of emphasis, a more precise definition of terms, the fuller development of an existing methodology. However, a significant change of direction may come about as the result of a very small first move. In this case, the alterations which were made were adjustments to slight but progressive changes in the habits of thought of a generation. These scholars deserve credit principally for making an effort to meet a need which they themselves felt rather than recognized. The work of the earliest twelfth-century scholars consists in large measure of an experimental shifting of ground in an attempt to relieve the pressure under which they now found themselves. Their work has something of the quality of Godwin's, as William Hazlitt describes it: 'Mr. Godwin's faculties have kept at home, and plied their task in the workshop of the brain, diligently and effectually. [When] Mr. Godwin is intent on a subject . . . he works it out as a matter of duty, and discards from his mind whatever does not forward his main object as impertinent and vain.'[12] The majority of these scholars were men of limited vision and painstaking mind, but by industrious effort they 'leave more than one monument of a powerful intellect behind'.

2. The Old Disciplines

i. *Trees of Knowledge*

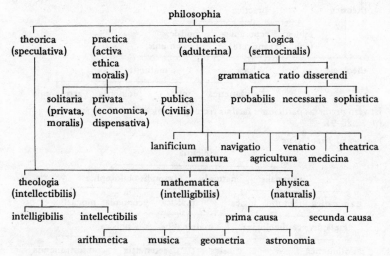

A modification:

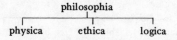

aliquando physica large accipitur aequipollens theoricae

philosophia

physica   ethica   logica

Hugh of St. Victor: *Didascalicon, Epitome Dindimi in Philosophiam*

Several twelfth-century scholars tried to set out a complete conspectus of learning in diagram form. Some of the results may be seen here.[1] Although there is a substantial measure of agreement among them, they are not identical. But they are suf-

[12] William Hazlitt, 'Coleridge', *The Spirit of the Age*, ed. G. Richards (Oxford, 1911).
[1] They may be reconstructed from Hugh of St. Victor's *Didascalicon*, ed. C. Buttimer (Washington, 1939), and his *Epitome Dindimi in Philosophiam*, ed. R. Baron, *Opera Propaedeutica* (Notre Dame, 1965); from the *Ysagoge in Theologiam*,

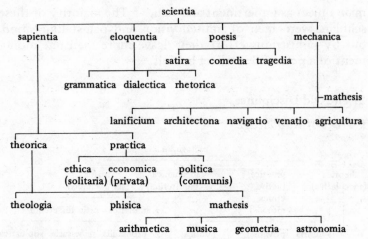

Ut vero predictas particiones facilius recolligas subiectam intuere formulam
(p. 72.28–9).

Ysagoge in Theologiam

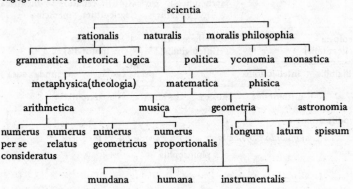

Dialectica Monacensis

ficently alike to suggest that they represent a remarkably close
general consensus of opinion on the range of studies which
comprehended all human knowledge. They tell us something

ed. R. Martin, *Écrits théologiques de l'école d'Abelard*, SS Lov. 14 (1934),
where an actual diagram is given, p. 73; and from *LM* II[ii], pp. 459–60. A fuller
tree of knowledge for Hugh's and Abelard's 'schools' is given in R. W. Southern,
Mediaeval Humanism, charts I and II, but the versions given here are those which
deal with the academic and related disciplines only, and which are to be found *in
toto* in the texts cited.

else, too: the academic scene was evidently being surveyed as a whole, with a view to determining the relative position and standing of the traditional disciplines.

Hugh of St. Victor was able to give a little general guidance on most of them in his *Didascalicon,* in the form of short encyclopaedia articles. But we should not be misled into thinking that all these subjects could be studied in the schools. Had anyone wanted to take his study of *practica* (*mechanica*) further, he would have found that the branches of learning were not all equally adequately catered for in the schools.[2] The greatest interest and value of these *schemata* for our purposes perhaps lies in this: they tell us where the liberal arts were felt to stand in relation to the whole scheme of learning.

Hugh himself acknowledges in the summary he made for 'Dindimus' that the seven liberal arts are supreme: 'Of these we call arts, the diligence of the ancients discerned seven, in which studies the tools of all philosophy might be learned'.[3] Only these seven had textbooks and a long tradition of study in the schoolroom, and even of these, not all were equally well equipped to make the transition into the new schools because several of them had been badly neglected for centuries. One significant difference between the trivium and quadrivium subjects emerges. The mathematical subjects of the quadrivium are regarded as 'theoretical' or 'speculative'. The trivium subjects of grammar, logic, and rhetoric are seen as 'arts of language'.

These disciplines are still, in some cases, studied as academic subjects, though some have changed their names. Others grouped together here have moved apart. The art of *economica*, or the running of a household, has little in common now with the formal study of personal morality on the one hand (*solitaria* or *moralis*) or the study of government and public administration on the other (*publica* or *civilis*). We should not readily list these three and only these three under the heading of 'practical' studies. To the list of mechanical arts it would now be necessary to make a number of changes.

[2] See *Theological Tractates,* pp. 4–8, for Boethius' division of philosophy in the *De Trinitate.* Nine arts were distinguished by Varro, but the seven medieval liberal arts were selected by Cassiodorus and Isidore.

[3] *Epitome Dindimi in Philosophiam,* p. 204.435.

These are no longer studies of the same general type. Working with wool (*lanificium*) would have to be expanded to take in the work of all the textile industries. *Navigatio* would have to include the piloting of aeroplanes and perhaps driving of trains and public service vehicles, as well as the navigation of ships. Hunting has become a sport (*venatio*) and *armamenta* (armaments), the business of governments and industries, rarely of craftsmen.

Some lines of descent may be traced from ancient to modern disciplines. From grammar has come the study of linguistics and of languages. First Greek was added to Latin in the sixteenth century, then modern and other ancient languages much more recently. The old grammarians who taught parsing from the classical poets began a tradition which led to the study of the literatures of all ancient and modern languages. *Poesis,* the writing of poetry and plays, of 'literature' in general, is now the work of creative artists, and only occasionally treated as an academic discipline, but the study of existing poetry and plays has fallen under the umbrella of literary criticism. Out of rhetoric has come the study of law, and the arts of composition (for which manuals existed in the twelfth century for letter-writing, poetry-writing, and the composition of sermons). Logic has lost its medieval pre-eminence, and become part of philosophy; it is no longer a subject with which every schoolboy is familiar.

Of the mathematical arts, music and astronomy have become quite different kinds of study, in which mathematics plays only a limited part. Arithmetic and geometry are still staple ingredients of mathematics, but they form only two branches of the syllabus, and it would seem absurd to divide geometry into the study of length, breadth, and depth as the author of the *Dialectica Monacensis* does.

These changes are of more than curiosity interest because the processes by which they have taken place reflect greatly altered social requirements and cultural attitudes since the twelfth century. The most rapid and dramatic changes are the most recent. By stretching it considerably the old scheme can still be made to fit. Physics, chemistry, and biology might go into *phisica,* natural science, and history into *poesis,* engineering under *mechanica,* sociology under *publica* perhaps, but it would be absurd to suggest that the founders of these new disciplines looked back to their remote ancestors for detailed help in deciding upon the boundaries of their subject-matter and the methods which would be appropriate for the study of the new subject.

What began in the twelfth century was an open-ended process. A few simple principles were established in an effort to make the traditional disciplines suitable for study in the schools, to make them, for the first time, recognizably academic disciplines. But these were the cardinal principles and they have worn well. They lasted unaltered for several centuries and they are still important because the continuity of development has never been broken.

ii. Textbooks

John Henry Newman prefaced his *Discourses on the Scope and Nature of University Education* with a definition of a university. It is, he says, 'a place of teaching universal knowledge'. He thus suggests 'that its object is, on the one hand, intellectual, not moral; and on the other, that it is the diffusion and extension of knowledge, rather than the advancement'. Newman's immediate concern was to re-establish the proper relation of what he calls the 'the Church's assistance' to the work of a university, and the place of both religious training and the academic study of theology in a university. These matters did not have the same urgency for medieval scholars, or at least, not in the same way. But the preliminary definition he gives is intended to convey the very 'essence' of a university, 'independently of its relation to the Church'. These 'essential' elements were already present in the twelfth century, before we can properly speak of the schools as universities at all. Schools were becoming 'places', not mere meetings of masters and pupils; and certainly their primary function was to teach. Bernard of Chartres wrote almost nothing (or almost nothing which has survived). Much twelfth-century writing, like the commentaries on Boethius' theological tractates with which we shall be much concerned, consisted of textbooks for teaching purposes. Most masters gave up the greater part of their time to imparting existing knowledge rather than to composing original works. A

twelfth-century school was already a 'place of teaching'
chiefly given up to 'the diffusion and extension of knowledge'.

Such schools were also concerned with what Newman calls
'universal knowledge'. An academic discipline must be of
general interest; it must go beyond local concerns and have
an international, if not a universal appeal. This is precisely
what the study of the liberal arts provided from the first in
the twelfth century. This international and universal
character could be preserved in practice only because masters
everywhere relied heavily upon the same textbooks. They
provided a common core for the work of all the schools.
Existing knowledge expanded, certainly, as the texts were
glossed, and enlarged commentaries were written, but in none
of the liberal arts did the new work lose contact with the old,
and there is ample evidence that a common community of
thought was maintained as one master's views were compared
with another's. Thanks to the renewed interest in the textbooks, students began to gain much more than the smattering
of their subject which was to be had from the encyclopedias of
Isidore or Cassiodorus or the Carolingians. Two further
requirements of an academic discipline were thus fulfilled:
the common subject-matter proved capable of development,
and it proved teachable to generations of pupils.

As to Newman's emphasis on the intellectual character of
the work of the universities: the liberal arts had always been
disciplines of the mind. This was perhaps a legacy of the
Hellenistic preference for the intellectual aspects of education; it still comes more naturally to think of academic work
as an activity of the mind rather than of the body. It is
primarily book-work.

By the fourteenth century the university syllabus listed set
texts to be covered by every student in preparation for the
degree of bachelor or master of arts. He had to hear a fixed
number of lectures on each. A glance at the *index auctorum*
of a good modern edition of the work of a twelfth-century
author will show how comparatively limited was the range of
sources on which he was able to draw. But the instinct to
found the syllabus on close detailed study of set texts was
there already; it resulted in immensely detailed, if sometimes
not very perceptive, examination of the words of the

authority, line by line. Newman does not emphasize the importance of textbooks because it was so integral a part of his own training to study set books that it seems scarcely worth mentioning. Methods of studying set books change from age to age. Their role in preserving academic continuity does not.

In the first half of the twelfth century additions to the range of textbooks which had been available to scholars of the earlier Middle Ages were few: chiefly some of the 'new logic' of Aristotle.[4] But textbooks which had been available earlier and which did not await the efforts of an Adelard of Bath or a Hermann of Carinthia to bring them to the West from the Arab world, now suddenly came to notice after being neglected by all but a few scholars who had a specialist interest. Boethius' *Arithmetica* is a case in point, as is Chalcidius' *Commentary* on the *Timaeus*. For the formation of the new theological discipline, Boethius' 'theological treatises' were of the first importance. The influence these newly rediscovered textbooks exerted has tended to be obscured by the more dramatic effects of the introduction of fresh works in translation from the Arabic and the Greek in the twelfth and thirteenth century. But it was the old Latin works which provided the foundation for the comprehensive re-establishment of the disciplines of the liberal arts.

The first stage in finding a place for a discipline in the schoolroom is to devise a means of teaching it effectively. The first sign of the active use of textbooks in the schools is the proliferation of copies accompanied by glosses or commentaries, and of glosses and commentaries written out on their own for use in conjunction with plain texts. The most substantial and common 'textbooks' of all were the Bible and the Fathers. But before we consider their place in the new academic discipline of theology we must look at the textbooks of the arts.

Donatus in the fourth century and Priscian in the sixth

---

[4] On the transmission of these textbooks, see A. van de Vyver 'Les étappes du développement philosophique du haut moyen âge', *Revue belge de philologie et d'histoire* 8 (1929), 425–52. See Abelard, *Dialectica*, pp. xvi–xix on the likelihood that Peter Abelard knew something of the new logic. For English scholars who were responsible for bringing Arabic science back from Spain, see *Mediaeval Humanism*, pp. 170–1.

provided the basic textbooks on which grammatical studies were founded for centuries. A number of later writers attempted to compose manuals along the same lines. In the eleventh century the glosses on Priscian began to show a response to the needs of a new kind of schoolroom. Between 1050 and 1150 formal *glosule* came into being. The old discipline was made newly academic by Manegold of Lautenbach and Anselm of Laon and other masters, who worked through the text patiently furnishing explanations of difficult terms and paraphrases of the rules, and their work was used in several schools. This kind of composite, if not co-ordinated, creation of a commentary upon a textbook by a series of masters was something new. The reading of the poets, which had formed the backbone of the teaching of grammar in monastic schools became increasingly distinct from the new concern with the theory of the subject.[5]

The same interest in theory animates the new work on the dialectical textbooks. Here the position was a little different. For the old logic, the beginner's books, the *Isagoge* of Porphyry, Aristotle's *Categories* and the *De Interpretatione*, were covered by Boethius' commentaries; Cicero's *Topics* and Boethius' commentary, together with Boethius' monograph *De Differentiis Topicis* were also known. Much of the new work of the twelfth century consisted in the writing of short manuals which were designed to turn Boethius' reflections into manageable handbooks for the schoolroom. Adam of Balsam, Peter Abelard, the elusive Garlandus, and the authors of a number of anonymous manuals, all tried to supply this need.[6] As to the new logic: during the middle years of the century the *Sophistici Elenchi* appeared in the schools,[7] and

---

[5] The classical study of 'The Studies on Priscian in the eleventh and twelfth centuries' is still R. W. Hunt, *MARS* i (1941-3), 194-231 and ii (1950), 1-56. See, too, K. M. Fredborg, 'The dependence of Petrus Helias' *Summa super Priscianum* on William of Conches' *Glose super Priscianum*', *Cahiers*, 11 (1973), 1-57, 'Tractatus glosarum Prisciani in MS. Vat. lat. 1486', *Cahiers*, 21 (1977), 21-44; see too, *Lanfranc of Bec*, pp. 46-7. The Roman grammarians and their followers are collected in H. Keil, *Grammatici Latini* (Leipzig, 1855-80), 8 vols.

[6] Garlandus' treatise, the *Dialectica*, is edited by L. M. de Rijk (Assen, 1959); see, too Abelard, *Dialectica* and the *Logica Modernorum*, ed. L. M. de Rijk (Assen, 1967), 2 vols.; Adam of Balsam, *Ars Disserendi*, ed. L. Minio-Paluello (Rome, 1956).

[7] S. Ebbesen, 'Jacobus Veneticus on the *Posterior Analytics* and some Early 13th Century Oxford Masters on the *Elenchi*', *Cahiers*, 21 (1977), 1-9.

before 1200 the Aristotelian *Topics* and the *Prior* and *Posterior Analytics* were available. The study of dialectic therefore had to encompass a larger body of texts than that of grammar. It also had to accommodate new textbooks within the syllabus.

Masters who taught dialectic had, in addition, to find ways of explaining to their pupils the difference between the grammarians' approach to language and that of the dialectician. As we shall see, there was a considerable area of overlap between the two disciplines in their technical vocabulary and in their common concern with the theory of language. Amidst all these additional difficulties the textbooks provided a reassuring certainty, a solid core of subject-matter which gave the discipline stability under pressure.

Rhetoric was still the most neglected of the trivial arts; where it was studied it was taught from Cicero's *De Inventione* and the *Rhetorica ad Herennium*. Both these textbooks were designed in the first place to be school manuals, and they suited twelfth-century purposes admirably in their relatively mechanical treatment of the branches of the subject. Quintilian's *Institutio Oratoria* was little known, and it was in circulation only in a very truncated form.[8] The new 'rhetorical arts' of letter-writing, the writing of poetry and — in the thirteenth century — of preaching, had no place in the teaching of rhetoric as a theoretical discipline.[9] The emphasis of the eleventh- and twelfth-century commentators on the two 'Ciceronian rhetorics' was upon the skills of argumentation they taught. In many respects rhetoric was taught as though it were a branch of dialectic.[10] This is not surprising in view of the concentrated effort which was being put into the teaching of dialectic, and into the reconciliation of all the disparate elements it was found to contain when the corpus

---

[8] On Quintilian, see P. Boskoff, 'Quintilian in the Late Middle Ages', *Speculum,* 27 (1952), 71–8.

[9] M. Dickey, 'Some commentaries on the *De Inventione* and the *Rhetorica ad Herennium* of the eleventh and twelfth centuries', *MARS* vi (1968), 1–41. K. Fredborg, 'The commentary of Thierry of Chartres on Cicero's *De Inventione*' *Cahiers,* 7 (1971), 1–36; 'Petrus Helias on Rhetoric', *Cahiers,* 13 (1974), 31–41; 'The commentaries on Cicero's *De Inventione* and the *Rhetorica ad Herennium* by William of Champeaux', *Cahiers,* 17 (1976), 1–39.

[10] M. Dickey makes this point, op. cit.

of material about argument in the rhetorical and dialectical textbooks was systematically examined in the schools.

There is some evidence that Boethius' *Arithmetica* was coming to be more widely known in the first half of the twelfth century. Its general influence appears to have been confined to the first chapters and to a few definitions and principles which were thought to have a theological application.[11] Euclid's *Elements* were available in a Latin text – in fact in more than one version[12] – and music could be learned from Boethius' *Musica*. For astronomy there was Macrobius on *The Dream of Scipio,* and Chalcidius on the *Timaeus.* But it would be misleading to suggest that any of the quadrivium subjects had the popularity of grammar and dialectic, or even of rhetoric. The use that was made of these textbooks was eclectic. These subjects were rarely studied in any depth in their own right, and they were fully-fledged academic disciplines only by courtesy, because they held a traditional place in the scheme of the seven liberal arts. But they, too, owed their academic respectability to the textbooks on which they were based.

Boethius' *opuscula sacra* occupy a somewhat anomalous position; although they came to be studied as textbooks in the schools with increasing interest in the middle of the twelfth century, they never found a place in the syllabus of the traditional academic disciplines. This must be put down to their subject-matter. The *De Trinitate* is, as Boethius himself acknowledges, an attempt to take a little further what Augustine had said in his own book on the Trinity. The *De Hebdomadibus* is about the relation of individual goods to the highest good. The *Contra Eutychen* deals with the heresies of Eutyches and Nestorius concerning the Person and Nature of Christ. Their subject-matter is therefore theological, although much of the content requires a considerable knowledge of the liberal arts to make it comprehensible. They were of enormous importance in bringing about the new perceptions of the purposes and scope of theology which

[11] See my article 'Introductions to Boethius's *Arithmetica* of the tenth and the fourteenth century', *History of Science,* xvi (1978), 22–41.

[12] M. Clagett, 'The mediaeval translations from the Arabic of the *Elements* of Euclid, with special emphasis on the versions of Adelard of Bath', *Isis,* 44 (1953), 16–43.

made it an academic discipline. They helped in significant ways to bridge the gap between the liberal arts and speculative theology.[13] They were soon overshadowed by the range of texts of Aristotle newly available in the thirteenth century; but for the twelfth century their influence was indispensable in encouraging scholars to see more clearly the size of the questions with which they were dealing.

A further anomaly was presented by the presence of disciplines for which no ancient textbooks were available, in the traditional *schemata* of subjects for study. Hugh of St. Victor gives a list of the authorities on each of the secular arts in his *Didascalicon*. He borrows the greater part of it from Isidore and makes no comment on the availability of the books they wrote in his own day. His intention is rather to give a historical account of the discovery and transmission of each art. Arithmetic, for example, was discovered by Pythagoras; Nicomachus wrote about it in Greek, and first Apuleius and then Boethius translated his work into Latin. Ham, son of Noah, is credited with the invention of astrology, which was first taught by the Chaldeans; Josephus, we are told, says that Abraham first learned astrology among the Egyptians. Two areas of study in particular were poorly served by traditional textbooks of the kind which lent themselves to study in the context of a school syllabus. One of the ancient divisions of human knowledge distinguishes *logica, physica,* and *ethica.* Only *logica* is adequately catered for. Hugh identifies Thales of Miletus and Pliny as the principal authors on *physica.* Socrates is the inventor of ethics. The best Hugh can do for a textbook here is to say that Plato wrote about the nature of justice in his *Republic* and that Cicero wrote a *Republica* in Latin His account certainly does not yield a set of working textbooks for the study of these two major subjects. The books Hugh mentions were rare or unobtainable in Latin as yet, and he omits others, such as Chalcidius on the *Timaeus,* which were being read in the schools of his own day. In the absence of standard textbooks for commentary the study of 'ethics' and 'physics' developed in a curiously piecemeal fashion in the schools of the twelfth century, sometimes

[13] *Theological Tractates.*

making great strides where an individual scholar wrote a book of his own, as Abelard did in his ethics, the *Scito Teipsum*. Sometimes *physica* touched on the subject-matter of theology, as we shall see, and here, too, advances were made. But for the most part, the unsatisfactory state of affairs with regard to the textbooks acted as a disincentive to scholars to develop these subjects as formal academic disciplines.[14]

There appear to have been at least the beginnings of a notion of academic respectability in Hugh's mind. His intention is to describe the subjects which are worthy of study, the authors who have written on them and some of their books. He is careful to exclude explicitly anything which might be a source of spiritual or intellectual peril to the reader. He is animated perhaps by rather the same desire to separate canonical from uncanonical, *authentica* from *apocrypha*, which had encouraged Cassidorus and Isidore and some of Hugh's own contemporaries to make lists of Christian writings which may be regarded as reliable. When he comes to do the same for secular authors he perceives a special danger in magical and astrological studies. These were beginning to revive with the increasing interest of the day in the more respectable mathematical and a scientific subjects. Hugh explains carefully the difference between the mathematics of the quadrivium and the *mathematica* which is another name for astrology. He keeps these comments apart from his treatment of the traditional disciplines. Undoubtedly his strongest motive in all this is his concern for the spiritual welfare of the reader. Magic is dangerous and evil. But it is also, to the twelfth-century eye, academically unsound and unscientific,[15] and that is something new.

[14] *Didascalicon*, III, 2 *PL* 176.765-6, ed. C. Buttimer (Washington, 1939) pp. 49-52. *Peter Abelard's Ethics*, ed. D. Luscombe (Oxford, 1971).

[15] *Didascalicon*, VI, 15, *PL* 176.810; Buttimer, pp. 132-3. L. Thorndike, *A History of Magic and Experimental Science* (New York, 1929), II.13-14 makes the point that magic 'is treated by itself' by Hugh partly at least because he sees it as a subject which should not be 'included in philosophy'. The revival of interest in astrology and magic in connection with the new enthusiasm for mathematics proper is attested by M. L. M. Laistner, 'The Western Church and Astrology, *Harvard Theological Review*, 34 (1941), 251-75. On the twelfth-century Bernardus Silvestris on astrology, see C. S. F. Burnett, 'What is the *Experimentarius* of Bernardus Silvestris? A Preliminary Survey of the Material' *AHDLMA* xliv (1977), 79-125.

3. The New Discipline

i. Theologia

Cassidorus and Isidore and the Carolingian encyclopedists had helped to make the terms used to describe the liberal arts so familiar that no twelfth-century scholar could be in any doubt as to what to call the subject in which he was engaged when he was studying grammar or arithmetic. But for the studies we should now group under the heading of 'theology' there was as yet no generally accepted term. The student of dialectic might be forgiven for being confused about the area of study in which he was engaged when he found this *questio gravis*: 'Was the Virgin made free from original sin at the point when she herself was conceived, or when she conceived Christ?'[1] among a series of purely logical problems in a set of school exercises. When Lanfranc and Berengar had explored the application of dialectic to theology they had kept chiefly to problems concerning the sacraments.[2] In Anselm's day the range was much wider, and by the twelfth century no topic of modern academic theology had been left unexplored by the dialecticians, as if its subject-matter properly fell within the scope of an academic discipline.

There are strong indications that theology had a place of its own among the academic disciplines by the end of the century. In a twelfth- or early thirteenth-century text, the *Logica cum sit nostra,* one of the first points to be discussed is how, if 'dialectic is the art of arts and the science of sciences', theology, too, may be called 'the science of sciences.'[3] One master of dialectic provides this definition of an academic discipline when he tries to explain in what the art of dialectic consists:

There are, he says, two kinds of practitioner of this art: Who are they? There is one who performs according to the art, who disputes by the rules and precepts of the art; he is called a dialectician, that is, a 'disputer'. He whose work concerns the art is he who teaches the art and expounds the rules and precepts of the art. He is called a master or 'demonstrator'. . . . What is his purpose? To teach the art. What is his task? To expound the rules and precepts of the art and to add new

[1] *LM* II[ii], pp. 735–48 *Quaestiones Victorinae.*
[2] M. Gibson, *Lanfranc of Bec,* p. 102.
[3] *LM* II[ii], p. 417.24–7, *Logica cum sit nostra.*

ones, if they can be appropriately added.[4]
He thus distinguishes between the teaching of the art, which
is the academic's first concern, and the practice of the art,
which, although it should never be entirely separated from
the teaching, is something quite different.

On this view of things, the master's first duty as an
academic is to teach it to others, to study logic rather than
to argue, to study poetry rather than to write poems, to read
and write about history rather than to make history. Yet: 'In
every art is taught that which it is the art itself to do' (*in
omni arte docetur id quod faciendi ipsa est ars*)[5] and 'Every
art exists for the purpose of making it easy to do that which
it is the art itself to do' (*omnis ars est ad id ut ex ea sit facile
id quod faciendi ipsa est ars*).[6]

It is important then that the academic study should not
become dissociated from the practice of the skill or art itself;
but it must remain teachable, and it is teachable only in so
far as it can be reduced to a system of rules. 'An art is a
collection of many principles directed to the same end.'[7] 'An
art is, as it were, a finite compendium of something infinite
. . . if you consider it you will find it small in size, but if you
apply yourself to its contents you will find it full of force.'[8]
Theology was never to become merely one of the arts, a
study equivalent in scope and standing to dialectic or grammar.
But it was to borrow from the arts the preoccupation with
what can be taught by rule, and with what can be reduced to
a manageable compass, which distinguishes the traditional
disciplines and which makes them suitable for the schoolroom.

There was nothing new in regarding the study of God as
something which might be approached by the conventional
procedures of learning. Augustine's *De Doctrina Christiana* is
about the way in which the arts of language of his own day
might be used by Christians in studying the Bible and in
teaching others. He finds it necessary to emphasize that his

---

[4] *LM* II[ii], p. 77.11-25, *Abbreviatio Montana.*
[5] *LM* II[ii], p. 147.17-18, *Ars Emmerana.*
[6] *LM* II[ii], p. 147.21-2.
[7] *LM* II[ii], p. 417.9-13, *Logica cum sit nostra.*
[8] Ibid.

reader is not to expect an advanced academic treatment from him, just because he is known to have been a teacher of rhetoric himself.[9] Augustine does not want to make theology an academic discipline like rhetoric. His work is especially concerned with the position of the Christian who is not highly educated and who cannot make use of the rhetorician's skills. He outlines a programme of 'Christian learning' which everyone may use.

This deliberate subordination of the scholarly and technical to the needs of the general reader continued within the monastic tradition into the medieval period. Early in the twelfth century Rupert of Deutz speaks of *sacrum studium* with a double sense of 'holy learning' and 'holy zeal'.[10] The expression *sacra eruditio* is also found. But the 'learning' involved, although it may take place in part in a monastic or cathedral schoolroom, and although it may have a formal character lacks the comprehensive, systematic organization and the established and extended syllabus of an academic discipline.

If we are to argue that twelfth-century scholars perceived for the first time that it might be possible to treat theology as an academic discipline (for limited purposes) we should expect to find a first indication in their discussion of the name by which they are to call it. The term *theologia* only gradually came to have the universality as a title for an academic discipline which *grammatica* or *rhetorica* had enjoyed at least since Roman times. Even for Aquinas the expression *sacra doctrina* still comes naturally to mind, although Rivière contends that *theologia* was 'l'usage normal de son temps'.[11]

It is not difficult to see why this should have been so. Twelfth-century scholars were looking for a single term which would embrace aspects of a study which was already immensely rich and varied, and which there was no precedent for regarding as a unified body. The syllabus of study of grammar or of dialectic had developed under an existing heading and had therefore retained a certain homogeneity of

[9] *De Doctrina Christiana, CCSL* 32 (1962), IV.i.2.
[10] See p. 61 for a discussion of the context of this expression.
[11] J. Rivière, *'Theologia', Revue des sciences réligieuses,* xvi (1936), 47.

labelling at least. The masters of theology of the twelfth
century were trying to settle on a name for two distinct and
not easily reconciled existing approaches to the subject-
matter — that of the study of the Bible and that of speculative
theology (where Scriptural passages serve principally to pose
problems or to furnish proofs for use in problem-solving).
Religio will not do. When Anselm of Havelberg cries that
churchmen are confronted by a *nova religio* because there are
so many innovations in the Church of God (*tot novitates in
Ecclesia Dei*)[12] he sees *religio* as something altogether broader
in its scope than academic theology, embracing the work of
the Church at large. Expressions such as *sacra pagina, divina
pagina, studium sacrae scripturae*, referred primarily to the
study of the Bible, although, *faute de mieux*, they are often
used for speculative exercises, too. Anselm's three treatises
'pertaining to the study of Scripture',[13] are about truth,
freedom of will, and the fall of Satan respectively. Peter
Lombard relates *sacra pagina* to *doctrina* and discusses its
contribution to 'all learning'.[14] Sometimes *divinitas* is tried
as an alternative general term. The author of the *Ysagoge in
Theologiam* describes his work as a *divinorum summa,*[15] a
complete handbook to divine matters.

   Out of a period of relative confusion about terminology in
the first half of the twelfth century, *theologia* can be seen to
be gradually making its way to its ultimate position as 'l'usage
normal' to describe the study of theology as an academic
discipline. The discipline it covered was very different in its
scope and conception from that which the ancient Greeks
would have recognized (if we can speak of *theologia* in such
terms at all among the Greeks).[16] But the Greeks left the
legacy of the word itself, along with terms for the theologian
himself (Latinized as *theologus*) and the verb 'to theologize'
to describe the activity of doing theology.[17]

---

[12] *PL* 188.1141-3, Book I of Anselm's *Dialogus* is edited by G. Salet (Paris,
1966).   [13] *Anselmi Opera Omnia,* I.173.2.
   [14] Petrus Lombardus, *Sententiae, Spicilegium Bonaventurianum,* IV (Rome,
1971), p. 55, Book I, Dist. i, Ch. i, para. i.
   [15] *Ysagoge in Theologiam,* p. 64.18.
   [16] F. Kattenbusch, 'Die Enstehung einer Christlichen Theologie', *Zeitschrift
fur theologie und Kirche,* ix (1930), 161, 169.
   [17] θεολογία, θεολογεῶ, θεολογos.

Rivière has suggested that Peter Abelard was the principal scholar to give a lead here, chiefly perhaps because of the title he gave his *Theologia Christiana.*[18] Certainly St. Bernard described Abelard as *theologus* as though he thought he had set himself up as a master in a new discipline *Habemus in Francia novum de veteri magistro theologum*[19] ('we have in France an old master turned new theologian'); he mockingly calls him: *theologus noster.* But Pseudo-Dionysius is referred to as *theologus* by some of Abelard's contemporaries,[20] and the term was certainly not confined to Abelard.

We shall come closer to the origins of the new approach and the new sense of theology as an academic discipline if we look, not at Abelard, but at a group of commentaries edited (since Rivière wrote) by Father Häring: the work of Gilbert of Poitiers, Thierry of Chartres, Clarenbald of Arras, and others on Boethius' *opuscula sacra.*[21] Abelard himself was not, it appears, one of the scholars who took a special interest in these works, and they remained, during his lifetime, something of a specialist study. Nevertheless, Thierry of Chartres and Gilbert of Poitiers did a great deal to popularize them as suitable for commentary in the schoolroom, although they continued to be regarded, with some justification, as obscure and difficult; they certainly lent themselves best to the close, patient study of the text in which these masters excelled. This method helped to focus attention on specific words, and particularly terms which seemed to refer to important notions and which had, at the same time, a certain novelty.

The textbook which confronted the problem of the definition of an academic *theologia* most directly was Boethius' *De Trinitate.* In his *Prologue* he refers to the innermost discipline of philosophy: *intima philosophiae disciplina.*[22] This falls into three: *ethica, speculativa* and *rationalis.*[23] In

---

[18] Rivière, op. cit., p. 50.   [19] *PL* 182.1055.

[20] *Thierry of Chartres,* p. 246.63.

[21] Gilbert of Poitiers, *Clarenbald of Arras,* and *Thierry of Chartres.*

[22] *Theological Tractates,* p. 4. Boethius is not the originator of these classifications; something similar is to be found in Proclus' commentary on the first book of Euclid's *Elements,* and elsewhere in Neoplatonic writings. See, too, *Thierry of Chartres,* p. 125.26–9, Aristotle *Met.* VI, 1025b–1026a. Zeno divided philosophy into logic, ethics, and physics.   [23] *Theological Tractates,* p. 4.

Chapter II he explains that *speculativa* may be divided into three branches, *naturalis* or natural science, *mathematica* and *theologia*.[24] Theology thus emerges as a subdivision of one of the three principal subdivisions of philosophy — and, incidentally, as a *disciplina*,[25] a subject of academic study at least in Boethian terms, if not in quite the way it was to develop in the twelfth century.

Boethius takes us a little further than this into the definition of *theologia*. Having 'placed' the study of theology, he describes its scope. It deals not with form and matter in their embodiment in moving and corporeal things, as natural science does, nor, like mathematics, with pure form (which also has corporeal associations), but with the motionless, distinct and incorporeal divine substance', for the substance of God lacks matter and motion'.[26] This working definition did very well for those branches of theology with which Boethius is concerned, and to which Abelard largely restricts himself in the *Theologia Christiana* — the study of the Divine Nature and the Trinity. It was another matter to extend the term to include the theology of redemption, sacramentology, and the many other matters which Honorius Augustodunensis brings together in his comprehensive handbook, the *Elucidarium*, early in the twelfth century. Honorius did not yet, perhaps, see theology as a whole. He has written in answer to 'certain little questions' (*quaedam quaestiuncula*),[27] and his chief concession to the demands of the schoolroom has been to arrange them in an orderly fashion. Yet Honorius was much-travelled and a great eclectic. He knew what questions were being asked among his contemporaries. When we set his work, for all its comparative superficiality, beside Abelard's it is clear that Boethius' definition of theology had to be greatly stretched if it was to meet the needs of the twelfth-century schools. The new theology had to include the study of the Bible, with which Boethius is not at all concerned, as well as a great many matters of doctrine and practice, some of central importance, some peripheral, but all of them

----

[24] Ibid., p. 8.   [25] *Thierry of Chartres*, p. 130.92–5.
[26] *Theological Tractates*, p. 8.
[27] *L'Eucidarium et les lucidaires*, ed. Y. Lefèvre, *Bibliothèque des écoles françaises d'Athenes et de Rome*, clxxx (1954).

demanding a place in a complete syllabus of theological studies by the twelfth century.

Abelard himself drew upon Augustine in forming his conception of *theologia*;[28] here he had access to a tradition which took an altogether larger view of the scope of theology, but which had disadvantages to equal those of Boethius' definition, if of an exactly opposite kind. Where Boethius' definition was too narrow for twelfth-century purposes, Augustine's was too broad. Augustine grew up in the late-classical world. He knew that the pagan idea of theology included the study of myths, the stuff of the ancient poets. The pagans recognized a political role for theology — the proper conduct of public worship was regarded as an important contributing factor in maintaining the strength and stability of the state. Moreover, since some thinkers have regarded the world itself as divine, the study of the natural world may itself constitute a form of theology.[29] Tertullian describes the three branches of theology like this (after Varro): 'One branch is physics, with which the philosophers deal, another myth, which is the concern of poets, the third rational which each people chooses for itself'.[30] Some of these notions had a place in the pagan world for which there was no exact parallel in the twelfth century; it was not perhaps difficult for medieval thinkers to set aside what Augustine had to say about 'poetic' and 'civil' theology. *Naturalis theologia*, however, posed special problems for them because it touched on the subject-matter of their own secular arts and philosophy,[31] and because the questions it raised were of pressing contemporary interest.

Augustine provided Abelard with a good deal of help on the specific problem of deciding the relation between philosophy and theology.[32] This twelfth-century scholars saw as

[28] Compare Augustine, *De Civitate Dei*, VIII, 2, and *Theologia Christiana*, p. 148.541.

[29] See Kattenbusch, op. cit.; P. Batiffol, '*Theologia, theologi*' *Ephemerides Theologicae Lovaniensis*, V (1928), 205–20; A. H. Armstrong, *St. Augustine and Christian Platonism* (Villanova, 1967).

[30] Tertullian, *Ad Nationes*, II. 1.

[31] *De Civitate Dei*, VIII contains Augustine's most extended thoughts on these matters.

[32] *Theologia Christiana*, II, *passim*, where the emphasis is principally on matters of ethics.

the main issue, without some resolution of which theology could not take its place among the accepted disciplines of the schools. It is possible, says Augustine, to be a philosopher who takes no account of the idea of God, but he argues that the highest philosophies are those which have attempted to be theologies, too. Natural theology in particular he regards as the attempt of pagan philosophers to think about God by the light of natural reason. He proposes to examine how far philosophy can go by such means, and to test the effectiveness of philosophical methods for the theologian's purpose. In order to do so, he leaves out of consideration a good many philosophical topics which he feels to be irrelevant because they have nothing to do with theology. He does not try to oppose or compare the two disciplines point by point or to maintain that there is any full-scale correspondence in their differences. But for Augustine *theologia* is far from being a mere subdivision of *philosophia*. It is the measure against which philosophy's highest achievements are to be tested. It is a study of an intrinsically higher order than philosophy, as it was for Philo of Alexandria[33] (who would probably have found himself in some sympathy with Hugh of St. Victor's statement that the 'lower wisdom' of secular studies, rightly ordered: *recte ordinata*, leads to higher wisdom (*ad superiorem conducit*)).[34] Hugh of St. Victor saw the human sciences which made use of reasoning and which were primarily concerned with the things of the natural world, as disciplines of a more lowly kind, whose purpose was to serve as a means of approach to a higher understanding of the divine. William of Conches, with a similar sense that the human sciences are straightforwardly serviceable for the purpose, describes theology as a *ratio de divinis,* reasoning applied to the divine[35] (*Theos enim est deus, logos ratio*).[36]

But side by side with the new sense of the magnificence of theological knowledge in comparison with the knowledge attainable by philosophy alone, the Boethian scheme is still to be found. In his commentary on the *Timaeus* William of

---

[33] See H. Chadwick, *Philo of Alexandria, Cambridge History of Later Greek and Early Medieval Philosophy* (Cambridge, 1967).

[34] *De Sacramentis Ecclesiae,* Book I, prol. i, *PL* 176.185.

[35] William of Conches, op. cit., p. 61.2, the *Accessus in Timaeum.*

[36] Ibid., cf. *Thierry of Chartres,* p. 70.86–7.

Conches speaks of the parts of philosophy, among them *theologia*.[37] It was still the usual practice of the day for a schoolmaster to introduce his pupils to the study of a new book by means of an *accessus*, a list of standard explanations of such matters as the authorship, the title, the author's purpose in writing the work, its value, and the place it occupied in the scheme of studies, that is 'under what division of philosophy it falls' (*cui parte philosophiae supponatur*). *Philosophia* retained its meaning as a term to describe the carapace under which all learning was gathered.

The keynote of all these early attempts to define the scope of the discipline of theology, however, is an emphasis on its concern with the search for knowledge about God. Peter Abelard says that an enlightened pagan philosopher, a lover of wisdom not human but divine, is admirable in so far as he turns his thoughts towards God.[38] A philosopher may try to acquire any kind of knowledge and be rated a lover of wisdom, although the highest *sapientia* is a knowledge of God. But a theologian must by definition want to know about God. It is in accordance with this principle that Augustine looked at the schools of philosophers he knew and grouped them by their beliefs. Broadly, he says, there are two views of the divine to be found among them. Some men believe that the universe itself is divine[39] — a view which is given some house-room in the *Timaeus*. Others have moved beyond to the idea that the divine must transcend all things in the material world, and that the world is a creation of a higher being. He sets aside all those who hold the former view and considers the others, because they come closer to the Christian position in their idea of God.

He points out that among the Platonists three views are to be found which bring them nearer to the Christian position than any other pagan philosophers.[40] These are the idea that God is the first cause of everything which exists. The 'natural philosophers' have made this discovery. Secondly, God is the

[37] William of Conches, op. cit., p. 62, para. VI.

[38] *Theologia Christiana*, p. 147.538.

[39] Augustine *De Civitate Dei*, VIII, 5. The study of the *Timaeus* became popular in certain schools about the same time as that of Boethius' theological tractes.

[40] *De Civitate Dei*, VIII, 5.

principle of reason and the source of all rational thought. This is the discovery of 'rational philosophy' or logic. Thirdly, the notion that God makes the rules of right living underlies 'moral philosophy' or ethics.[41] His purpose is to find a place for philosophical studies in Christian thought; if those philosophers who lived before Christian times lived now, they would have found their system of thought completed and perfected by Christian teaching. If philosophy has a place lower than theology, in its higher forms it is in general sympathy with its aims, and indeed the two might be said to become one. The tenor of Augustine's account is optimistic. In so far as a philosopher seeks to know God he is studying theology and Augustine makes no distinction between the methods of thought involved at this level; in this sense, theology is philosophy for Augustine.

It is not possible for his twelfth-century successors to take so bold a view, or indeed so simple a view, because the tendency of their scholarship was to subdivide, to look for differences of method and content. They discovered a great many specific points on which the views of the *philosophi* proved difficult or even impossible to reconcile with Christian teaching.[42] Contemporary thinkers found that the *philosophi* were still very much with them, in the persons of scholars who found their opinions forceful; *philosophi dicunt* has a certain immediacy about it in twelfth-century writings.[43] Augustine's attempt to find common ground between theology and philosophy raised at least as many questions as it settled for medieval thinkers. Where Augustine saw consensus among the most able of pagan philosophers they began to find what Calvin calls a 'shameful diversity' among thinkers who tried to learn about God through reason and the human sciences alone.[44]

In his discussions of natural and civil theology and mythical or poetical theology Augustine suggests that there may be more than one kind of *theologia*. Pseudo-Dionysius had

---

[41] On Augustine's Christian philosophy in general, see R. Holte *Béatitude et sagesse* (Paris, 1962). This study is primarily concerned with the teleological aspects of the thought of Augustine and the philosophers on whom he draws.

[42] William of Conches op. cit., p. 62, para VI.

[43] Cf. Gilbert of Poitiers, p. 127.52, p. 128.80.

[44] Calvin, *Institutes*, I. v. 12.

implied something rather different in his teaching about the many theologies to which Thierry of Chartres refers.[45] He had suggested that there might be a theology of God himself, a theology of created spirits and a pagan theology (which must be treated with contempt).[46] The mid-twelfth-century *Ysagoge in Theologiam* teaches that the first elements of theology have to do with the human nature (*natura humana*) the more advanced aspects with angelic beings (*provectus in angelica*) and only the consummation of the study of theology with the divine nature (*consummatio autem in divina*).[47] The lower theologies are all theologies in the Boethian sense because they deal with spiritual beings and thus with incorporeal things;[48] but they are not all theologies in the sense common to Augustine and Boethius, that they are directed towards knowing God. Also from Pseudo-Dionysius comes the idea that theology may be either affirmative or negative, that it may try to tell us what God is or be able to say only what he is not. 'The theology of negation denies that any word can apply to God.'[49] Affirmative theology concedes that some things may properly be said of him.[50] Almost as soon, then, as the term *theologia* came into use in the schools as a relatively technical term to describe an academic study, its reference was being further subdivided in the cause of still greater precision of usage. A great deal more might be said about the implications of the 'many theologies', but for our immediate purposes the importance of this development is plain enough: it is a sign that the word *theologia* was being employed by scholars who wanted to give it an academically acceptable frame of reference and to make it a more exact technical term. A determination to avoid confusion and blurred meaning is evident; this is perhaps an inevitable concomitant of the attempt to impose a single label on a study at once so vast and complex and so ancient in its various traditions.

[45] *Thierry of Chartres*, p. 246.55.　　　　[46] Ibid.
[47] *Ysagoge in Theologiam*, p. 64.3.　　[48] *Thierry of Chartres*, p. 126.33-4.
[49] *Thierry of Chartres*, p. 309.23.　　　[50] *Thierry of Chartres*, p. 502.68-9.

ii. Theology and the Three Traditions

The study of the Bible; a speculative theology which was dependent to a considerable extent upon the secular *philosophia* and in particular upon the liberal arts;[51] and a polemical or missionary theology designed to refute the views of unbelievers. These were the ingredients of the new academic theology. They are in many ways significantly different in their purposes and in the methods appropriate to them, as theologians have always found. For twelfth-century thinkers the most urgent task was to decide the ways in which these branches of theology could legitimately[52] throw light upon one another and, accordingly, to superimpose a working organization of material upon them, so that they could be systematically studied. The urge to find a principle of organization was present in Hugh of St. Victor when he wrote the *De Sacramentis Ecclesiae*, in Rupert of Deutz and Peter Lombard and Alan of Lille and a dozen other scholars who attempted to write comprehensive theological textbooks of one kind or another. These books are so very different in form and structure that their variety alone would tell us that this was a period of experiment. But they all have in common the intention of making the study of theology orderly, and each of these authors has some concept of theology as a distinct discipline.

The Bible was the great central textbook here, but the writings of the Fathers ran it close in importance and interest in the schools. By far the largest and most solid of the three traditions was that of the study of *sacra scriptura*. Aquinas sets out ten points at the very beginning of the first book of the *Summa Theologica,* where he considers the scope and purpose of the discipline. The first nine lead up to what he sees as the principal consideration: how are we to expound Holy Scripture? The study of the Bible and the Fathers never lost its pre-eminence in the process of organization of the subject-matter of theology which went on throughout the twelfth century. The tradition was far too strong for that, and also perhaps too bulky in the sheer quantity of material

[51] Rupert of Deutz, *CCCM* XXIV (1972), p. 2041.
[52] Ibid., p. 2040-1.

which was available to students of Scripture from patristic times and later. For the Fathers themselves, and the early medieval scholars who came after them, theology was concerned with the study of the Bible and there was no topic of dogmatics which could not be subsumed under that heading.[53] There was little need to accommodate a further tradition of speculative theology as twelfth-century scholars found it necessary to do.

Aquinas did not find it possible to construct an order of study which would be helpful to beginners and which, at the same time, followed the sequence of the Bible itself. He begins with a treatise on the existence and nature of God, and goes on to look at the Trinity, creation, angels, the work of the six days of creation, man, and the divine ordering of the universe, before passing on to other matters. This pattern of study conforms in part to the sequence of events in Genesis, but it cannot be made to do so altogether if it is to keep to the hierarchical arrangement of the material which seems appropriate to Aquinas. Systematic commentary, beginning with Genesis, cannot be adjusted easily to the needs of a speculative theology which is concerned with topics of doctrinal theory, and where the order of treatment is dictated by logic rather than by the Bible. Twelfth-century scholars produced a number of alternative schemes, some more consistent than others, and some quite disorderly in their treatment,[54] but all prompted by an attempt to find a way round the discrepancy between Scriptural order and the order dictated by the demands of the classroom for a means of teaching methodically.

This discrepancy at first resulted in some relatively piecemeal attempts to deal with one question at a time: the Sentences of the School of Laon, for example, or the *quaestiones* with which Abelard interrupts the sequences of his *Commentary on Romans*.[55] But as they increased in

[53] On the notion of 'Biblical theology' see Ebeling, *Wort und Glaube*, Vol. I (Tubingen, 1963), p. 79 ff.

[54] With Honorius' *Elucidarium*, which has already been mentioned as an early attempt to bring all theology together, might be compared Simon of Tournai's *Disputationes*, ed. J. Warichez, *SSLov.* 12 (1932).

[55] On these developments, see B. Smalley, *The Study of the Bible in the Middle Ages* (Oxford 1952). On Anselm of Laon, and the *Sentences* of the school, see O. Lottin, *Psychologie et morale aux xiie et xiiie siècles*, V (Gembloux, 1959).

number these questions came to be considered collectively
and not individually, and attempts were made to arrange
them systematically. The need for organization which marks
the early development of an academic discipline begins to be
apparent.

At the same time, scriptural commentators, too, were
beginning to look at their task as a whole. Side by side with
explorations of the possibility of constructing a sensible
topical arrangement of issues of dogmatics went a new
systematic approach to Bible study. Hugh of St. Victor went
about this by making use of secular studies as an aid. His
Didascalicon is intended to make the reader a more competent
student of Holy Scripture by giving him a training in the
liberal arts; it is designed to teach him systematically all that
he needs to know if he is to avoid elementary misunderstandings and develop sound habits of working when he reads the
Bible. In his *De Sacramentis Ecclesiae* Hugh composed a
work which comes close to being a theological *summa,* but it
is not like Aquinas' *Summa Theologica*; there is no question
of its being anything but complementary to the study of the
Bible.[56]

Perhaps no one tried to review the study of the Bible as a
whole from so original a standpoint as Rupert of Deutz. This
monastic scholar of the early twelfth century divided the
subject-matter of the Bible into three, so that each section
represents the work of one of the Persons of the Trinity. The
conception is historical, or at least chronological, in that
Father, Son, and Holy Spirit are envisaged as presiding over
successive ages.[57] Rupert's arrangement does not in fact
simply follow the books of the Bible in order. It may be that
he originally intended that it should, since he follows such
an arrangement closely throughout until he reaches the work
of the Holy Spirit in Book 34. Then, having concluded his
brief study of the Gospels, he is obliged to mingle material
from Old and New Testament books, making special use of

[56] He intends both approaches to work together at the level of close reading
and detailed solution of specific difficulties.

[57] Rupert of Deutz, *De Trinitate et Operibus Eius,* ed. R. Haacke, *CCCM* XXI–
XXIV, XXI, p. 122. On Rupert's life and work, see D. M. Magrassi *Teologia e
storia nel pensiero di Ruperto di Deutz* (Rome, 1959).

Romans (Book 37) in order to finish his plan. Even if the scheme as he originally conceived it could not be worked out with the elegance and simplicity he might have wished, it is, in its essence, very straightforward. He has made the experiment of providing an organizing principle which will be readily understood by any reader, which is workable and flexible for the author himself, and which has the additional merit of accommodating both what the Bible says about the nature of God and what it teaches about him through historical events. Thus Rupert includes a study of the doctrine of the Trinity and an enquiry into God's actions in the world in a sequence of Bible-study. This cannot be called an academic theology in any sense Aquinas would have recognized, though it had some following in the work of the succeeding centuries.[58] But Rupert's attempt to bring everything the Bible says about God to order, to organize and subdivide his material, has been prompted by that urge to arrange large bodies of material for study which was soon to show itself as the characteristic pattern of development in the schools of the twelfth century. One of the first requirements of an academic study is that its subject-matter shall be looked at as a whole by those engaged in it, with a view to its reduction to some sort of order. In that sense, Rupert of Deutz must be rated one of these early forerunners, a man of grand vision, who did not yet perhaps see what kind of a study theology was to become, but who felt the first pressure of the need to make it an integrated discipline and tried to meet it.

Rupert seems undaunted by the size of such an undertaking. The desire to achieve a broad view of the whole has provided the motive force for a very ambitious exercise. Peter Lombard, too, possessed the ability to organize his material, together with the desire to provide a book which will be all-embracing, which such an undertaking requires. At the beginning of his *Sentences* he says that he has put together the opinions of the Fathers in a short book (*brevi volumine complicans Patrum sententias*) so that it will not be necessary for his readers to search through many volumes. He hopes to

[58] On Rupert's immediate influence, see H. Lubac *Exegese medievale* (Aubier, 1961), 2 vols., II^i p. 227.

save them labour.[59] But he has done more. He has arranged the *sententiae* in an order which is independent of that of the books of the Bible and he has tried to provide easily-grasped principles of arrangement to make them accessible. He points out that every study has to do with things themselves or with symbols of things (*de rebus vel de signis*) and that the Bible is concerned with both. It furnishes a complete *doctrina* or body of learning in itself.[60] The thinking of the theologians (*theologorum speculatio*) has therefore only to keep to the rules indicated in Holy Scripture to arrive at the truth.[61] His scheme was so successful in making itself acceptable to succeeding generations that in Aquinas' youth the *Sentences* constituted the chief textbook on theology, after the Bible itself.

That may be put down in part to the way in which Peter Lombard had (as he had intended to do) made it unnecessary for most students to read the Fathers for themselves at all. His textbook had the appeal of a convenient reference-book to works which would otherwise have been important reading matter in themselves. He cannot be said to have written a *summa* of theology in Aquinas' sense. But side by side with the development of the *glossa ordinaria*, the standard school commentary on the Bible which he himself helped to fix in its twelfth-century form,[62] the handbook of *Sentences* kept the study of Scripture in the central position it had always occupied and encouraged the taking of a grand view of the whole of the Bible rather than a concentration upon individual books. St. Bernard speaks of the definition of faith as the first threshold of theology (the *primum limen*),[63] as several of his contemporaries do; this was the point of departure for a study of dogmatics in which numerous questions and answers of varying degrees of importance had to be dealt with systematically. It is exactly this phenomenon which Aquinas says has made him feel so strongly the need for a unified treatment.[64] Peter Lombard was trying to meet a

---

[59] Petrus Lombardus, *Sententiae, Prologue*, para. 5.
[60] Ibid., Book I, Dist. i, ch. i, para. i.   [61] Ibid., Book I, Dist. i, ch. i. para. ii.
[62] See B. Smalley, op. cit., p. 64.   [63] *PL* 182.1061.
[64] *Summa Theologica, Prologue*.

need which had become clear to him as he taught — the need of a student in a busy school for a convenient work of reference. Rupert's monastic readers did not have to contend with the pressure of an ever-growing syllabus of studies. He could allow himself a leisureliness of treatment denied to Peter Lombard and his pupils.

Rupert's very different conception of the purpose of 'doing theology' is made plain in the letter he addressed to Bishop Thietmar with his commentary on the Song of Songs. He sees exposition of the Bible as a form of preaching 'The bells of the divine words are golden', he says (*Nam verba divina tintinabula sunt aurea*).[65] By commenting on Scripture Rupert is making its sound ring out. He hopes the sound is pleasing.[66] He is engaged in the first of the three forms of exegesis which St. Jerome had distinguished: the homily, the commentary, and the *scholia* (or detailed notes on especially difficult passages). This desire to preach was the inspiration of Augustine's homiletic scriptural commentaries and of Gregory the Great's *Moralia* on the book of Job. The spirit of Rupert's grand new view of Scriptural commentary as a whole is still close to the monastic tradition of *lectio divina* from which it proceeds, and which is founded on patristic exegesis. He praises Thietmar for being *studiosus et intentus . . . lectioni divina,*[67] zealous and industrious in holy reading.

There was an element of the devotional in the monastic study of the Bible which is far less in evidence in the academic study of Scripture in the schools. 'The faithful mind', says Rupert, 'dwells on the word of God.'[68] There 'ought to be a great fervour' in the work.[69] For monastic scholars the *studium sacrae scripturae* continued to be a 'zeal' as well as a 'study', a passion as well as an investigation. There is every reason to suppose that some of the academic theologians of the later twelfth and thirteenth centuries saw it in this light still, yet the element of fervour necessarily became a mere

---

[65] Rupert of Deutz, *Commentary on the Song of Songs,* ed. R. Haacke, *CCCM* XXVI, p. 3.10–11.   [66] Ibid., p. 4.57.

[67] Ibid., p. 3.9.   [68] Prologue, ibid., p. 5.18.

[69] Prologue, *De Victoria Verbi Dei,* ed. R. Haacke, *MGH, Quellen,* V (1970), p. 4.5.

adjunct to a syllabus which dealt with what can be known and learnt by the rational methods which lend themselves to systematic teaching. Mystical and devotional writing increasingly became the province of monastic scholarship and the clarifying and fresh organization of the subject-matter of Holy Scripture for study in the schools involved some loss of an element indispensable to the purposes of *lectio divina.*

For the strongest influence in forming the new conception of orderliness and rational method in the treatment of Scripture and dogmatics we must look to the liberal arts. The author of the *Ysagoge in Theologiam* emphasizes that the *scientiarum instrumenta*, the instruments of the sciences, are definition, division, and argumentation or comparison.[70] With the aid of this scientific method it is possible to arrange and work upon the subject-matter (*subiectam artare materiam*) of any discipline. It is proposed that the same instruments should be used in *theologia,* that they shall be borrowed for use in what is already being treated as another academic discipline. By this means, argues our author, an orderly treatment of Holy Scripture and all the questions it raises may be attempted, and a clear explanation provided.[71]

The use of the *artes* was by no means as uncontroversial as it is made to appear here. Bernard writes in a letter to Cardinal Stephen that Peter Abelard had been introducing beginners in dialectic who can barely grasp the first elements of the faith (*qui . . . prima fidei elementa vix sustinere possunt*)[72] to the mystery of the Holy Trinity. Abelard himself, he claims elsewhere, is an old master of the arts turned new theologian (*novum de veteri magistro theologum*),[73] himself a rank beginner in the higher study, who presumes to teach what he does not yet understand. Bernard's objection is not principally to Abelard's conception of the scope of the subject or of the way in which it may be organized, but to the specific errors into which he is led when he applies the techniques of the *artes* to the study of Holy Scripture. Had the *artes* done no more than suggest methods of arranging and dividing the material for consideration there might have

---

[70] *Ysagoge in Theologiam*, p. 64.7-11.   [71] Ibid., p. 64.25.
[72] *PL* 182.537, *Letter* 331.   [73] *PL* 182.1055, *Letter* 190.

been less difficlty. But they taught scholars to argue, and Bernard's particular objection is that they provided a ready but specious facility in handling deep questions. Without a solid foundation of years of reflective study of Holy Scripture Peter Abelard merely 'raves' about the Bible (*nunc in Scripturis sanctis insanit*).[74] The two methods of approach, the tradition of slow absorption through *lectio divina,* and that of rapid over-all mastery through the study of the *artes,* ground against one another with increasing force as the detailed implications of their differences became apparent. The study of the *artes* provided not only a stimulus to orderliness but also a good deal of contradiction of purpose.

The emotional energy which was generated in this way makes itself felt in the Prologue to Peter Lombard's *Sentences.* The work was, he says, conceived as a defensive exercise against propounders of false doctrine,[75] as much as a convenient reference book for students with a limited knowledge of patristic writings. The 'unbelievers' or *dialectici haeretici* of the schools caused as much anxiety as the self-confessed heretics and holders of other faiths to whom most of the better-known scholars of the day addressed themselves in at least one treatise. The opposition to orthodox teaching on all fronts posed a threat to the survival of a tradition of sound doctrine which it is difficult for us now to assess. It was not perhaps as great as that which faced the Christians of the first centuries whose task was to lay down the lines of that tradition. The task of the twelfth-century scholar was to maintain it, and to find means of accommodating newly-perceived difficulties in the general scheme. But it is not necessarily easier to keep to a road than to find it in the first place, and dialecticians had a way of altering the signposts of thought which made it difficult for many of their pupils to lay hold on a reassuring sense of direction.

The academic theologians of the twelfth century developed their academic methods in the face of a strongly-felt threat to orthodoxy. Yet the effect of the existence of unbelievers was far from being a negative one. We are dealing with a

<hr/>

[74] Ibid.   [75] *Prologue,* p. 4.

polemical or missionary rather than an apologetic theology. Perhaps the most positive result of the abrasive contact of the three branches of theology with one another was the way in which it encouraged the development of the clear thinking and precision of language which traditionally identify the academic discipline — and which are, indeed, what make it a discipline.

4. Method

It was said that Gilbert of Poitier's teaching was difficult for beginners to understand (*novis obscurior*) but that to more advanced students he seemed to give a full and sound treatment (*sed provectis compendiosior et solidior videbatur*).[1] This was worthy of remark because few of his contemporaries made the same difficulties for the beginners among their pupils. A great deal of effort went into making the subject-matter of the arts clear and straightforward. Above all that meant being methodical. This presented no special difficulty to the master who lectured on the textbooks of the liberal arts if he confined himself to the rather limited procedure of following the text and explaining each obscure point and unfamiliar word as it arose. The Scriptural commentator could do much the same for Scripture. But these relatively straightforward procedures appeared less satisfactory at the beginning of the twelfth century than they had done a hundred years earlier, because questions were now being raised — even in the elementary schoolroom it seems[2] — which could not be settled quickly and without reference to other texts and other masters' opinions. One response to this was to pause long enough in the exposition to treat each problem separately as a question or *quaestio*.[3] But what was involved was something more than a mechanical difficulty which made it necessary to interrupt the flow of exposition.

It was also a methodological difficulty increasingly often

[1] *Historia Pontificalis*, p. 27.
[2] Abelard gives an example from his own days as a pupil, Abelard, *Dialectica*, p. 59.
[3] Abelard's *Commentary on Romans* in interrupted by a series of *quaestiones* of this kind. On the development of the gloss and the *quaestio* see B. Smalley, *The Study of the Bible in the Middle Ages* (Oxford, 1952), Chapter 2.

presented by the comparison of one text with another. In the later twelfth century, in the *Sentences* of Peter of Poitiers, for example, it is possible to see the beginnings of the technique the scholastic theologians of the thirteenth century evolved to meet this difficulty. Peter introduces questions with some such expressions as: 'It is asked whether' or: 'It is often asked'. He then gives a set of explanations to show that a given view 'seems to hold' or 'does not seem to hold' (*quod videtur, quod non videtur*).[4] This is not as yet systematically done, but it was becoming urgently necessary to devise a method which would allow comparisons to be made between the viewpoints of different authorities, or between the rules and principles of the different arts, or between the principles of secular studies and the study of the Bible.

Descartes wrote a *Discourse sur la Méthode,* a treatise on *the* method. When it becomes clear that a problem of method exists, the first need is to determine whether a universal method may be applicable to all kinds of study or whether each has its own peculiar rules. At the beginning of the *De Hebdomadibus* Boethius tries to define the nature of an axiom. It is, he says, the self-evident notion which everyone understands and accepts as soon as he hears it. These are, he suggests, 'common'; they are *communes animi conceptiones*.[5] But there are two kinds of axiom, those which are mere commonplaces, and those which seem axiomatic only to educated people who understand how they have been derived from the fundamental axioms which are obvious to everyone. Gilbert of Poitiers is quick to identify these more advanced axioms with the rules or principles of the liberal arts. Each art, he suggests, has its own kind of axiom: rhetoric has topics or commonplaces, dialectic has major premises, geometry has theorems, and so on.[6] These self-evident notions are not dead statements; they do not constitute an end in themselves, rather they are useful instruments for the student of the art in question. Out of them the peculiar methodology of each art develops. They are, in other words, the rules of the arts, the laws which distinguish them from one another,

---

[4] *Sententie Petri Pictavensis*, ed. P. S. Moore, M. Dulong (Notre Dame, Indiana, 1943), I. xv, and see p. xix on *regulae*.
[5] *Theological Tractates*, p. 40.   [6] Gilbert of Poitiers, p. 189.67–p. 190.75.

and which are not transferable without qualification or modification.

Alan of Lille took Gilbert's account a little further in his *Regulae Theologicae,* in order to show how the same view of the distinctiveness of different methods may help to place theology among the traditional disciplines. Theology too has its rules. These are pre-eminent over all others in their difficulty and subtlety (*sui obscuritate et subtilitate caeteris preeminentes*).[7] They are essentially more difficult rules, of another order than the rules of the secular arts and pagan philosophy. Indeed they carry a categorical necessity which is even greater than the obviousness of other axioms (*necessitas theologiarum maximarum absoluta est et irrefragibilis*),[8] both *in se* and *quoad nos.* Like the laws of other disciplines they are instruments of argument. Cicero defines an argument as that which creates belief,[9] and Alan emphasizes that this is exactly the function of theological laws (*fidem faciunt*).[10] The beliefs they create are not open to modification by deed or action or by anything in nature. Therefore theological method carries more weight of conviction than any other.

But while the rules of the liberal arts are not difficult to discover from the traditional textbooks, the laws of theology are not so easily found. Alan has had to formulate them himself, restating principles he has borrowed from the arts for the purpose, and arguably he has not entirely succeeded in fulfilling the promise of his high claims for them. Before he begins, he concedes that theological axioms are mysterious; they are *paradoxae, aenigmata, emblemata,* grasped, in so far as they are grasped at all, by the most refined acuteness of the mind (*puriore mentis acumine comprehenduntur*). They are self-evident only to the deepest levels of the mind (*intus in mente latentia*).[11] The theory of distinctiveness of method serves well enough to locate theology among the other disciplines in a general way, but only Alan attempted to work out its implications in a comprehensive theory in the twelfth

---

[7] *PL* 210.621–2.   [8] Ibid.
[9] Cicero, *Topics,* II.8.   [10] *PL* 210.622.   [11] Ibid.

century, and he found that immense practical difficulties stood in his way.

Gilbert of Poitiers was concerned rather with the particular difficulties which arose when the methods of one discipline were adapted for use in another. John of Salisbury explains that he believed that the disciplines were interrelated (*connexae*) and that they could serve the theologian directly, but he was anxious to confine the rules of each discipline to matters for which they were appropriate (*et cohibebat omnium regulas infra proprii generis limitem*).[12] The authors of a number of school textbooks on logic shared Gilbert's interest in the *regulae* and *principia* proper to each discipline. They tell us that a rule (*regula*) is so-called because it governs or directs the practitioner of an art. A principle (*principium*) derives its name from the fact that it is the first thing to be learned in the art. A maxim (*maxima*) is named after the great force of necessity (*maxima necessitas*) it carries. A precept (*preceptum*) is so-called because it instructs the practitioner of the art what he is to do. A topic (*locus*) is a subdivision or 'place' in which a section of the art is contained.[13] A knowledge of the rules gives the beginner a great sense of security, and as long as the rules proper to each art were confined to it, the new developments in method served exactly the purpose for which they were designed. They made it easier for beginners to learn. But the temptation to try out the rules of one discipline in another was strong, especially when it became possible to treat theology as an academic discipline.

If we are to argue that a methodical approach is the key-note of the new development we must look for evidence that twelfth-century scholars were seeking a special method for the use of theologians. Thierry of Chartres does so by comparing theological method not with the methods of individual arts but, more generally, with philosophical method. On some matters, he says, the philosophers agree with Holy Scripture (*philosophi cum sanctis scripturis concordant*); on others they do not.[14] Abelard points out that there are false

---

[12] *Historia Pontificalis*, p. 27.
[13] *LM* II^{ii} p. 357.12-6, *Introductiones Parisienses*; p. 379.2-8, *Logica ut dicit*.
[14] *Thierry of Chartres*, p. 74.91-4.

philosophers (*pseudo-philosophi*, who may be compared with the false theologians or heretics); they being philosophical reasons against Christians and they can be met only on their own ground, for they will accept only philosophical reasoning.[15] The methods of the two disciplines had to be set side by side for comparison if only because the *philosophi* were still making their presence felt in contemporary discussions.

In Thierry of Chartres's commentaries on Boethius there are a number of references to 'philosophizing' and 'theologizing' which suggest that the techniques appropriate to each were clearly distinguished in Thierry's mind. He accuses the man who 'claims falsely that there are many unities' of 'not philosophizing correctly'.[16] Theologians who philosophise about God (*theologi qui de Deo philosophantur*)[17] are likely to go astray because they are attempting to use the methods of one discipline in the context of another. Thierry and his pupils refer to 'speaking theologically' (*theologice loqui*),[18] 'thinking theologically' (*ita theologice de Trinitate sentendiendum est*),[19] and, again, 'speaking theologically' (*theologice dicere*).[20] The last is of particular interest because Thierry believes that this is what Hilary of Poitiers taught; he does not see the notion of 'speaking theologically' as anything new.

In their analyses of Boethius' arguments in the theological tractates Thierry of Chartres and Gilbert of Poitiers discuss theological and philosophical 'reasons'. Thierry explains at one point that Boethius is using 'Arguments taken from theological sources [or topics], that is, he draws his arguments from theology (*sed deinceps utetur ad hoc argumentis sumptis ex locis theologicis, i.e. trahet argumenta ex theologica*). He defends them (*secundum theologicas rationes*).[21] The idea that theological, mathematical, and physical *rationes* carry different weights in different contexts is frequently put

---

[15] *Theologia Christiana,* p. 297.1033-7.   [16] *Thierry of Chartres,* p. 90.19.
[17] Ibid., p. 543.74.   [18] Ibid., p. 224.42.   [19] Ibid., p. 224.41.
[20] Ibid., p. 501.58; cf. *PL* 10.51, and Augustine *De Trinitate,* VI.10.11.
[21] Ibid., p. 137.43-5.

forward to explain an anomaly,[22] as is the principle that
philosophi and *ethici* and *logici* and *theologici* use words in
different ways.[23] *Philosophi* and *theologici* with their modes
of reasoning are contrasted with one another directly.[24] We
are usually expected to understand the difference without
explanation. Although this tendency to assume a knowledge
in the reader indicates that the distinction was quite commonly understood — at least among the pupils of Thierry and
Gilbert themselves — it leaves a good deal obscure to the
modern reader. Thierry says that he speaks *secundum theologicas rationes* when he says that there are three Persons in
the Godhead and yet there is no plurality. He pauses to
explain that 'theological reasons' are subject to 'theological
considerations' (*secundum considerationem theologice*), but
the nature of theological considerations in general is not
made plain. Thierry restricts himself to an account of the
differences between the mathematical laws governing plurality
and those which operate in the case of the Trinity.[25] Thierry,
like many of his immediate contemporaries, has far more to
tell us about the details of his development of specific pieces
of theological method than about its essential differences
from philosophical and other methods. The process seems to
have been not unlike that which John Bunyan describes in
his *The Authors Apology* before *Pilgrim's Progress*:

> For having now my Method by the end,
> Still as I pull'd, it came; and so I penn'd
> It down; until at last it came to be,
> For length and breadth the bigness which you see.

What is lacking in broad vision is made up for in per-
serverance, and Thierry and his fellows were to make it
possible for later generations to see the issues involved more
largely, and to attach more than a nominal significance to the
recognition that theological method is different from philosophical method.

In the *Dialectica* which has traditionally been ascribed to

---

[22] Gilbert of Poitiers, p. 89.12; p. 294-90.   [23] Ibid., p. 243.12.
[24] Ibid., p. 194.78-87.   [25] *Thierry of Chartres*, p. 154.19-p. 155.22.

Augustine[26] a distinction is made between the *facultas dialecticae* and the *dialectica disciplina*, skill in dialectic and the formal discipline of dialectic. The author's meaning is made a little clearer by an example. The speeches of Cicero, he says, are examples of rhetorical skill (*rhetoricae facultatis*) but they do not directly teach rhetoric (*non in his docetur rhetorica*).[27] They are not, in other words, manuals of instruction. In Cicero himself *facultas* seems to have the sense of a natural gift (*facultas ab natura profecta*). He contrasts it with the gift developed by study and practice, with *ars, studium*, and *exercitatio*.[28] (Not until the thirteenth century did *facultas* come to refer to an academic institution, or to the department of such an institution in which a particular discipline or group of disciplines was studied — the 'faculty of arts' or the 'faculty of theology'.) Twelfth-century usage is much closer to that of earlier writers. When Gilbert of Poitiers says that *facultates* 'differ according to the kind of thing with which they are concerned: that is, natural, mathematical, theological, civil, rational',[29] he sees the faculties as specialized skills. Thierry of Chartres, too, thought that when Boethius distinguished natural science from mathematics and theology he meant it to be understood that each study required a different skill.[30] But these are by no means untrained native skills; *facultas* is already something more than plain ability. A discipline is involved.

Moreover, this is a discipline which is taught by rote and rule, not learned by imitation. Twelfth-century students worked from the ancient manuals of rhetoric, rather than from Cicero's orations. The aim of their training was not primarily to make them performers in the discipline concerned, competent in framing arguments, able to make a stirring

---

[26] For a recent study of this work, see J. Pépin, *S. Augustin et la Dialectique* (Wetteren, 1976). On *facultas* see B. Geyer, '*Facultas theologica*: eine bedeutingsgeschichtliche Untersuchung', *Zeitschrift fur Kirchengeschichte*, 75 (1964), 133–45.   [27] *PL* 32.1411.

[28] *De Inventione*, I.i.2. Compare Gerhoch's quite different sense of *facultas* in his *Letter to Pope Hadrian*, ed. N. M. Haring (Toronto, 1974), p. 23. The word has a non-technical sense, too, in the twelfth century.

[29] Gilbert of Poitiers, p. 115.2-6.

[30] *Thierry of Chartres*, p. 68.15; p. 71.11.

speech, able to write correct Latin (although many of them derived these benefits from it), but to give them a mastery of the theory of the subject. The treatment of method was not, therefore, designed to develop a knowledge or practical methods of putting the subject-matter of the discipline to use. It served chiefly to show what kinds of differences existed between the disciplines at a theoretical level, to suggest what kinds of question might be helpful and what kinds of question were simply irrelevant to the concerns of a particular discipline. The moulding and polishing of a native ability to do something, gave way to the refinement and development of the theory of the way it should be done. *Facultas,* in its ancient sense, became *disciplina.* And the *facultates* which had been turned into disciplines became, in the thirteenth century, institutions in their own right. There could scarcely be a more striking illustration of the way in which the built-in laws of the traditional disciplines imposed a structure upon the development of the schools as institutions.

The methods proper to each discipline were distinguished; but they were also borrowed and exchanged for one another, in the hope of solving the apparently intractable problems which arose in those borderline areas where grammar overlapped with dialectic, dialectic with rhetoric, dialectic with arithmetic. *Nomen* and *verbum* are parts of speech yet nouns and verbs are the building-blocks of a dialectical proposition. Arguments by analogy (*inductio, exemplum*) are properly the province of the rhetoricians, but they may be used in dialectic, too, and the rhetoricians adapted the formal syllogism for use in the more informal and variable enthymeme. Quantity is one of the dialectical categories, but arithmetic is concerned with quantity, too, with magnitude and multitude, with discrete and continuous quantity. The more deeply the disciplines were studied the more difficult it became to ignore these difficulties and to keep the study of a given subject within bounds. Indeed there was no reason to do so. These are extremely interesting questions of common terminology and borrowed method.

Such comparisons and contrasts became more interesting still when they were extended to the new discipline of theology. Aquinas points out that God is a being who does not belong to a class.[31] The study of what can be known about him must therefore contain elements which are quite peculiar to theology and which have a kinship with other studies only by courtesy. But even if the whole of the theologian's work must be carried out by analogy, as some writers have insisted, it must make use of the aids provided by the most highly developed human arts and sciences. Habits of thought are persistent, and a man with a trained mind will not find it easy to approach a new problem in a way which owes nothing to his training. He is more likely to try to modify or adapt his training to make it applicable to the job in hand. That is what Christian theologians had done from the beginning. The teaching of the Bible had been supplemented from the first by explanations and interpretations. A complete, internally consistent, doctrinal system was fashioned in the first Christian centuries with the aid of the most sophisticated secular disciplines. There has always been philosophy in Christian theology. The experiments of twelfth-century scholars were not, therefore, entirely new, and in many respects they were timid and repetitious if they are compared with the boldness of Augustine or Boethius in attempting a reconciliation between secular and holy learning. But cautiously and systematically these scholars set about making so thorough a reconciliation that the secular arts could be applied to theological problems at every point where there was a natural or traditional point of contact, not by pioneers in the history of thought only, but by pupils who were still almost beginners — as Aquinas' readers of the *Summa Theologia* were. They reduced great problems to manageable dimensions, subjected them to simple procedures and wrought out of a vast complex of discussion something which is recognizably a body of academic disciplines.

Peter Abelard opens his commentary on Romans with the statement that 'every divine scripture is designed, like a rhetorical oration, to teach or to move' (*omnis scriptura divina more orationis rhetoricae aut docere intendit aut movere*).[32]

[31] Aquinas, *Summa Theologica,* I, Q.3, Art.5.
[32] Abelard, *Comm. Rom.,* p. 41.5–6; cf. Augustine *De Doctrina Christiana,* IV. xvii. 34; Cicero, *Orator,* 21.69.

He has asked himself why the Epistle to the Romans was written and what kind of commentary may be appropriate to it. His Prologue takes the form of a much extended *accessus,*[33] or formal introduction, in which he considers the *intentio* and the *modus tractandi,* the purpose and method of treatment of the writers of Scripture, just as he would have done if he had been examining a work of one of the *philosophi.* In trying the place the Epistle according to principles established by Augustine in the *De Doctrina Christiana* and to relate it to the more ancient tradition of classical rhetoric, he has attempted to show the place it holds in an academic tradition, and to match his own commentary to it. This is an indication of a newly emerging awareness that different kinds of study require different approaches.

'Theology has two modes of treatment proper to it, for sometimes in reasoning about the divine a man employs examples sought in external evidence, but sometimes he perceives the divine Being devoutly, without the help of created matter.'[34] In his commentary on Boethius' *De Trinitate,* written in the middle of the twelfth century, Clarenbald of Arras feels his way towards a distinction between the method of the academic theologian, who must learn to weigh external evidence, and the approach to God of the contemplative, who experiences God directly within himself in ways which are, of their nature, inaccessible to others. He and his contemporaries were beginning to see that theology may, in a strictly defined sense, constitute an academic discipline, and that in so far as it does so, it must be treated in ways proper to other academic disciplines, where the rules of argument and the laws of evidence and organization of material provide the guarantees of soundness of procedure. Clarenbald attempts to define the relation the academic disciplines of his day bear to one another in the hope of deciding the proper place for theology among them. He is prompted by Boethius to see the problem as one which turns on the difference between theology and philosophy, but even though he draws upon traditional definitions, he finds it difficult to arrive at a

[33] On the *accessus,* see R. B. C. Huygens, *Accessus ad Auctores* (Leiden, 1970).
[34] *Clarenbald of Arras,* p. 70, para. 14.

satisfactory solution. This was largely because the use of the
term *theologia* to describe an academic discipline was new,
and it was not yet quite clear what the subject-matter and
methods of that discipline comprised, although it was obvious
that it involved rather more than Boethius had envisaged in
the *De Trinitate*.

Étienne Gilson has argued that it was only with the coming
of the full tide of the influence of Arabic science and philosophy in the thirteenth century that the problem of defining the
respective kinds of knowledge proper to secular learning and
philosophy and to theology came to be acutely felt. He cites
Grosseteste, Roger Bacon, Albertus Magnus, as examples of
scholars who for the first time 'conceived the work of the
theologian in a way distinctly recognisable'.[35] They had, he
says, 'a clear awareness' that 'theology was specifically distinct
from philosophy and that faith was a mode of cognition
specifically other than natural reason'.[36] Certainly it is true
that these principles could be stated in the thirteenth century
with a clarity which was not yet possible in the twelfth. But
Clarenbald of Arras saw the difference, and a number of his
contemporaries felt the need to make the distinction.

[35] E. Gilson, *Christian Philosophy in the Middle Ages* (London, 1955), p. 275.
[36] Ibid., pp. 277–8.

II   The Study of the Bible
and the Liberal Arts

1. The Middle Way

In two of the most noisy and notorious conflicts between
academics and the Church authorities in the twelfth century,
Peter Abelard and Gilbert of Poitiers in turn faced Bernard of
Clairvaux, the Church's appointed defender of the faith, in
public trial. John of Salisbury's account of Gilbert's trial has
the impartiality and fair-mindedness which are characteristic
of his historical writing at its best, but in the cause of balance,
he perhaps oversimplifies the difference between the old
scholarship and the new. Both Gilbert and Bernard, he says,
'were most learned and eloquent, but in different branches of
study' (*Erant tamen ambo optime litterati et admodum
eloquentes, sed dissimilibus studiis*).[1] Bernard was an outstanding preacher whose knowledge of Holy Scripture was so
thorough that he was almost incapable of speaking in any
words but those of the Bible. (It is plain from Bernard's
surviving sermons that John is not exaggerating.) But Bernard,
he says, knew much less about secular learning (*seculares
litterae*). This was an area in which no one could compete
with the Bishop of Poitiers. Gilbert, on the other hand, did
not have so ready a command of Scripture. His strength lay
in his knowledge of the Fathers and the secular authors.[2] We
will let Bernard speak for himself on his knowledge of the
arts a little later. For the moment the importance of the
contrast lies in John of Salisbury's recognition that there are
two distinct ways of being learned.

John of Salisbury is careful to present the facts in such a
way as to minimize the acrimoniousness of the conflict. His re-
collections of conversation he himself had had with the partici-
pants, and his descriptions of what was said about them and
by them, are all made to suggest that the trial was conducted in
a calm and reasonable frame of mind on all sides. But we

---

[1] *Historia Pontificalis*, p. 27.   [2] Ibid.

know that Bernard was an impassioned speaker and that Gilbert himself could be fiery when stirred. 'You would do best to find him roused', says John, 'so that he would illuminate you with the fire of his mind and warm you with his power.'[3] Other authors deal with conflicts between the new academic and the conventional monastic scholar in a more aggressive tone. William of St. Thierry and others concentrated on the particular offences of individuals. Gerhoch of Reichersberg and Geoffrey of Auxerre and Walter of St. Victor in his diatribe againtst 'the four labyrinths of France' splutter their disapproval of the new theological scholarship in general.[4]

Underlying the fear and anger and resentment such encounters produced in the combatants is, however, a problem which is not easily resolved even in cold blood. John of Salisbury puts his finger on it when he describes the differences between Bernard's learning and that of Gilbert of Poitiers. It is not easy for a man to understand what he does not know. The old school of the study of the Bible had not required any extensive knowledge of the secular arts — nothing, in fact beyond a little elementary grammar. But the new breed of academic theologian approached ancient mysteries with a new confidence, with the aid of techniques which were unfamiliar and even incomprehensible to traditional biblical scholarship. They assumed that the knowledge they had would serve as well in theology as it did in the liberal arts. Bernard accused Abelard of precisely this attempt to set himself up as a theologian when his expertise as a scholar lay in dialectic, and even the gentle Anselm, himself no enemy of dialectical method sensibly applied, accused the *dialectici haeretici* of approaching the study of the Bible without reverence, and without respect for a proper procedure

---

[3] Ibid.

[4] The only major general biography of Abelard is still J. Sikes, *Peter Abailard* (Cambridge, 1932). For a more recent bibliography, see D. Luscombe, *The School of Peter Abelard* (Cambridge, 1969). On Gilbert, see H. C. van Elswijk, *Gilbert Porreta, SSLov,* 33 (1966). Geoffrey's *Libellus* is in *PL* 185.595-618; Gerhoch of Reichersberg's *Letter to Pope Hadrian about the Novelties of the Day* is edited by N. M. Haring (Toronto, 1974); Walter of St Victor's *Contra Quattuor Labyrinthos Franciae* is edited by P. Glorieux *AHDLMA* xix (1952), 187-335. William of St. Thierry's *Epistola ad Fratres de Monte Dei, PL* 184.

which was different from their own.[5]

Before we look at the results of this new consciousness of differences of method which was to occupy academic theologians for several generations, something must be said about the quite uncontroversial spirit in which many monastic scholars applied their knowledge of the arts to the study of the Bible. Angry words capture the attention in a way that ordinary working practices do not, and work of this kind has often gone unnoticed. It was not an approach which was to prove fruitful of new ideas, and it soon gave way to more searching exercises on the part of scholars who saw the areas of conflict more clearly. But for earlier twelfth-century scholars the arts often formed a perfectly acceptable aid to Bible study.

Peter Abelard and Gilbert of Poitiers were exceptional in their knowledge of dialectic, but they were also notorious for other reasons. The opprobrium attached to their work in the arts did not touch Richard of St. Victor, for example, daring though his theology sometimes was, and widely though his influence extended. Thierry of Chartres, although he was a scholar with a rare command of the technicalities of the arts, and used them widely in his own theological commentaries, was never brought to trial for heresy. It was not, strictly speaking, the use of the *artes* in itself which caused disquiet, but the way in which it could give rise to dangerous misunderstandings. Abelard and Gilbert of Poitiers made no concessions to their weaker pupils,[6] and it is beyond question that their opinions were sometimes misrepresented when they were reported.[7] It is not difficult to understand how real or supposed errors of doctrine made by outstanding masters of the art of dialectic came to be attributed to the influence of dialectical studies, and dialectic itself came under suspicion. Frequently there were good grounds for such suspicion, and dialectic certainly brought scholars into conflict with orthodox opinion even where it was not abused. But if we look only at the real or imaginary points of con-

[5] *Anselmi Opera Omnia,* II.9.21–2; cf. *PL* 185.1055, Bernard's Letter 190.

[6] See Geoffrey of Auxerre, *PL* 185.609.

[7] On this history of the Abelardian, *Capitula Haeresim* see M. Buytaert, *Petri Abelardi Opera Theologica,* CCCM XII, pp. 458–467.

flict we shall fail to see that for a good many of Abelard's immediate contemporaries the use of the arts in Scriptural commentary was relatively uncontroversial. It required caution but it was not intrinsically objectionable. It was open to abuse, but there was a proper and acceptable place for it.

Hugh of St. Victor saw no difficulty if the arts were regarded as the handmaids of theology — that is, if they were kept in their proper place as its servants. In his *Didascalicon* he sets out a programme of preliminary study of the arts which is quite unambitious in its treatment of technical problems. The emphasis is placed on thorough mastery of a general method of approach to the reading of the Bible. Hugh's pupil is to learn first to look at the grammatical structure of each passage, so as to understand the 'letter' (*littera*); then he is to examine the surface meaning of the words, their obvious sense or *aperta significatio*; finally he is to look beneath the surface for the deeper meaning or *sententia*.[8] In this way he will avoid making mistakes of interpretation through careless misunderstandings, and he will find his knowledge of the arts of language useful because it will help him keep to proper procedures in his interpretations. The arts are not allowed to obtrude. They pose no questions on their own account.

The contrast between the atmosphere in which the arts were studied in this way in monastic schools and the contentious atmosphere created by Gilbert of Poitier's teaching, is plain enough. There can be few more neglected or more informative instances of this quiet absorption of the methods of the *artes* into the technical procedures of Scriptural commentary than the work of Rupert of Deutz. This Benedictine contemporary of Hugh of St. Victor would have been substantially in agreement with him on the wisdom of his practice of teaching the liberal arts to young men who were beginning to study the Bible. He gives an account of the usefulness of the arts in his enormous work on the study of Holy

---

[8] *Didascalicon*, III.ix, *De Ordine Legendi*, PL 176.771 and ed. C. Buttimer (Washington, 1939), pp. 58–9.

Scripture, *On the Holy Trinity and his Works.* Rupert teaches his system of Bible study partly by theoretical discussion and partly by means of example. He tries to demonstrate the value of the arts, rather as Augustine had done in the *De Doctrina Christiana,* by looking for instances of stylistic and other technical devices in the text of the Bible itself. Cassiodorus had done much the same in his *Exposition of the Psalms* and so had Bede in his *De Schematibus et Tropis.* Both Hugh of St. Victor[9] and Rupert of Deutz approach the study of the *artes* in the expectation of finding them straightforwardly helpful.

When Rupert describes the passage in Revelation which tells of John's receiving the book from the angel (10: 9–10) he says that John 'read the book as he devoured it and devoured it as he read it, with the eye of his mind' (*et intellectuali oculo sic librum et legendo devoravit et devorando legit*).[10] He reached for his pen even as he read (*sumpsit calamum*). Rupert sees John's hunger as a yearning to understand the divine mysteries so that he could pour out again in writing what he had learned, and show all those who were in error where the truth lay. Rupert himself wanted to learn so that he could teach, not what was new and controversial, but what was eternally true. There is no hard-edged intellectual curiosity about him, but a gentler habit of mind. He prefers to encourage his readers to chew the food of the mind slowly and to digest it slowly,[11] to absorb the *artes* thoroughly, for they can only be of help to him in his study of Scripture. Rupert had no specialist knowledge of any of the arts. He possessed a good knowledge of the elements of grammar and dialectic, a competence in rhetoric (he had read the *De Inventione*) and, as we might expect, very little knowledge of the quadrivium subjects. What he knew could be acquired by anyone who had access to a good library within a monastic context.[12] H. Silvestre[13] has listed a number of citations

[9] Buttimer gives footnote references which make clear Hugh's debt to Augustine. [10] H XXIV., 1954.622–3.

[11] This is the characteristic exercise of *lectio divina.*

[12] For an *index auctorum* to Rupert's reading, see H XXIV.2195–217. See, too, the account of Rupert's life in H. Haacke's edition of the *De Victoria Verbi Dei, MGH, Quellen,* V (1970), F. de Lubac, *Exégèse Médiévale* (Lyons, 1959–61), 2 vols., II i.219–228, D. M. Magrassi, *Teologia e storia nel pensiero di Ruperto di Deutz* (Rome, 1959), 17–22, H. Silvestre, 'Les Citations et reminiscences classiques dans l'oeuvre de Rupert de Deutz' *Revue d'Histoire Ecclésiastique,* 45 (1950), 140–74.

13. Op. cit.

of classical and late-classical poets in Rupert's writings, together with some items from Boethius' *Consolation of Philosophy* and from Cicero. Although he does not consider Rupert's knowledge of the textbooks of the *artes*, he shows convincingly that Rupert was well-read. His reading gave him an appetite for learning of a typically monastic kind.

Hugh of St. Victor, too, although he taught in a school in close proximity to the most academically adventurous schools of Paris and northern France, was not attracted by the possibilities of using the arts in controversy. He has something new to say about methods of learning by heart, for example, or about the best way to practise a newly-acquired skill.[14] But in the *Didascalicon* he has almost nothing to say about the technicalities of the arts beyond what the older encyclopedias contain[15] and even his more technically detailed treatises on grammar and practical geometry[16] show that speculative explorations of the possibilities of applying the technical devices of the arts to the study of Scripture had little appeal for him. He wrote functional manuals. He preferred consolidation to speculation. The monastic tradition of the study of the arts was, on the whole, unpretentious, and in many houses in the twelfth century it amounted to little more than a grounding in grammar. Even in the more advanced school run by the Augustinian canons of St. Victor it was always so firmly subordinated to the purposes of *lectio divina* that it gave rise to little new development within the fields of the arts themselves. There is no tension here to stimulate fresh thought.

In Book VII of the part of the *De Sancta Trinitate* which is devoted to wisdom (the work of the Holy Spirit) Rupert deals at length with the function of the arts.[17] He first looks at the arts as a whole, and then he works his way through the

---

[14] See R. W. Southern, 'Aspects of the European Tradition of Historical Writing: 2 Hugh of St. Victor and the Idea of Historical Development', *Transactions of the Royal Historical Society*, 21 (1971), 159–81; and Grover A. Zinn Jr., 'Hugh of St. Victor and the Art of Memory', *Viator*, 5 (1974), 211–34, on some of Hugh's novel ideas.

[15] He makes considerable use of Cassiodorus' *Institutiones* and Isidore's *Etymologiae*.

[16] R. Baron, ed., *Opera Propaedeutica* (Notre Dame, 1966).

[17] H.XXIV, Book XXXIX of the *De Sancta Trinitate*.

arts in order. The desire to see things as a whole and to look for a principle of organization which will make it possible to reduce a great complex of study to manageable order, was not confined to the new academics. Hugh of St. Victor wrote the *Didascalicon* and the *De Sacramentis Ecclesiae* to meet such a need, and Rupert attempted to take a grand view of the way in which the whole Bible may most constructively be studied. Indeed, it was from the Victorine tradition, which spoke to both cloister and school, that the leaders of the progressive organization of the study of the Bible in the middle and later twelfth century came: Peter Comestor, Peter the Chanter, Stephen Langton.[18] Peter of Poitiers says in his *Prologue* to the *Sentences* that he has striven to bring debatable matters to order and to arrange in an orderly manner what is disorderly in the study of Scripture (*Disputabilia . . . in seriem redigentes, inordinata in ordinem redigimus*).[19] The groundwork of the organization of subject-matter which made theology an academic discipline by the end of the twelfth century was laid within the monastic tradition, but it was only in the sharper air of the public schools that it went beyond a mere arrangement of material and brought about an encounter between disciplines.

We find Rupert of Deutz approaching his task of organization by defining his terms, making as he does so the ancient distinction between knowledge and wisdom. 'We must clearly distinguish what is knowledge (*scientia*) and what is wisdom (*sapientia*).'[20] Aquinas defines his terms, too, but Rupert makes a habit of testing his definitions upon passages of Scripture, while Aquinas looks to a wide range of sources for his definitions. Where Aquinas seeks to organize what he has to say according to a logical order, Rupert prefers a historical or chronological order (for the treatment of Scripture) or a conventional order (for his remarks on the arts). The principles of organization which were being worked out in the schools and universities were more rigorous in the intellectual demands they made than those with which monastic scholars felt most comfortable.

---

[18] B. Smalley, *The Study of the Bible in the Middle Ages,* pp. 196-7.
[19] *Sententie Petri Pictavensis*, I, p. 1.15.
[20] H.XXIV. 2039.26.

Rupert is careful to match his terms exactly to his subject-matter; but he does not see them as technical terms, as the academic theologians were beginning to do. 'The knowledge of all good and legitimate arts is *notitia,* but *sapientia* (wisdom), is of one thing only, that is God.'[21] This knowledge of the arts, or *notitia,* he consistently refers to as *scientia.* *Scientia* may be divided into *literalis* and *illiteralis.* 'Literal arts' are those which are learned from books.[22] Non-literal arts, such as sculpture and the mechanical arts, are learned in other ways. Of literal knowledge some is *liberalis,* some *illiberalis.*[23] Medicine, for example, is literal and illiberal, in Rupert's view, although he knows that not everyone will agree with this classification. *Philosophia* is literal and liberal. It is divided into *logica* (the arts of language: grammar, dialectic, and rhetoric) and *physica* (arithmetic, geometry, music astronomy).[24] These are the branches of the secular arts which are recognized by the *magistri,*[25] the masters who teach the liberal arts. (Rupert's classification has something in common with Hugh of St. Victor's less economical treatment in the *Didascalicon* in that it allows a place in the scheme of learning for the mechanical arts,[26] and it bears some resemblances to the other 'trees of knowledge' we have met.)

St. Paul warns against the deceitfulness of philosophy in Colossians 2:8. Rupert has shown that the liberal arts are subdivisions of philosophy. He now confronts the question: 'Is it legitimate to use the liberal arts in the study of the Bible?' There seems to him to be not one *philosophia* but two, one vain and deceitful, the other solid and true (*gravis et vera*).[27] Paul's reservation, he argues, is about the *philosophia* devised by men; that which is studied *secundum Christum,* according to Christ, as the apostles and evangelists teach, is sound and helpful. Rupert has defined *philosophia* in Biblical terms. He

---

[21] Ibid., p. 2039.33.   [22] Ibid., p. 2040.53-5.   [23] Ibid., p. 2040.58.
[24] Ibid., p. 2040.64-8.   [25] Ibid., p. 2040.68-9.
[26] The plan of the *Didascalicon* is also repetitive in that Hugh is forced to return to certain topics as he proceeds with his scheme of study.
[27] H.XXIV, 2041.82.

leaves no room for the accusation that he has given more weight to the secular *auctores* than to the authority of Scripture, and he does not anticipate any further difficulty if the arts are rightly used. 'The anger of God', he feels, is not directed against the work the grammarians, dialecticians, and rhetoricians do, 'but this he blames in them', that 'they do not seek the fruit of wisdom' from their studies, or glorify God in them. That is the purpose for which God gave the arts to men.[28] Rupert sees in wisdom a moral aspect which mere knowledge lacks, for many knowledgeable men live without heavenly wisdom, and it is clear that their learning does not govern the way they live their lives.[29] Knowledge in itself is neutral. Only the purpose for which it is used makes it good or bad.

The arts are more than a convenience of human devising for Rupert and therefore they cannot in any case simply be dismissed from consideration by the student of Scripture. It is essential that their proper place should be defined. Perhaps no difference of opinion on the subject of the arts was more important than this among twelfth-century scholars; it divided those who argued that the arts ought to be left out of account altogether because they are merely man-made, from those who held that a place must be found for them because God made them. Rupert describes the arts as handmaids of the court of Heaven, who served their mistress Wisdom unsatisfactorily at first, running wildly about, chattering and undisciplined. But when God set them to work they learned to speak about their Creator sensibly and they are now reliable servants.[30] This is a happy image, but it is doubtful whether Rupert had any real conception of the difficulty of reconciliation he hoped that it would meet. He was able to conceive of the problem so simply only because he had no more than a partial awareness of the controversies to which it might give rise. He expects to find no difficulty which cannot be put down to deliberate misuse of the arts on the part of unbelievers, or to misunderstanding. The tone of most of what he has to say about the value of the study of the arts for the

---

[28] Ibid., p. 2042.119–29.   [29] Ibid., p. 2041.98–101.
[30] H.XXIV, 2048.382–2049.394, S. of S. 4:11 and 2:14.

student of the Bible is optimistic. 'If a man uses [dialectic] legitimately' (*si quis legitime utatur illa*),[31] it will prove the truth of faith in accordance with the word of God. Rupert speaks of legitimate knowledge (*licita scientia*)[32] too, and his emphasis throughout is on the legitimacy with which the arts may be used. Heretics use them illegitimately, but there is nothing intrinsically objectionable about their use by right-minded Christians.[33]

As a rule, Rupert makes no great technical demands on his reader. But he shifts the discussion on to more technical ground when he deals with something which can be recognized 'externally' (*foris*), that is, according to the rules of human reason and the principles of the liberal arts. From these he distinguishes the spiritual intimations, the *rationes divinae* which a man understands inwardly (*intus*).[34] The separation makes it possible to confine statements of a kind the arts can usefully make about the study of Scripture to passages where they are applicable, and to leave out of consideration there matters which they cannot touch on — matters of devotional feeling and holy mystery. Rupert explains, for example, that *scientia* is broader than *sapientia* in certain respects. They differ, as Porphyry would put it, as greater and lesser (*ut maius et minus*). We signify more by the noun 'knowledge' than by the noun 'wisdom' (*plura scientiae quam sapientiae nomine significamus*),[35] because the word *scientia* is a general term, a *generale nomen*. He looks, too, at the way *scientia* may be divided if we regard it as a genus. All these principles of elementary dialectic are to be found in Porphyry's *Isagoge*.[36] Rupert's instinct is to make the arts serve their purpose in the study of the created world and the secular branches of knowledge, where these are relevant to

---

[31] Ibid., 2047.321.   [32] Ibid., p. 2048.369.   [33] Ibid., p. 2042.143.
[34] H.XXIV, 2043.162-3.   [35] Ibid., p. 2042.145.
[36] Boethius' Commentary on Porphyry's *Isagoge* is printed in *PL* 64.9-158, and in *Corpus Scriptorum Ecclesiasticorum Latinorum*, 48 (Leipzig, 1906). A translation of the *Isagoge* with some notes has been made by E. W. Warren, *Pontifical Institute of Mediaeval Studies: Mediaeval Sources in Translation*, 16 (Toronto, 1975).

Bible study, and to avoid employing them upon intimate
spiritual matters. Their legitimacy of use, as we have seen,
depends upon their being kept strictly within their proper
bounds. Rupert does not find it difficult to decide where
those bounds lie. The academic theologians of the day were
beginning to find it far from easy.

The way in which Rupert carried out his rule in practice
becomes clear if we look at what he has to say about each
of the arts in turn. When Rupert writes about the function
of grammar in Scriptural commentary and *lectio divina* he
has almost nothing to say about the way in which it may be
used to make fresh discoveries. His main concern is to show
how readily grammatical rules may be accommodated to the
interpretation of Scripture. He borrows from Isidore a brief
list of the 'divisions' of the art of grammar,[37] but he does not
try to extend or adapt the technical principles. He says
explicitly that 'it is not the business of the present study to
describe and distinguish' the branches of grammar (*describere
ac distinguere praesentis negotii non est*).[38] His emphasis lies
the other way. He gives Scriptural examples of *fabulae* and
schemata and *metra* to show that there is nothing out of
keeping in applying grammatical categories to the study of
the Bible. Grammatical aspects of all kinds, from parts of
speech to forms of composition and devices of style are,
Rupert argues, already present in the text. We bring no alien
discipline to bear when we identify them and give them their
proper grammatical names. This is the tenor of Augustine's
teaching about the use of the arts in the *De Doctrina
Christiana* and perhaps few monastic scholars would have
quarrelled with Rupert here.

Rupert was well able to go beyond these elementary
details in his handling of specific textual problems. In the *De
Victoria Verbi Dei* he considers the implications of the phrase
antiquus serpens in Revelation 12:9.[39] The *serpens* or
serpent cannot be as old as the Devil himself, says Rupert,
because the *reptilia* were made on the sixth day of creation.

---

[37] Isidore, *Etymologiae,* ed. W. M. Lindsay (Oxford, 1911), I.ii.i; I.v.4.
[38] H.XXIV, 2050. 444.
[39] *De Victoria Verbi Dei,* ed. cit., p. 56, Book II.2.

Antiquus has been added as an adjective[40] to make it clear
that it is the Old Serpent who is referred to, a being older
than the form of a serpent in which he appears in *Genesis*.
'But how old is the Devil?' asks Rupert. He is very old, but
not as old as God. We should therefore expect to find a
difference between the reference to God as 'the ancient of
days' (*antiquus dierum*) in *Daniel*, and the description of
Satan as *antiquus serpens*.[41] The serpent is called *antiquus*
adjectivally (*adiective*) and is thus merely described as old;
God is called *antiquus* with reference to his proper substance,
and the adjective is used as a substantive.[42] The difference
Rupert identifies readily as a grammatical one. In the expression *antiquus dierum* the adjectival noun is given in place of
a proper noun (*ut hoc ipsum adiectivum vice proprii nominis
ponatur*).[43] In *antiquus serpens, antiquus* is merely an
adjective. The grammarians call the first device *autonomasia*
and identify it as a trope in which something else is predicated
in place of a noun.[44] This information Rupert may have
drawn directly from Donatus,[45] but in any case it represents
a far more advanced knowledge of grammar than he can have
got from Isidore or any other encyclopedist. The approach is
altogether more technical than that which he adopts in his
general treatment of grammar in the *De Sancta Trinitate* and
altogether more specific. Grammar is being used here as a
means of solving problems and not merely as a source of convenient labels for the features of the Biblical text which the
conscientious reader will wish to have identified for him. The
grammatical technicality has been made the basis of a philosophical distinction.

This explanation is much closer in the level of technical
expertise required and in its attempt to resolve a problem of
interpretation by a technical device of secular studies, to the
kind of principle put forward by Abelard or Gilbert of

[40] In Roman grammatical theory the adjective is not a separate part of speech
but a kind of noun.
[41] *De Victoria Verbi Dei*, ed. cit., p. 56.7–13; cf. Dan. 7:9.
[42] *De Victoria Verbi Dei*, ed. cit., p. 56.19–22.
[43] Ibid., p. 56.12.   [44] Ibid., p. 56.15–17.
[45] *Donatus Ars Grammatica*, ed. H. Keil, *Grammatici Latini*, IV (Leipzig,
1864), p. 400.15.

Poitiers. But Rupert is confident that any demonstration that a technical device is present in Scripture can only make explicit the soundness and precision of expression which he is sure is already implicit in the text. He uses the arts only to prove the Bible's words to be consonant with orthodox doctrine.

This is very much the spirit in which Anselm treats a small group of problems raised by Biblical texts in his 'three treatises pertaining to the study of Holy Scripture', the *De Veritate*, the *De Libertate Arbitrii*, and the *De Casu Diaboli*. Anselm examines the expression *servus peccati*, the servant of sin' (John 8:34) in several chapters of the *De Libertate Arbitrii*. He shows his pupil how to determine the exact sense of *servus* so that it may be seen that when Scripture calls man the 'slave' of sin it does not imply that he has no power to act by his own free will. If a man is a slave, how is he free? And if he is free, how is he a slave? A man is free in so far as he cannot be made to turn from rightness (*rectitudo*) against his will. He is a slave in that he cannot by his own power be freed from sin. By a process of definition Anselm finds a means of resolving the paradox along these lines.[46] He, too, begins with the assumption that reasoning can only support the Bible's teaching and he is able to show by reasoning that the supposition is correct. Both Anselm and Rupert argue that it is only by making technical errors in the use of the arts themselves that the *dialectici haeretici* can make out a case for their opinions. A heretical dialectician is an incompetent dialectician,[47] and the case against him must be argued by discovering where he has gone wrong on his own ground.

Rupert's knowledge of rhetoric is surprisingly broad; he had evidently had an opportunity to read the *De Inventione* of Cicero. It has recently become clear that the *De Inventione* and the *Rhetorica ad Herennium* were by no means as generally neglected as had been thought.[48] But these text-

[46] *Anselmi Opera Omnia*, I.222-4, Chapters X-XII.
[47] *Anselmi Opera Omnia*, II.9-10.
[48] M. Dickey, 'Some Commentaries on the *De Inventione* and the *Rhetorica ad Herennium* of the eleventh and twelfth centuries', *MARS*, vi (1968), 1-41, K. M. Fredborg, 'The Commentary of Thierry of Chartres on Cicero's *De Inventione*', *Cahiers*, 7 (1971), 1-36, and 'The Commentaries on Cicero's *De Inventione* and *Rhetorica ad Herennium* by William of Champeaux', *Cahiers*, 17 (1976), 1-39.

books were still very far from being as common as the textbooks of grammar and dialectic in Rupert's day. Rupert
draws directly upon the *De Inventione* for an account of the
branches of rhetoric; in the *De Sancta Trinitate* he gives more
space to this art than to any other.

It was natural enough for Augustine to see rhetoric as the
most important of the arts when he gave an account of their
place in Christian learning in the *De Doctrina Christiana.*
Rhetoric was the supreme art in the late Roman world, and
all other studies served its needs. But in Rupert's time it was
the most neglected of the trivium studies. It was impossible
for his contemporaries to glimpse the majesty and power of
expression it gave its classical exponents. If Rupert had learnt
from Augustine that rhetoric has a place in Christian learning,
he had no opportunity to understand the qualities of the art
as Augustine knew them. He refers, it is true, to 'orators
whose business is in the law-courts or the political arena,[49]
who speak by their own wits and not at the prompting of the
Holy Spirit. But his knowledge of such orators was almost
certainly not taken from life.[50] In any case he places all his
emphasis on written, not on spoken rhetoric, on criticism, not
on composition. He turns Augustine's powerful defence of
the quality of a Christian oratory directly inspired by the
Holy Spirit in men who have no formal training in the art of
speaking, into a rather tame summary of Cicero's elementary
textbook with cross-references to Scripture. Nevertheless,
Rupert's achievement is considerable because it is original as
well as imitative, if not ambitious. From a poor, thin
rhetorical tradition he has fashioned something of substance.

He begins with conventional definitions. Rhetoric is the
art of speaking well and it has five parts (*inventio, dispositio,
elocutio, memoria, pronuntiato*).[51] Of these, only *inventio*
is fully covered in the *De Inventione* and it is this with which
Rupert proposes to concern himself, limiting what he has to
say to 'true orators' (*rhetores veri*). These are the writers of
Scripture, who address themselves to men of God.[52] Cicero

[49] H.XXIV. 2052–496.
[50] See M. T. Gibson, *Lanfranc of Bec,* Chapter I for a discussion of forensic
oratory in the eleventh century in northern Italy.
[51] H.XXIV. 2051.483, 490.   [52] Ibid., 2051.492–4.

lists six parts of *inventio,* or the process of discovering and framing arguments which will make a case convincing.[53] These are the *exordium,* or opening, the division, the confirmation, the confutation, the conclusion.[54] Rupert gives Cicero's definition of each.[55]

Then he looks at the Bible to see whether the writers of the Scriptural text followed proper technical procedures in their own compositions. The textbook rule allows the orator to use an *exordium* if he wishes, or to begin with the *narratio* and omit any formal opening. 'Moses', says Rupert, 'did not use an introduction but began straight away with the narrative, saying, "In the beginning God created heaven and earth". Neither Joshua nor Judges has an introduction, nor the Book of the Kings, but they, too, begin with a narrative.'[56] This, Rupert argues, is not a matter of chance or the result of ignorance (*non autem casu aut inscitia*) 'for where it seems profitable no one knows better than Moses when to use an opening, and no one is better able to do so; he can make not only men but the heavens and the very earth attentive and eager to listen, when he says: "Hear, O heavens, what I say, and let the earth hear the words of my mouth".'[57] Rupert is not claiming that Moses was technically expert in rhetoric, but simply that he is not to be rated the inferior of any secular orator who has learnt rhetoric from a human master. Moses has been taught to write well by the Creator of the very art of rhetoric, for he is divinely inspired.

Rupert consistently compares the work of secular authors unfavourably with that of the writers of Scripture. On *narratio,* for example, he says, 'How brief and clear is every narrative in Holy Scripture? We think, and we are certainly not mistaken, that the most accurate narrative among all the secular authors, is shapeless, uneven and wretchedly obscure by comparison.'[58] His argument gains force from the fact that he is able to support it by examples from the classical

[53] Cicero, *De Inventione,* ed. H. M. Hubbell (London, 1968), I.vii.9.
[54] Ibid., I.xiv.19.   [55] H.XXIV.2051-2.
[56] Ibid., p. 2052.529-32.
[57] Ibid., p. 2052.532-7; cf. Deut. 32:1; *De Inventione* I.xv.20.
[58] Ibid., p. 5052.565-9.

poets (here, two passages from Horace),[59] as well as from
Scripture. But its cogency lies chiefly in Rupert's sureness of
touch in handling the detailed technicalities of the art he is
describing. To claim a general superiority of argument for the
Bible is one thing. To explain that 'the most complete and
perfect argument . . . is that which has five parts: proposition,
reason, confirmation of the reason, elaboration (*exornatio*)
and conclusion (complexio)' is another, when he is able to
find several examples in Scripture to support what he says
and to base his exposition directly upon the teaching of the
De Inventione.[60] Rupert believed the arts to be God-given.
Cicero's *De Inventione* and other textbooks like it represent
human attempts to set out the rules God has invented. To
compare the actual practice of secular and Scriptural
auctores with the teaching of the textbooks is therefore the
closest Rupert can come to objective comparison against
an absolute standard.

The substantial section of the *De Sancta Trinitate* which
deals with rhetoric reveals a good deal incidentally about
Rupert's attitudes, the assumptions on which he has based
his attempt to apply the study of the arts to the study of the
Bible. It demonstrates again his confidence that this approach
can only be beneficial, that it will always bring to light the
hidden excellencies of Scripture and make its truth even
clearer, because the first and most important purpose of the
arts is to assist the reader of the Bible. But it reveals significant limitations, too. It is Rupert's habit to avoid areas of
potential conflict. Earlier in the *De Sancta Trinitate* he shows
that he understands the difference between dialectical and
rhetorical arguments: 'This is a valid argument than which a
stronger, more true and more reliable is not to be found
among the secular orators or the dialecticians.'[61] But in the
discussion of the 'most perfect argument' which we have just
met, Rupert does not enter into Cicero's own discussions of
the conflicting opinions of rhetoricians and dialecticians on
this point. He does not analyse the difference between an
enthymeme and a syllogism. He treats the arts, as far as he is

---

[59] Ibid., p. 2053.575–80; Horace, *Ars Poetica*, 240–2; *Serm.* I.10.71-3.
[60] H.XXIV. 2055.623–30; *De Inventione*, I.xxxiv.58-9.
[61] H.XXII. 1811.1152.

able, as though they are self-contained units whose rules are internally consistent. Had he allowed himself to make comparisons between the arts as he applied them to the study of Scripture, he would have begun to encounter the deep difficulties they gave to Abelard and others, at exactly the points where the teaching of one art was difficult to reconcile with that of another. Yet these problem areas were potentially the areas of growth and development precisely because they forced scholars to examine technical differences more closely. Ironically perhaps, in avoiding any possibility of abusing the arts and keeping to safe paths, Rupert restricted himself to some of the more limited aids the arts could give him.

When he comes to dialectic, Rupert enters on what was already the most controversial ground in the application of the arts to the study of the Bible. It is, as a rule, the *dialectici* who are called *haeretici* and not the *grammatici* or the *rhetores*. But again, a determination to avoid conflict is apparent. 'Surely,' he says, 'he who has studied the art of dialectic will not hesitate to come within the walls of Holy Scripture at the first door?'[62] There can be nothing objectionable in applying the elements of dialectic to the beginning of Genesis because the technical terms and principles involved are already present in the Scriptural text. No imposition of a distinct system of thought is required. For some of his contemporaries and for future generations the coincidence of terminology was to be a source of immense difficulty. Augustine himself had not found it easy to explain the discrepancy between the *substantia* and *relatio* of the Persons of the Trinity and the rules which govern substance and relation in the Aristotelian categories: the same difficulty had been troublesome to Boethius.[63] But for Rupert there is nothing but pleasure in the recognition that 'the first elements of the beginning of this Scripture' (*prima incipientis huius Scripturae elementa*)[64] are like the first elements of dialectic itself: the *genus* and *differentia*, the *species* and *proprium* and *accidens* of Porphyry.[65] These

[62] H.XXIV. 2060.827-9.
[63] Augustine, *De Trinitate*; Boethius *De Trinitate*, in particular.
[64] H.XXIV. 2060.831-2.
[65] *PL* 64.9-158; *Corpus Scriptorum Ecclesiasticorum Latinorum*, 48.

first principles of dialectic seem difficult to the secular scholar (*pro magnis et arduis habent*),[66] but to the student of Scripture they are elementary. It is entirely fitting that this should be so.[67] Rupert expects to find that the secular arts and the teaching of Scripture shall fit together in this way, with a natural harmony, and with the arts as humble handmaids. He goes so far as to say that a knowledge of the Aristotelian categories (*praedicamentorum doctrina*) is necessary to the student of the Bible.[68] His expectation, evidently, is that it will not prove a stumbling-block.

The elementary notions of dialectic Rupert finds in Genesis are these: In Genesis 1:11-12 there is a reference to the fruit-tree yielding fruit after its kind. The *lignum*, or tree, Rupert explains, is the *genus*, and when Moses says that it is *pomiferum* or *faciens fructum*, fruit-bearing, he gives the *differentia*. When the *genus* is joined to the *differentia* we can say what *species* it is: a fruit-tree. He also looks at the classification of creatures. Dialectic defines man as a moral, rational animal. But:

Much better and more correctly are *genera* and *species* and *differentia* arranged in order according to this most noble Scripture than Porphyry arranges them; when he had arrived at the definition of an animal by subdividing, he went on to subdivide 'animal' according to the *differentiae* 'rational' and 'irrational', 'mortal' and 'immortal'. But this most holy sequence or reading divides in such a way as to show that there is one kind of animal without a living soul which dwells in the water, and another which dwells on the earth. And first three divisions are given of what dwells in the water, and so on.[69]

Rupert works his way systematically through the differences between Porphyry's classification and that of Scripture, so as to demonstrate by measuring each against the technical procedures Porphyry lays down (which are taken as absolute) how much more satisfactory is the Bible's version. All the common expressions of elementary dialectic, *genus, species, differentia, accidens, substantia,* and the examples commonly used, *rationalis, animal, mortalis, color* receive painstaking attention. A dialectician might argue that Rupert's classifica-

---

[66] H. XXIV.2060.832.
[67] Ibid. p. 2060.823-5.
[68] Ibid., p. 2060.854-6.
[69] Ibid., p. 2061.890-8.

tions have a different purpose, that Porphyry, following Aristotle, was concerned with classifying the objects in the world for philosophical purposes and Rupert wanted to find a logical order in creation which would glorify the Creator. But Rupert has retained the rules of dialectic and made them serve his own ends with considerable skill, because he sees them as absolute if imperfect laws of a divinely appointed art.

He gives relatively little space to the syllogism, although he acknowledges it to be the device which is most important of all and most distinctive to dialectic (*Huius artis utilitas et virtus tota ostenditur in syllogismis*).[70] The profitableness and power of this art is demonstrated fully in the syllogism. He merely provides a series of brief examples, as he did for the five-part argument of rhetoric, and ends with a comfortable assurance that 'Holy Scripture is full of both perfect syllogisms, such as both dialecticians and rhetoricians employ, and enthymemes, that is the incomplete syllogisms whose brevity especially pleases the rhetoricians.'[71] Here again he can be seen to avoid — almost instinctively — an area of discourse where the study of the arts may pose as many difficulties as it resolves. There is no difficulty in finding parallel examples. But to discuss the validity and force of Scriptural arguments extensively in technical detail would be to enter another area altogether.

Earlier in the *De Sancta Trinitate* he makes a cautious attempt to do something of the kind. He discusses the technical force and the formal type of the argument which is used in Matthew 12:25-6; 'Every kingdom divided against itself is brought to desolation; and every city or house divided against itself shall not stand. And if Satan cast out Satan, he is divided against himself; how then shall his kingdom stand?' Rupert identifies this — in the most general terms — as a *syllogismus*. He asserts that this is a *validum argumentum*, a valid argument, than which none more forceful, true, or reliable is to be found among the rhetoricians (*oratores saeculi*) or among the dialecticians. He takes up in some perplexity the fact that the conclusion takes the form

[70] Ibid., p. 2066.1054.   [71] Ibid., p. 2066.1076-9.

of a question. If this were to be taken to imply that there is any doubt about it, 'the wise King of the Kingdom of Heaven would be arguing so strong a case in vain'. We are forced to conclude that there are those for whom this is not a self-evident truth. *Sed rem tam grandem unde poterimus probare?* ('But how can we prove so great a matter?') Only by resorting to the authority of Scripture, Rupert suggests.[72] His use of technical terms of the art of argument here is not extensive, and he does not pursue the technical discussion very far. But he has evidently approached the task of assessment and analysis with general principles in mind which he owes to the study of the *artes* and which have helped him to think clearly about the argument in hand. Any tension between the purposes of students of the *artes* and those of students of Holy Scripture here is slight.

It would be very surprising if Rupert displayed any extensive knowledge of the quadrivium subjects. These were still largely the province of those with a special interest in mathematical matters, until well after Rupert's time.[73] For arithmetic he tells us only that arithmetic is the *numerorum ratio*;[74] he mentions the Pythagorean theory that number is the organizing principle of the universe and that if it is taken away everything perishes (*tolle numerum in rebus omnibus et omnia pereunt*).[75] But this is a view too commonly found in the Fathers and in contemporary writings for it to indicate any expert knowledge on Rupert's part. Rupert's idea is that 'we must know about number so as not to be confused by it. Take away secular calculation and everything will be wrapped in the blindness of ignorance'. We shall be no different from other animals, if we do not know how to count.'[76] Rupert,

---

[72] H. XXIII.1811.1152-65.

[73] There is evidence of increasing interest in Boethius' *Arithmetica* in commentaries of the tenth, eleventh, and twelfth centuries, but few masters seem to have lectured on the quadrivium subjects even from this textbook. William of Champeaux and Thierry of Chartres are notable examples. Abelard mentions his master's teaching in his *Dialectica*, p. 59, and there is a good deal of mathematical material in *Thierry of Chartres*.

[74] H. XXIV.2066.1080.

[75] Ibid., p. 2067.1094, cf. Boethius, *Arithmetica*, ed. G. Friedlein (Leipzig, 1886), p. 12.14-15.

[76] H. XXIV. 2067.1093-4, and 2067.1094-6.

like William of Malmesbury, found practical arithmetic forbidding and largely incomprehensible.[77] But he grants it a
place and makes a sketchy attempt to relate it to the study of
Scripture by pointing out that there are many numbers in the
Bible, whose significance cannot be understood without a
knowledge of arithmetic. Rupert is attracted neither by the
discussions of the mystical significance of numbers (although
he had probably read the commentary on *The Dream of
Scipio* of Macrobius)[78] nor by number theory, nor by the
computation of dates, to give more than a cursory account of
arithmetic here.

His knowledge of geometry is practical rather than
theoretical, which is again to be expected. 'There are many
geometrical terms in Holy Scripture, that is: finger, palm,
cubit, foot, pace, *stadium, miliare,* and others like them.'[79]
These are the terms of practical geometry. The elements of
geometrical theory to be found in Boethius' *Arithmetica* and
in Gerbert of Aurillac's *Geometry* of the late tenth century[80]
do not come to Rupert's mind; there are no references to
point and line and surface, no plane figures, no solids, but
only a discussion of the origins of the art in the measuring of
the earth among the ancient Egyptians and a reference to the
instructions given to Noah for building the Ark.[81] Rupert has
strong reservations about this art. The most he will concede is
that it is *acceptabilis,* made acceptable by this passage in
Genesis,[82] and by the building of the tabernacle and the
Temple.

Of music both practical and theoretical Rupert knows
rather more, and he is accordingly happier about its usefulness
to the student of Scripture. He is able to cite numerous
Scriptural passages touching on music, singing, instruments
and the power of music to inspire 'a love of the coming

---

[77] William of Malmesbury, *De Rebus Gestis Regum Anglorum,* ed. W. Stubbs,
Rolls Series, xc (1887), p. 195.
[78] H. XXIV.2213, *index auctorum.*   [79] Ibid., p. 2067.1098-100.
[80] See my article, 'The sub-Euclidean Geometry of the Earlier Middle Ages up
to the mid-twelfth century', *Archive for the History of Exact Sciences,* 16 (1976),
105-18.   [81] Gen. 6:14-15, H. XXIV.2067.1119-27.
[82] H. XXIV.2067.1121.

Kingdom of God'.[83] He notes an example of the usefulness
of a knowledge of musical theory in understanding the Bible.
'God said, "If I find in Sodom fifty just men . . ."' and so
on.[84] The series of numbers which follows as Lot ask God to
spare Sodom for the sake of fewer and fewer just men, bear
a harmonic ratio to one another, Rupert explains. 'He
reduces the number proportionately so that he omits none
of these proportions which make musical sounds.'[85] The
numbers are not arbitrarily chosen. They represent the
harmonic proportions. The explanation demands no knowledge of music beyond what Cassiodorus provides although
Rupert may have drawn on Boethius' *Musica*.[86] Similarly, a
reading of the encyclopedias would have furnished all he has
to say about the technical aspects of astronomy, and he is
able to add material from Scripture to show how often the
stars and the heavens are mentioned there.[87]

The tone of these sections on the quadrivium subjects is a
little apologetic. Rupert has not been excited by them as he
has by the study of rhetoric or dialectic. This must be put
down to the fact that he knows a good deal less about them.
Where he knows more he sees a wider range of possibilities in
the application of the arts to the study of the Bible. Perhaps
in the last analysis this is the root of the difference of
approach between a monastic scholar such as Rupert — and
even Hugh of St. Victor — and that of Peter Abelard and
Gilbert of Poitiers who saw further possibilities of application
because they knew more than Rupert, at least about grammar
and dialectic. Greater knowledge not only added to the
excitement which is briefly evident in Rupert's account of
the role of rhetoric or dialectic. It also added to the risk of
conflict between the rules of the arts and the teaching of the
Bible. Where there was potential for growth in this area, there
was also a potential area of debate and disagreement.

Rupert is able to end his account in the *De Sancta Trinitate*
by saying that where they are introduced, the arts co-operate

[83] Ibid., p. 2068-9.   [84] Gen. 18:26 ff.
[85] H XXIV.2069.1187-8.
[86] Boethius, *Musica*, ed. G. Friedlein (Leipzig, 1867), I.18, Cassian, *Institutes*,
ed. R. A. B. Mynors (Oxford, 1937), II.5.7.
[87] H XXIV.2069-70.

or work together with the study of the Bible (*tunc artes liberales ad cooperandum eidem scripturae fuisse intromissas*).[88] That is what they were made for. It is doubtful whether he could have written with the same unassertive confidence had he possessed the technical knowledge of Thierry of Chartres. Writing a decade or two later, Thierry emphasizes how important it is to distinguish those things in which the *philosophi* agree with Holy Scripture, from the points of disagreement. We must concentrate on the areas of agreement, and keep away from what leads us from the path of the truth.[89] Thierry does not suggest that points of disagreement can always be put down to abuse of the *artes*. Some conflict is unavoidable and the reader's best defence is to be technically well-informed. Rupert sees no need for conflict if the arts are kept in a subordinate position and if the reader judges what to use by its tendency to confirm or support what the Bible says. If they are used in that way they will always co-operate.

2. Conflict

So it was that when Bernard set about refuting the heretical assertions he believed Abelard to have made in his theological writings, he did so in his own terms, and from the standpoint of the monastic scholar. One of the results is clear enough if we set Bernard's arguments beside Abelard's: Bernard's account gains a good deal of its forcefulness from the persuasiveness of his language; his arguments themselves are relatively simple in conception and often in their form. Before we look more closely at the nature of the difference, it may be helpful first to ask why Bernard should have chosen to respond as he did. It has been argued that he simply did not possess Abelard's command of technical skills, and that he could not have matched him at dialectic. This is no doubt true; but it is evident from the passages where technical terms and methods make an appearance in Bernard's writings that he felt himself quite at ease with them, and had no hesitation in employing them when it seemed necessary. He

[88] Ibid., p. 2070.1230–1.
[89] *Thierry of Chartres*, p. 74, para. 18.91–4.

was certainly not entirely ignorant of his opponent's weapons. We must allow for an element of deliberate choice in Bernard's limited use of a method of argument which would appear to put him at a technical disadvantage in comparison with his opponent.

Bernard saw very clearly a problem which Simon of Tournai was later to frame in his commentary on the 'Athanasian' Creed. (The Latin *fides* allows these and other twelfth-century scholars to blur a distinction between 'faith' and 'belief' which would now be much more troublesome.) 'In Aristotle an argument is a reason which creates faith or: 'a belief' (*ratio faciens fidem*). But in Christ an argument is faith creating reason (*fides faciens rationem*).[1] There is apparently a fundamental irreconcilability between the view that reasoning leads to faith and the view that a sound faith is the only test of reasonableness; it has often been remarked that this was a difficulty which was especially pressing to twelfth-century thinkers, and there is nothing new in pointing it out here. But we can perhaps go a little further if we see the concern of Bernard and many like him as lying, not in deciding between the two, but in finding a means of reconciliation between them. He explains in Chapter III of his treatise against the errors of Abelard that a sound religious instinct will guide a cautious man through the difficulty of deciding what is proper to the individual persons and what is common to the Godhead as one (*novit pietas fidei caute inter personarum proprietates et individuam essentiae unitatem discernere*).[2] Faith holds a middle way, 'and does not turn to the right, by confusing the Persons, or look to the left, by dividing the substance'.[3] In his emphasis on finding a middle way (*medium iter*) Bernard speaks for the orthodox in any generation, but particularly for his own. To answer extremism with extremism would not serve the best interests of the faithful, and Bernard's principal anxiety is that no one should

[1] Simon of Tournai, 'Commentary on the so-called Athanasian Creed', ed N. M. Haring, *AHDLMA,* xliii (1976), 147, cf. Cicero, *Topics,* ed. H. M. Hubbell (London, 1968), I, 8. On the Council of Sens of 1140 and Bernard's encounter with Abelard, see J. Sikes, *Peter Abailard* (Cambridge, 1932), pp. 219–48 and D. E. Luscombe, *The School of Peter Abelard* (Cambridge, 1969), pp. 103–42.

[2] *PL* 182.1060, *Letter* 190.

[3] Loc. cit.

be led astray from the middle way, the orthodox position, by any argument of a kind which will unbalance his judgement.

The maintaining of balance in doctrinal discussions was one of the most testing of the difficulties which faced his contemporaries, and Bernard himself goes about it not at one level only, but at several. His guiding principle is plain enough; he asks himself whether a particular argument will help or hinder faith. In *Letter* 337, to Innocent II, Bernard says that he is concerned about the wide spread of popular theologizing. Discussions are going on in towns, villages, and castles, not only in the schools, but before the general public.[4] He is concerned that simple men, who are not sufficiently learned to judge these arguments for themselves, may be dazzled by them, and led astray in their own thinking. There is always an audience for what is topical, and theological problems seem to have had an attractiveness for the twelfth-century public which is matched today only by popular interest in politics and public affairs in general. This attractiveness was dangerous because it was so general and because it was felt not only by those who took a professional interest in such matters but also by ordinary people. When Bernard looked for ways of meeting the challenge he considered the needs of a wide public. It is perhaps for this reason that he aims at bold effects in his arguments against Abelard; his tone is often mocking and his style rousing and full of ridicule.

But empty mockery would not meet the objections of scholars and silence them, even if it helped to change public attitudes. Bernard had to argue an informed case. Yet mockery of Abelard and his like for failing to argue correctly according to their own rules was a powerful weapon, and Bernard unhesitatingly made use of it, much as Anselm a generation earlier had mocked the arguments of the dialectician Roscelin to show that he had failed to employ dialectical procedures correctly, and that the very grounds on which he rested his challenge were unreliable. 'I should fill a great book if I wished to write down the absurdities and

[4] *PL* 182.540.

offences against the faith which follow',[5] he says of the
logical implications of Roscelin's arguments. Such charges
require substantiation. Bernard was certainly not a logician
of Anselm's calibre, but Bernard, like Anselm, wanted to
argue that the dialecticians did not know their own business,
and in order to do so, he had to show himself better able to
argue than they.

He rested his case on Abelard's movement from the field
of the *artes,* especially dialectic, to a field which Bernard
obliquely identifies as 'theology'. This former master has
become a *novus theologus,* he says.[6] He has, he says, removed
his pupils from the breasts of dialectic, where they have been
suckling, and although they can scarcely manage to deal with
the first elements of the faith, they have attempted to discuss
the mystery of the Holy Trinity at his instigation.[7] Bernard
has nothing to say directly about Abelard's competence as a
dialectician, but he implies that he and his pupils have been
too hasty in approaching higher things. This is exactly
Anselm's warning to the dialecticians of his own day in the
De Incarnatione Verbi.[8] The force of Bernard's argument lies
in his notion of the scope of theology. It is the study of Holy
Scripture upon which Abelard has embarked in this over-
confident manner (*nunc in Scripturis sanctis insanit*).[9]
Bernard himself, and others to whom he would concede the
right to discuss theological topics, have a thorough knowledge of the Scriptures and of the comment aries of the
Fathers, which can only be got by slow, patient reading. His
distaste is that of the monastic scholar whose mind has been
formed by *lectio divina,* for the approach of the men of the
schools which seeks to handle with crisp decisiveness matters
in which Bernard perceives mysteries too profound to be
susceptible of such treatment. His objection to Abelard's
work therefore rests on a conception of the scope and nature
of theology rather different from Abelard's own. Abelard
sees theology as a speculative exercise and Bernard sees it as

---

[5] *Anselmi Opera Omnia,* II.19.12–13.
[6] *PL* 182.1055, Chapter I of *Letter* 190.   [7] *PL* 182.537, *Letter* 331.
[8] *Anselmi Opera Omnia,* II.7.9–10.   [9] *PL* 182.1055.

a matter of careful reflection on Scripture and patient comparison of the teachings of patristic writers. Bernard can therefore claim with some authority that Abelard is inadequately equipped at a technical level to discuss Holy Scripture, and that the expertise he possesses has no bearing on the task he is trying to perform.

From this point of view Bernard himself appears not an inferior to Abelard in his technical competence in the *artes,* but his superior in the knowledge and skills particularly required in the theology of Scriptural commentary. Above all, he feels himself to be possessed of that fine sense of balance which is essential to his purposes if he is to maintain the cause of orthodoxy in the face of the arguments of extremists.

In the *Capitula Haeresum* Abelard was accused of having said that omnipotence was a special attribute of the Father.[10] The topic is certainly one which Abelard had discussed. In the *Theologia Scholarium* he comments on a reference of 'Maximus' (the Confessor) to the omnipotence of God the Father.[11] It is instructive to compare the arguments Abelard puts forward here with Bernard's view of what he had said and its implications, not because it makes the viewpoint of either plain, beyond dispute (even to contemporaries it was not clear exactly where any of those who took part in this dispute had got their versions of Abelard's teaching). The comparison is instructive because it shows how different their approaches were. Abelard takes the matter up at a technical level in the fashionable terms of contemporary dialectic: *Iuxta proprietates quippe trium personarum, quaedam specialiter ac tamquam proprie de aliqua earum dici vel accipi solent*[12] ('As regards the properties of the three Persons, some are said or accepted as a rule specially, and, as it were, "properly" of each of them individually'). But, Abelard goes on to explain, we do not doubt that when we attribute

---

[10] *Capitula Haeresum* no. 14, ed. M. Buytaert, *Petri Abaelardi Opera Theologica,* CCCM XII (Turnhold, 1969), p. 480, see ibid., p. 469 for other versions of this accusation. See, too, the discussion of this *capitulum* in D. Luscombe, *The School of Peter Abelard* (Cambridge, 1969), p. 115-19.

[11] Pseudo-Maximus of Turin *PL* 57.433-4, Homily lxxxiii.

[12] *Theologia 'Scholarium',* ed. M. Buytaert, *CCCM* XII pp. 419-23 (47-57).

sapientia or wisdom to the Son, the Father and the Spirit, too, and indeed the whole Trinity is Wisdom; when we call the Holy Spirit love (*caritas*) we recognize that the Father and the Son can also be said to be *caritas*. This paradoxical usage had only recently become a subject of general discussion. Anselm emphasizes the properties common to all three Persons, the justice, truth, blessedness, omnipotence of God,[13] and the properties which distinguish them: Fatherhood, Sonship,[14] as though there were no intermediate category of properties which may, in certain circumstances, be said to be especially the properties of individual Persons but which are nevertheless common to them all. Controversy now turned on the question of the exact reference of such terms to the Persons and the Godhead. It is this newly controversial middle category of properties with which Abelard is concerned.

The emphasis of his discussion is upon problems of usage. He looks at what is usually 'said or accepted' (*dici vel accipi solent*). 'Those things which pertain to power are as rule assigned to the Father' (*assignari solent*) 'for by his divine name, as it is said, power is especially designated' (*cum ex ipsius, ut dictum est, nomine divina specialiter potentia designetur*).[15] Abelard is using technical terms here in a manner which owes an obvious debt to his knowledge of grammar and dialectic. His training in the arts has encouraged him to look at the language which is being used in framing the paradox; he points out that this is a familiar and accepted usage, if a technical one. He also considers the reference and meaning of the terms as they are used in this context. These are divine names (*nomina divina*)[16] and the theologian must determine how they may be applied to God. If we think of 'power' in terms of the nature of God or in terms of the way he works, he says, we shall find that 'power' is especially the property of the Person of the Father (*Si itaque potentiam tam ad naturam subsistendi quam ad efficaciam operationis referamus, inveniemus ad proprietatem*

---

[13] *Proslogion* 5-6, *Anselmi Opera Omnia* I.104-5.
[14] *De Processione Spiritus Sancti, Anselmi Opera Omnia,* II.216-17.
[15] *Theologia 'Scholarium',* p. 420.573-6.
[16] Interest in the *divina nomina* was excited by the twelfth-century revival of the work of Pseudo-Dionysius.

personae Patris specialiter attinere potentiam).[17] This is the case because he can do everything equally with the other Persons, but of himself alone (*ipsa sola a se*) while the other two Persons exist from the Father and so they have from him the power to do what they will.[18] Abelard has proceeded by defining *potentia* and distinguishing the instrument of power (which is common to all three Persons), the act of power (which is carried out by all three Persons) and the source of power, which he feels to lie ultimately with the Father, who begets the Son and from whom, with the Son, the Holy Spirit proceeds. The device of defining by subdivision is to be found in Anselm, too. He treats the problem of the will in much the same way by showing that it comprises an instrument, a power, and an act.[19] The technique is certainly dialectical in inspiration.[20] Abelard's intention is to clear up obscurity in the use of language, in the hope that if he removes ambiguity of expression the paradox will disappear, too. Very similar assumptions in Anselm's work did not, however, lead to such controversial conclusions, and that is partly at least because Abelard was prepared to give serious consideration to ideas which Anselm either did not encounter, or dismissed as unfruitful areas of speculation. If he knew "Maximus" ' views on the omnipotence of the Father, it is unlikely that he would have been attracted by the problem they raised to reflect at length on the matter. The difference between Anselm's approach and that of Abelard does not lie in their use of technical devices to clarify linguistic and semantic questions, but in Abelard's readiness to let dialectic lead him to conclusions of sometimes doubtful orthodoxy.

Yet it is for his use of technical devices that Bernard attacks Abelard in *Letter* 190; mockingly, he calls him 'another Aristotle'.[21] Bernard, like Abelard, emphasizes the

---

[17] *Theologia 'Scholarium'*, p. 422-3, para. 57.   [18] Ibid.

[19] *Anselmi Opera Omnia*, I. 218-19; II. 280-2 *et alibi*.

[20] Boethius' commentaries on Porphyry's teaching about definition by division, and his own *De Divisione*, are both printed in *PL* 64; Marius' Victorinus' *De Definitione* is ed. T. Stangl (Munich, 1888). These works together with material in Cicero's *Topics* to which Boethius and Victorinus owe a great deal, formed the basis of the twelfth-century theory of definition.

[21] *PL* 182.1059.

importance of making it absolutely clear what is under discussion. 'Now realize clearly what he thinks, teaches and
writes' (*Adhuc advertite clarius quid sentiat, doceat,
scribat*).[22] Bernard renders accurately enough the terms in
which Abelard sets out the problem. 'He says that power
belongs properly and specially to the Father, and wisdom to
the Son' (*Dicit proprie et specialiter ad Patrem potentiam,
ad Filium sapientiam pertinere*).[23] 'But this is false', he says.
It is true that the Father is wisdom and the Son power, just
as it is true that the Father is power and the Son wisdom.
And 'what is common to both is not proper to each individually'.[24] Bernard's intention here seems to be to get to the
heart of the matter immediately by plain common sense. He
implies that Abelard is logic-chopping. Abelard, in his
Apologia, replies that Bernard is missing the point: 'You are
utterly mistaken, brother, in not understanding the force of
the words.'[25] But to conclude that Bernard is using a blunt
instrument while Abelard uses a sharp one is perhaps to mis-
understand Bernard's intention here. He is arguing for
common sense against a technical expertise which he sees to
be dangerous when it is applied to such issues as this.

It was impossible for him not to answer Abelard in the
terms of grammar and dialectic because no other means of
problem-solving was available to him which could handle a
problem couched in such terms. But his instinct was to keep
to a level which any educated man could follow easily. This
was Anselm's intention, too, and it is perhaps a mark of the
difference in quality of mind between Anselm and Abelard
that he was able to employ many of the devices Abelard uses
without making himself incomprehensible to the general
reader, while Abelard became more difficult to understand
as he became more technical. Bernard, like Abelard, sees
the problem as one of usage. There are certain terms, he says,
which are not used or said of the Persons themselves, but
of the Persons in relation to one another; thus each is peculiar
to one Person, and it is not common to any other. Thus, he

---

[22] *PL* 182.1058.
[23] Loc cit.
[24] Loc. cit.
[25] *Apologia,* ed. M. Buytaert, *CCCM* XI, p. 363.133.

who is the Father is not the Son and he who is the Son is not the Father. It is not in relation to himself but in relation to the Son that the Father is designated by the name of Father (*non quod ad se sed quod ad Filium Pater est, Patris nomine designatur*).[26] This specific application does not apply to *potentia* or *sapientia* or to other, similar terms. Bernard argues for an Anselmian simplicity of classification of the names of God, where there is no 'middle category'). As far as Bernard is concerned he has met Abelard's arguments briefly and effectively, without resorting to further technical complications, and indeed by simpler but perfectly adequate technical principles.

To drive home his victory he turns again to the old device of mockery. 'Let him choose what he will' he cries; let Abelard attribute wisdom to the Son and take it from the Father, or give it to the Father and take it from the Son; let him attribute kindness (*benignitas*) to the Holy Spirit and not to the Father, or to the Father and not to the Son. 'Or else let him cease altogether from making common names proper' (*aut certe desinat nomina communia propria*).[27] He speaks feelingly of the waste of words (*inani multiplicate verborum*) which such dialectical exercises involve, the weary labour (*hoc opus, hoc labor*),[28] involved in teaching us what relation obtains between Father and Son:

We hold, on your teaching, that 'animal' may be substituted for 'man', but not the other way round, according to the rule of your dialectic, by which a species may not be substituted for a genus, but a genus may be substituted for a species. When then you compare the Father to a genus and the Son to a species, does dialectic not demand by the same token that the Father may be substituted for the Son, but not the Son for the Father? Thus, too, it is necessary for the Father to be whatever the Son is, but not the other way round![29]

Bernard is certainly sufficiently well-informed on points of elementary dialectic to point out what seem to him obvious absurdities in Abelard's arguments. He does not hesitate to employ technical principles himself for purposes of ridicule.

---

[26] *PL* 182.1059.
[27] *PL* 182.1059. On the conventional character of this use of mockery, see M. T. Gibson, *Lanfranc of Bec*, p. 85.
[28] *PL* 182.1060.
[29] Loc. cit.

But he will not do so for positive purposes because he sees there the very danger of going astray to which he finds Abelard himself so prone.

The rhetorical forcefulness of Bernard's brisk summary of Abelard's errors, and his hearty condemnation of the means by which he has arrived at them, was intended no doubt to make his readers confident that their own common sense could be relied upon even where Abelard appeared to have greater technical skill than they could match. Bernard wants to prevent those who hear Abelard teach being blinded by his verbal and conceptual dexterity to the truths of orthodox faith.

But if we look at Abelard's reply in the *Apologia,* Bernard's confidence in his own technical soundness looks a little more questionable. Bernard, he says, is 'ignorant of that discipline which is the mistress of argument, and which not only teaches understanding of words, but is also able to discuss them once they are understood'.[30] He proceeds, a little offensively, to spell out for Bernard the basic principles of the discipline. 'It often happens that when certain words whose meaning is known . . . are put into a grammatical construction, the same words in juxtaposition have a different meaning, so that one meaning, in the whole construction, is true, and the other false.'[31] This is not, perhaps, intended as so blatant an insult to Bernard's understanding as it seems; Anselm had found it necessary to make much the same point in a quite uncontroversial context.[32] Abelard goes further. He asserts that this is as true for words applied to the Creator as it is for the discussion of created things.[33] Here he is making a claim of a very different kind, and begging a question of great importance to twelfth-century thinkers: that of whether or not the rules which govern human language can be taken to work in the same way when we talk about God. (We shall look at this question later.) But for the purposes of his reply to Bernard, he assumes that *habens filium, habens paternitatem* ('having a son' and 'having paternity') mean the same whether they

[30] *Apologia,* p. 363.133.   [31] Ibid., p. 363.142–6.
[32] *Anselmi Opera Omnia,* I.235.8–12.   [33] *Apologia,* p. 363.147.

refer to human or divine fatherhood.[34] As he goes on it becomes clear that his thinking about theological problems of language is on a quite different level from that of Bernard, that the two scholars are entirely at cross-purposes in their methods of approach. The conflict between practitioners of the arts and those, chiefly monastic, scholars who preferred to avoid technical devices in their discussion of theological problems was often not a confrontation face to face, but a battle in which weapons were never directly engaged because the enemies did not meet on the same field.

It would be an oversimplification to suggest that Bernard believed that no technical questions of usage would arise if the dialecticians did not look for them. But he certainly felt that they went too far in searching them out, even to the point of manufacturing difficulties such as those he finds quite illusory in Abelard's work. Abelard and his fellows, however, felt it equally dangerous to allow usages to go unexamined. They saw a greater risk of misunderstanding in loose and inexact expressions. 'Some words used of God which have the same meaning differ in meaning when they are in apposition to the same words', says Abelard (*Sic et [de Deo] nonnulla sunt eiusdem significationis verba quae sensum variant eisdem verbis apposita.*[35] 'God is divinity' (*Deus est divinitas*). We can say: *Deus est homo* (God is man) but not: *divinitas est homo* (divinity is man). *Deus est passus* (God suffered [in Christ]) is acceptable, but: *divinitas est passa* (divinity suffered), is not.[36] Similarly, *Deus est substantia Dei* (God is the substance of God'), but: *in Deo esse* (to be in God) is not the same thing as: *in substantia Dei esse* (to be in the substance of God).[37] The problems of signification Abelard touches on here are major problems of logic for which the study of dialectic was only beginning to find means of resolution in his day. His contention is that they are also real problems of a theological kind. They were relatively new in the way that they were framed, and especially in the way they demonstrated the difference

---

[34] Ibid., p. 363.149–50.
[36] Ibid., p. 364.160.

[35] Ibid., p. 364.155–6.
[37] Ibid., p. 364.165.

context may make to meaning. When the context was theological the difficulties were not only of another order, but also of pressing importance to theologians. Whether or not Bernard was right in his strong reservations about the wisdom of pursuing these lines of enquiry, the fact was that they were being opened up on all sides. The questions had already been posed, because dialecticians had already begun to look at the context of the expressions they were considering, and they had already perceived some of the special difficulties posed by trying to apply the rules of language to God. The possibilities for development were too exciting and the roots of the problems too profound for there to be any question of ignoring them in the hope that interest in such matters would die away.

It is easy enough to see that this was so when we look at the work of the next few generations of academic theologians. It would have been far less evident to Bernard, for whom these novelties seemed dangerous but ephemeral. In the conflict between monastic scholarship, with its emphasis on the simple helpfulness of the arts, and the work of the schools where the arts challenged received opinion, there could only be a short period of intense hostility as it became clear that scholars were at cross purposes. For perhaps half a century it was possible to maintain that the dialecticians' enterprise was simply misconceived, and to hope to quench curiosity with mockery as Bernard did. But frivolous as many of their questions were, the dialecticians were seriously engaged in the discussion of substantial problems at the very meeting-point of theological and philosophical knowledge. These were not matters which could be left in abeyance; although there continued to be many writers, particularly in the monastic tradition, who knew nothing of their implications, by the end of the twelfth century students of the arts could no longer make use of secular studies with the confident simplicity of Rupert of Deutz.

III   Speculative Theology and the Liberal Arts

1. The Tower of Speculation

Twelfth-century scholars studied the working of their mental processes in a way which has no parallel in earlier medieval thought, and they found that they needed a new vocabulary to describe the different modes of reasoning and reflection which they were beginning to recognize. The Latin language had a limited range of possibilities to offer. (Boethius refers in the *Contra Eutychen* III to the *inopia* or shortage of Latin terms which may be used to render Greek words denoting abstractions.) It is not surprising to find Boethius' own terms being pressed into service, since his theological tractates were responsible for much of the awakening of interest in the nature of abstract thought in the first half of the twelfth century. But there is perhaps a larger context. These Boethian terms and others newly coined were not introduced into the scholarly vocabulary of the day merely for their curiosity value. They were genuinely needed by thinkers who were alive for the first time since patristic days to the deep problems of epistemology raised by the features of natural language and its functioning. Thinking about the nature of thought naturally took the form of thinking about the *language* of thought for these scholars. In addition to the difficulties Aristotle had perceived, they were forced to make allowance for the difference it made to use language of a God of whom Aristotle had no conception. As twelfth-century scholars speculated like philosophers about theological problems, they began to fashion a speculative theology; to describe it they adopted the terms *speculatio* and *speculativus* which are first to be found in patristic writers and in Boethius, but which had no general currency after that until the twelfth century, when they were found to meet a new need for a means of describing the processes of abstract thought.

At the beginning of his *Sentences* Peter Lombard speaks of

the speculation of the theologians (*theologorum speculatio*)
as something which, if it is *studiosa* and *modesta,* will concern itself primarily with the interpretation of Holy
Scripture.[1] It is clear from Peter Lombard's reference to
speculatio that there is nothing out of keeping in using the
term 'speculative' of twelfth century theology. But this
'speculation of the theologians' was not, for him, speculative
theology of a kind which involved reasoning about theological
problems, but a form of Bible study. The most influential
development of twelfth-century theology was, however, the
evolution of what we should now more readily recognize as a
speculative theology side by side with improved methods of
studying Scripture. Many of the problems with which it was
concerned arose out of difficulties of textual interpretation
and it continued to be tied very closely to exegesis. But by
Aquinas' day speculative theology had sufficient substance
and independence to provide copious material for the *Summa
Theologica.* It has long been clear to many of his twelfth-
century predecessors that it required skills rather different
from those which had traditionally been employed in
Scriptural commentary – that it was an exercise of another
kind altogether in the methods of thought involved.

It is important not to place too much emphasis upon the
distinction between the study of the Bible and what we
would now call speculative theology when we are concerned
with a period in which they were so closely interdependent.
But there can be no doubt that a number of twelfth-century
scholars were aware of a difference between the two in terms
of methods of analysis and even of subject-matter. They
defined the difference increasingly clearly at the prompting
of their own need to 'place' their work in the scheme of
academic study. But it is doubtful whether they would have
been so ready to do so if they had their attention drawn to
the existence of a technical sense of *speculatio* and *speculativa*
in Boethius' commentary on Porphyry and in Boethius'
theological tractates.

Among monastic scholars of the late eleventh and early

---

[1] Peter Lombard, *Sentences,* Book I, Dist.I, c.1,2. I am grateful to the editor of
Classical Folia for permission to reprint my article '*Speculatio* and *speculativus*:
Boethius and the speculative theology of the twelfth centry', (1978), 69–78.

twelfth centuries *speculatio* seems to have had the general sense of 'gazing upon the divine'. Anselm, like Augustine, sees in the human mind a mirror of the Trinity. 'What is more obvious', he says, 'than that the more eagerly the rational mind strives to know itself, the more effectively does it attain a knowledge of [the divine Being], and the more it neglects to understand itself, the further it falls short of the vision of Him?' [2] (*tanto ab eius speculatione descendit*). This vision or gazing involves contemplation and it is, essentially, a devotional exercise. The hard-edged academic exercise of later twelfth-century speculative theology had been stripped of all such elements; it became an activity of the mind in which religious emotion had little or no place, and which, unlike the act of contemplation, could be taught and discussed in the classroom. Both senses are to be found in Aquinas, but they are distinct in his mind; the divorce of contemplation from abstract though of an academic kind was complete.

Cassiodorus opposed *speculativa* to *activa* in his *Variarum*,[3] by setting the contemplative against the active life. It would seem a considerable leap to equate the pairing of the Greek *theorica* and *practica* with that of the Latin *speculativa* and *activa* were it not done for us by Boethius in his commentary on Porphyry; he explains that there are two kinds of philosophy: 'one which is called theoretical, the other practical, that is, speculative and active' (*una quae theoretica dicitur, altera quae practica, id est speculativa et activa*).[4] Theoretical philosophy involves abstract thought, *practica* pratical skills.

The two pairs of terms are to be found in Hugh of St. Victor, in different parts of the *Didascalicon*. This encyclopedic work lays an almost equal emphasis upon spiritual and intellectual preparation. Hugh borrows from Boethius a reference to the *speculationum cogitationumque veritas*, truth of though and contemplation, and the: *sancta puraque actuum castimonia*,[5] holy and pure chastity of deed. Later,

[2] *Anselmi Opera Omnia*, 1.77.21.4.
[3] Cassiodorus, *Variarum*, ed. A. J. Fridh, *CCSL* 96 (1963), I.45.
[4] Boethius, *In Isagogen Porphyrii Commenta*, CSEL 48 (Leipzig, 1906), p. 8.1.
[5] Ibid., p. 7.22; *Didascalicon*, I.2, Buttimer, p. 7, and *PL* 176.743.

he considers the difference between an art, or mechanical skill, and a discipline, or skill of the mind. The *ars* involves practical skills: 'it is carried out by actual labour, for example, building'. The *disciplina* involves abstract thought; 'It consists in speculation and it is carried out by reasoning alone, for example, logic.'[6] Hugh of St. Victor was not, however, merely an eclectic; he gave some thought on his own account to the difference between theoretical and practical studies, particularly in the case of geometry, where the practical art of measurement had long been divorced from the theory of the subject as it was expounded by Euclid. He has even been credited with an important role in the introduction of the terms *theorica* and *practica* into Latin usage in the twelfth century.[7] Hugh has certainly done more than borrow the terms *speculativa* and *activa*; *theorica* and *practica* from Boethius. He has emphasized the special role of reasoning in abstract thought (*per solam. . . . ratiocinationem*) and thus brought the concept of a theoretical study a little more sharply into focus. At the same time he has separated it in some measure from the art of contemplation which he regarded as of the first importance for men of God, and in which more than reasoning is involved.[8]

Speculatio, or contemplation, must be directed towards God. It is the study of the divine (*studium divinitatis*) in which the *vivax mens,* the alert mind (or the reason) has a part to play.[9] The abstract thought required to master geometrical theory is of another order, because it demands nothing but reasoning, and is not concerned with the divine. The same is true for the arithmetical theory which was divorced, for the most part, from practical calculation in twelfth-century schools and for the logic Hugh himself gives as an example of a discipline requiring nothing but reason for its mastery. He is prepared, as we have seen to use the term *speculatio* for such theoretical *disciplinae*. But if we are to

---

[6] *Didascalicon,* II.1, Buttimer, p. 24.7–10 and *PL* 176.751.

[7] See R. Baron, 'Sur l'introduction en Occident des termes *geometria theorica et practica*', *Revue d'histoire des sciences,* 8 (1955), 298–302. Hugh's textbook on geometry is edited by R. Baron in *Opera Propaedeutica.*

[8] R. Baron, *Hugues de Saint-Victor: 'La contemplation et ses especes'* (Paris, 1955).

[9] Boethius on Porphyry, CSEL 48, p. 7.11.

speak of speculative theology we cannot restrict the definition
of *speculatio* to one which will embrace all such *theoretica*
equally well. We must accommodate the difference which is
made by the fact that this is a *studium divinitatis*. The contemplative resorts to the spiritual, to religious emotion and
devotional practices. But Hugh, again quoting Boethius on
Porphyry, is anxious to emphasize that the intellectual
discipline of *speculatio* involves only the mind and the understanding (which he sees as a faculty of the soul) and not the
senses.[10] The devotional element has not been explicitly set
aside, only the help the senses can give, the *practica* or *activa*
which are irrelevant to speculation. There is some emphasis
both in Boethius and in Hugh of St. Victor on the part the
powers of the soul, the *vires animae,* play.[11] They are seen as
the highest faculties of the understanding. The abstract
reasoning which thinking about God requires involves the
highest levels of mental activity. It is in this sense that it may
be said to have a spiritual component and to differ from the
abstract thought required to understand Euclid.

Such sentiments are to be found in a number of twelfth-
century writers. There was a widespread general recognition
that in so far as it was speculative, theology was a study of a
higher order than any other speculative or theoretical discipline. But because it was coming to be recognized as an
academic discipline in its own right, it was profoundly
influenced by the laws of thought which governed other
disciplines. Theology could be referred to in the thirteenth
century as the *ars artium* and the *scientia scientiarum* only
because it was possible to define its scope and its methods in
terms similar to those which were used for other disciplines.
So close had it become in some respects to all the other
disciplines, that there was some debate as to whether theology
or dialectic best deserved the title of 'art of arts' and 'science
of sciences'.[12]

If we are to argue that in becoming a speculative science,
theology approached the other disciplines in its methods, we

---

[10] *Didascalicon,* II.2, Buttimer, p. 25.1-14, *PL* 176.752; Boethius on
Porphyry p. 8.13.
[11] *Didascalicon,* I.3, Buttimer, p. 7, *PL* 176.743.
[12] Bodleian Library Oxford, MS. Digby 2 f.27, and see *LM* II¹, 416-26; 432-8.

must look a little more closely at the idea of *disciplina* in the
twelfth century. Again, a dual sense, a monastic and a
scholastic context, existed side by side. For Hugh of St.
Victor *disciplina* has a predominantly monastic sense. Discipline of life is inseparable from discipline of the mind. In a
chapter *On Discipline* in Book III of the *Didascalicon* he links
praecepta legendi with *pracepta vivendi*, the rules of reading
with the rules of living. 'Knowledge is not praiseworthy' if it
is marred by an ill-led life. 'And so he who seeks knowledge
must be careful above all not to neglect discipline' (*Et idcirco
summopere cavendum est ei qui quaerit scientiam, ut non
negligat disciplinam*).[13] William of Conches, in a not di-
similar way, sees two aspects, in the gift of sight *ad morum
instructionem,* to teach us to live well, and in the insight with
which we think about theoretical philosophy.[14]

But the term already had a technical sense in Boethius
from which developed its use as a term to describe an
academic discipline in twelfth-century schools. Boethius says
that mathematical studies must be conducted *disciplinaliter*.[15]
We have seen how he explains in his *De Trinitate* that there
are three *speculativae partes,* three branches of speculative
philosophy, *naturalis, mathematica, theologa.*[16] Natural
philosophy is concerned with the study of the natural world.
It is susceptible of rational enquiry (*rationaliter*). Mathematics
deals with the forms bodies take, but those forms cannot be
entirely separated from matter, and so mathematical thought
is not strictly abstract. It is carried out according to its own
proper rules (*disciplinaliter*). Theology deals with the divine,
and is truly abstract. Theological thought is handled *intel-
lectualiter.*[17] A discipline is thus an area of technical academic
study, even if Boethius does not here countenance its general
use to describe any branch of academic study. Moreover,
disciplina is seen as a form of *speculatio,* a method of philo-

---

[13] Buttimer p. 61.10–19; *PL* 176.773, Book III.12.

[14] William of Conches, *Glosa super Platonem,* ed. E. Jeauneau (Paris, 1965), p.
254.

[15] References to Boethius' text here are to Gilbert of Poitiers' version, reconstructed from his commentary by N. M. Haring in his edition of the Commentaries
on Boethius, p. 371.144–5, *De Trinitate,* I.2.

[16] Ibid., p. 371.5–13.　　　　　　　　　　　　　　[17] Ibid., p. 371.14–16.

sophizing. 'Come, now, let us speculate': *Age nunc ...
speculemur,*[18] says Boethius a little later in the *De Trinitate.*
The resources twelfth-century scholars needed in their search
for a technical terminology by which to distinguish speculative
theology as an academic discipline, and to clarify the
difference between speculative theological method and the
methods of the Scriptural commentator, were all provided by
Boethius here, in a treatise which was just coming to general
notice in the first half of the twelfth century at the time
when the need for such a technical terminology was beginning to be felt.

Thierry of Chartres says that it is the powers of the soul
which we use to understand abstraction. The particular
power (*vis anime*) we employ to understand the truth about
those things with which the mathematical disciplines are
concerned is called, he says, a *disciplina.*[19] Although *speculativa* include all forms of philosophy[20] which are concerned
with theory rather than practice[21] we must use different
powers of the soul for each of its three branches. 'And we
must know that we must use different powers of the soul
and different methods of comprehension in physics, mathematics and theology, so as to comprehend them all.'[22]
Although Thierry would not use *disciplina* for all three indis-
criminately, he sees each as involving a proper method which
we might loosely categorize as an academic discipline. Gilbert
of Poitiers says that rational speculation cannot be conducted
properly without the discipline which ensures its soundness
of procedure: 'The speculation of the "reason" cannot grasp
perfectly except by "discipline" what it is "to be" a something
said to "exist".'[23] For example, the 'reason' cannot understand what it is to be a body and to be coloured and to be
broad, unless it knows the 'discipline' which tells it what a
body is, what colour is and what breadth is. The process
involves abstracting such concepts from their concrete mani-

---

[18] Ibid., p. 376.1, *De Trinitate* I.5.
[19] *Thierry of Chartres,* p. 164.47-9.
[20] Ibid., p. 125.23.   [21] Ibid., p. 160.96.
[22] Ibid., p. 164.51.   [23] Gilbert of Poitiers, p. 84.74-6.

festations in individual bodies.[24] Gilbert's concern in this
passage is to show the relation between *physica* and *mathematica*, but he is making a statement of a more general kind
too, about the different ways in which each discipline or
mode of thought operates, and the different powers of mind
it requires. We are a long way here from the part the soul
plays in contemplative *speculatio* and much closer to a concept
of systematic thought such as that involved in the speculative theology of the later Middle Ages.

The strict delineation of the methods proper to a given
study is characteristic of the development of the academic
disciplines of the twelfth and thirteenth centuries. The way
in which this took place owes not a little to the direction
Boethius gave such explorations by his definition of *speculative* in the *De Trinitate* and his emphasis on the principle that
the object of speculation determines which method is appropriate. As Gilbert of Poitiers puts it in his commentary: 'And
this diversity of speculation comes from the diversity of
things which are perceived.'[25] Clarembald of Arras, too,
emphasises that once Boethius has listed the *speculative
partes* and explained their properties, he teaches his readers
how to speculate properly in each area.[26] The general view
of a discipline as a formal procedure is not confined to
mathematics even in Gilbert of Poitiers. He explains that
disciplina is *scola* in Greek, and gives it a broader sense in his
Prologue to his commentary on Boethius' *De Hebdomadibus*[27]
than that of the discipline of mathematics; he includes, for
example, the *logica disciplina*.[28] The most important element
in the twelfth-century concept of *disciplina* was its reference
to a formal body of methods proper to the study of a clearly-
defined type of material. *Speculatio* may be concerned with
any discipline of a theoretical kind, and theology had pride
of place among the disciplines, according to Boethius'
scheme, because no study was more highly abstract, more
wholly free of a concern with mutable and corporeal things.

[24] Ibid., p. 84.76–80.   [25] Ibid., p. 86.16–17.
[26] *Clarembald of Arras*, pp. 109–10.   [27] Gilbert of Poitiers, p. 183.10.
[28] Ibid., p. 190.87.

From the first half of the twelfth century, then, *speculatio* and *speculativa* were in use as terms to describe abstract thought on philosophical problems in general. When we speak of speculative theology in the terms of the time, we are speaking of philosophical theology. T. F. Torrance has said of modern thought in theology, science, or philosophy that its most marked characteristic is the search for 'appropriate methods and apposite modes of speech'.[29] Something of the same process may be seen at work in the twelfth century as scholars sought to divide and subdivide the speculative disciplines so as to give theology its proper place among them. The more clearly the methods and the technical terms and distinctive language of theology were defined, the more evidence became the fundamental differences of purpose between *speculatio* and the *studium sacrae scripturae*. As M. D. Chenu points out, for William of Auxerre and Thomas Aquinas in the thirteenth century, speculative theology was not only quite distinct from the study of the Bible. It was also a recognized science in its own right.[30] The difference lay partly in the organization of material. But a difference of thought is involved, too. *Speculatio* is abstract thought, purposeful, investigative thought which is governed by consciously-held principles concerning 'appropriate methods and apposite modes of speech'. As William of Conches puts it, it is *vehemens et assidua animi applicatio*[31] (a forceful and assiduous application of the mind).

It is never easy to determine whether a term has come into use to describe a novel phenomenon for which no name was available before, or whether the existence of a hitherto neglected term has influenced subsequent developments once it has come to notice. No doubt both processes have been at work here. The twelfth century commentators on Boethius' *opuscula sacra* found that Boethius had something to say on matters of strong contemporary interest to themselves, and that he provided a ready-made technical vocabulary in which the particular problems of methods of thought could be

---

[29] T. F. Torrance, *Theological Science* (Oxford, 1969), p. xiii.
[30] M. D. Chenu, *La Théologie comme science au treizième siecle* (Paris, 1943), p. 71–101. [31] William of Conches, ed. cit., p. 65.

discussed. Once the words *speculatio* and *speculativus* had
attracted attention they provided a focal point for further
discussion. What is beyond dispute is that these late Latin
words developed a new and extended meaning in the twelfth
century. *Speculativa* became something more than the
antithesis of *activa*; *speculatio* emcompassed more than its
older sense of 'contemplation'. And the outline definition of
the speculative disciplines which Boethius gives in the *De
Trinitate* lent a foundation to the structure of speculative
theology for which Boethius has not always been given
sufficient credit. His twelfth-century commentators looked
to him for technical terms as well as for instruction. Unless
we recognize the importance of such adoptions of terminology
at a time when it seemed to Thierry of Chartres that the
Latins were particularly short of words[32] we shall be in
danger of neglecting one of the most solid foundation-stones
of medieval scholasticism: the clarification of the technical
terms of each discipline, and in particular of the highest
discipline, theology.

2. The Problem of Knowledge

Three questions may be asked about the body of knowledge
which makes up the subject-matter of a discipline: 'What is to
be known about this subject?'; 'How do we know?'; and,
most fundamental of all, 'What do we mean by "knowing" in
connection with this subject?' For the beginner in each of the
liberal arts these questions could be answered simply, if not
very profoundly. The encyclopedias of Cassiodorus and
Isidore explain the main topics to be covered in studying
each discipline; they say something about the origins of the
discipline, and they suggest that 'knowing' rhetoric, for
example, means understanding the rules of oratory and
having some skill in using them. Hugh of St. Victor's pupils
apparently found answers like this reasonably satisfying even
in the twelfth century. But the advent of theology among
the conventional disciplines make it necessary for these
answers to be examined more searchingly. The majority of

[32] *Thierry of Chartres*, p. 237.68–9.

students were unlikely, perhaps, to be seriously worried by their inadequacy, but a few were more demanding. In the first decades of the twelfth century the converted Jew, Petrus Alphonsus, wrote a dialogue between a Christian and a Jew in which exactly this question of the way we know is raised. 'It is said that we know in three ways', he explains, by sense-perception, by what he calls a 'necessary reason' (*necessaria ratio*)[1] and by analogy, or *similitudo*.

The senses are specific, and knowledge proper to any one sense cannot be got in any other way. A blind man cannot imagine colours if they are described to him so that he merely hears about them (*solo auditu*). Such knowledge is to be had only by direct experience. The second kind of knowledge is directly recognized by the reason, as something self-evident; in this way we know that a body cannot at the same time be still and in motion. The last method of knowing involves a special sense of analogy or *similitudo*,[2] where we learn about something by its effect or result, or by some other sign of its existence. If we hear a voice, we know that someone able to speak is nearby. If we see smoke we know that there is a fire nearby. If we see a vessel, we know that someone made it, even if we did not watch him do so.[3] It is in this way that we know about God. It is the least direct and immediate of all the modes of knowledge which are available to us. Petrus Alphonsus has posed clearly and simply the difficulty in which he and his contemporaries increasingly found themselves when they began to ask what knowledge of his subject-matter the academic theologian could have. Knowledge about God did not lend itself to the convenient packaging to which the bodies of knowledge of the liberal arts had long been subjected.

In a sermon for the birthday of the Virgin St. Bernard tries to explain by means of an image the situation in which man finds himself when he seeks to know a God whom he recognizes to be beyond the reach of his understanding. In the beginning, he says, the Word was with God, a fountain

---

[1] *Necessaria ratio* is a concept of some importance in Anselm's thought, particularly in the *Cur Deus Homo*.

[2] Its more usual meaning in eleventh- and twelfth century writings is that of 'analogy'.   [3] *PL* 157.555.

pouring into itself. God's thoughts were his own, and we cannot know what they were. But since God became man, he says, 'He dwells through faith in our hearts; he dwells in our memory; he dwells in our thought', and he descends even to a level where we may form a mental image of him. The fountain thus overflows upon the minds of men. Until then, how could a man think about God unless he made an idol in his heart, asks Bernard?[4] Now that God has become man it is possible for human understanding to think about God and to envisage him in human terms without idolatry.

Bernard gives his readers a picture. Aquinas approaches the problem in more abstract terms because he is writing for an academic readership. He asks whether we have need of any other knowledge, since philosophy embraces all knowledge and Aristotle has shown that theology (as the Greek world understood it) is a branch of philosophy.[5] But he goes on to point out that the Bible has no place in this scheme, which is entirely the work of human reason. The knowledge about God to be found in the Bible is given directly by God, who inspired the writing of Holy Scripture. Thus this kind of knowledge is given by the object of the knowledge himself, and it is to be attained in no other way. Even the knowledge by *similitudo* of Petrus Alphonsus, the oblique knowledge gained from the evidence of God's work in making and sustaining the natural world, can tell us nothing about God except what he has made it possible to see reflected there. The subject-matter of theology in general is therefore unique in that only so much is revealed as the central object of study himself chooses to show.

The ordinary language and the ordinary modes of knowledge in which we deal when we study created things therefore apply to the divine only in a transferred or specially adapted sense.[6] In the *Summa Contra Gentiles* (I, 28–30) Aquinas explains that words used of God are metaphorical when they are derived from a normal usage in which they refer to a creature. A creature may be said to be 'like' God

---

[4] *Bernardi Opera Omnia,* ed. J. Leclercq and H. Rochais (Rome, 1968), V.282, 10–18.

[5] *Summa Theologica,* I, Q.1, art. 1, obj.2, cf. Aristotle *Met.* VI.1, 1026ª19.

[6] *Thierry of Chartres,* p. 60.5–6.

only in the sense that the creature has what belongs to God. God cannot be understood in terms of the creature. The student of theology is therefore forced to construct his analogies from a disadvantageous position, because he cannot clearly see that with which he wants to compare them. The struggle to get round this difficulty led to a search for a technical language which will serve the purpose of talking about God as well as possible. Ordinary language must be allowed special rules here. There can be no academic study where discourse about the subject of study is impossible, and one of the strongest indications that theology was being seen as an academic discipline was the attempt to make available to its students a language adequate for talking about God in this way.

There was a new sophistication of approach to the theory of language in Anselm and in Peter Abelard. The long-term implications of their work for the philosophy of language have only recently become fully apparent.[7] These scholars and others among their contemporaries examined the relation between the grammatical function and the dialectical function of a word in a statement or proposition, in an attempt to show where the two disciplines coincided and where they were distinct. The *Sententiae Parisienses,* which owe a good deal to Abelard, say that the skills of the philosophers in this kind of exercise were useless to them when they tried to talk about God. The dialectical laws of definition fail: 'The philosophers could not transfer any word to God which they could define, nor could they show what God was. 'Philosophi non potuerunt adaptare Deo aliquod vocabulum, quo possent diffinire vel ostendere quid Deus esset'.[8] This is because the *philosophi* could not say anything 'properly' of God (*proprie dicere de Deo*) according to the rule of the human or secular arts (*per regulam humanarum artium*).[9] The fundamental laws of grammar will not serve, either. The verb, we are told, is the most important part of speech because no statement is complete without a verb,

---

[7] D. P. Henry, *The Logic of St. Anselm* (Oxford, 1967).
[8] *Ysagoge in Theologiam,* p. 5.27.   [9] Ibid., p. 6.5.

and a verb can even serve as a noun: 'For every saying can be complete without the other [parts of speech], but never without a verb, for I can use a participle in place of a noun.'[10] But the verb in its ordinary grammatical sense cannot be used of God because a verb denotes time (*consignificativum temporis*) by its tenses, and God is eternal. Reflections of this kind are relatively commonplace. The difficulty of handling the knowledge God gives us of himself in terms available to us in human language presented a pressing problem in specific and detailed ways, and the developments in technical language which were helpful in the secular arts often compounded the peculiar difficulties of the academic theologian in treating his own subject-matter by clear-cut and generally accepted rules.

William of St. Thierry says that the first task of the theologian is to define what is to be believed.[11] Because he works in an academic discipline, the academic theologian is concerned primarily with the subject-matter of faith. The act of believing, the religious emotion or spiritual perception involved in faith is another matter, as William James emphasizes,[12] and as Hugh of St. Victor, Clarenbald of Arras, and other twelfth-century thinkers saw very clearly. In a later generation Bonaventure describes in his *Itinerarium Mentis ad Deum* the ardent love (*ardentissimus amor*),[13] the desires (*desideria*),[14] and the steps of ecstasy (*esctaticos excessus*)[15] by which the soul reaches a condition of faith. Bonaventure was unusual among later medieval theologians in trying to unite the spiritual experience of faith with the academic discussion of its subject-matter in a single system of knowledge. The attempt was not commonly made because the development of an academic theology made the difference between the activity of faith (the act of knowing God) and the subject-matter of faith (the question of what can be known about God) increasingly plain.

[10] Ibid., p. 7.3.   [11] *PL* 180.249 *De Contemplando Dei.*
[12] William James, *The Varieties of Religious Experience* (1901, reprinted London, 1960), p. 48.   [13] *Opera Omnia*, V.295, para. 3.
[14] Ibid., p. 296, para. 3.   [15] Ibid., p. 295, para. 3.

Yet Boethius taught that theological ideas have a special inwardness. While the ideas of natural science are *exteriores* and those of the most abstract of the sciences (mathematics) are *interiores,* he says, those of theology are *intima.*[16] Gilbert of Poitiers, too, concedes the mystery of the *secreta theologice.*[17] But it was the depth and remoteness and obscurity of theological concepts in an intellectual sense which concerned academic theologians, not their spiritual profundity. It was the sheer difficulty of theological epistemology which absorbed their interest, not the spiritual experience of the act of faith. It was only those aspects of knowledge about God which lent themselves to the new technical procedures which became the subject-matter of academic theology. The field of study was to be immensely broadened in comparison with Boethius' definition of *theologia* in the *De Trinitate* and considerable adaptations of Augustine's use of the term were to be made, but theology was not to encompass all the 'varieties of religious experience'. These distinctions are still with us.

It is sometimes possible to arrive by painstaking effort at a knowledge or a skill for which one has little natural talent, and which others can achieve quickly and easily. The new academic theology offered a method of making some progress in the knowledge of God by procedures open to any educated man, even if he had no exceptional spiritual gifts. Rupert of Deutz says that the Word of God is known not in one way but in two (*non tantum uno modo cognoscitur sed duobus modis*).[18] He is known from his works (*ex operibus*) and from himself (*ex semetipse*); wonderfully is he known from his works, but far more wonderfully from himself (*magnificentius ex semetipso*)![19] The second mode of knowledge is reserved for a few (*Hec talis cognitio sive experimentum valde paucorum est*).[20] Anyone could set about methodically learning what could be learned about God from the created world and from the Bible. To know him in any other

---

[16] Gilbert of Poitiers, p. 67.43, *Theological Tractates,* p. 4.

[17] Gilbert of Poitiers, p. 54.32.

[18] *De Victoria Verbi Dei,* ed. H. Haacke *MGH Quellen,* V (Weimar, 1970), p. 7.22.   [19] Loc. cit.   [20] Ibid., p. 8.21.

way is recognized here as a rare gift. There is a sense in which the twelfth-century development of an academic theology can be seen to grow out of a common-sense recognition of the limitations of human powers of knowing about God. It concerns itself with what can be managed by straightforward, sound technical procedures, with what can be closely supervised and kept within the bounds of orthodoxy. The experience of knowing God 'directly' remains a private affair, and although in the later Middle Ages St. Bonaventure and Meister Eckhart, like Hugh of St. Victor in the twelfth century, saw no great divide here, the main stream of academic theology flowed in only one channel.

The twelfth-century clarification of the difference between theology and philosophy (and particularly between what might be called a 'theological epistemology'[21] and the philosopher's epistemology) was not arrived at as the result of a new insight on the part of a single thinker, or even as the result of a concerted effort. For every scholar who can be identified as moving one way along the line of development, there are others who have not been caught up in the change. But as a result of patient investigation of the textbooks in the light of new habits of thought, the fact that there was an epistemological difference became increasingly clear to a number of scholars. The arrival of new works on the academic scene provided an important stimulus, but certainly not the only stimulus. We shall understand the aims and achievements of these scholars best if we look for the working together of the ideas and assumptions they drew from an increasingly wide range of technical studies, and try to reconstruct the community of thought in which they worked.

Because of the way in which contemporary scholars normally went about their work, their general reflections are, as a rule, tied closely to the specific difficulty out of which they have arisen. Although these were men of intellectual enterprise and their aspirations were great, their first concern was with detailed comparison and contrast. Their academic theology was conceived in relation to and in contradistinction

---

[21] See F. Guisberti, 'A Treatise on Implicit Propositions', *Cahiers* 21 (1977), 47-8.

from what they knew of an existing philosophical system of some sophistication, that of the ancient world; it was only by borrowing from that system that they could give their own new academic study a comparable standing. Theirs is a thology defined in the terms of philosophy, but at a detailed level and perhaps without profound originality of conception. They were not, for example, apparently struck by a point which was clear to Philo of Alexandria and which is noted by Charles Hartshorne: the intrinsic repugnance between the Platonists' view of God as supremely abstract and the Christian conception of God as a personal deity.[22] They looked at Platonic teaching without a sense of the difference of inspiration which made it alien to Christian theology; they exercised their caution instead over the specific doctrinal differences *philosophia* might give rise to.

F. R. Tennant makes a distinction between the 'psychological' epistemology of faith and the 'higher logic aloof from psychology', with which philosophers are concerned.[23] By means of such devices modern scholarship can sometimes provide a form of words — if no more — to help illuminate difficulties which greatly troubled twelfth-century thinkers. Their method of working discouraged them from allowing broad distinctions to obfuscate particular problems by generalizing them. The twelfth-century discovery of the scope and limitations of theology as an academic discipline was, for this reason, strictly limited at first. But it had the advantage of ensuring that the foundations were very thoroughly dug and that the theology of the thirteenth century and after rested on a solid base. It is to this very concern with detail that we owe the durability of the main principles upon which academic theology was organized for many centuries, and some of the principles which have governed it ever since.

3. The Arts of Language

John Stuart Mill credits the study of logic with the power of

---

[22] C. Hartshorne, 'The God of Religion and the God of Philosophy', *Talk of God* (*Royal Institute of Philosophy Lectures*), 2 (1969), p. 153.
[23] F. R. Tennant, *Philosophical Theology* (Cambridge, 1928), p. 290.

forming sound habits of mind: 'I am persuaded that nothing, in modern education, tends so much, when properly used, to form exact thinkers, who attach a precise meaning to words and propositions, and are not imposed on by vague, loose, or ambiguous terms.'[1] He sees the qualities which are to be desired in a trained mind in very much the light in which twelfth-century scholars were beginning to see them. Exactly this concern with precision in the use of words was bred by the increasingly widespread and detailed study of the arts of language of the trivium and the mathematical arts of the quadrivium in the twelfth-century schools.[2] By thinking hard about the words they were using the scholars of the day began to see more deeply into the philosophical and theological problems with which they were dealing. As Jolivet has put it, 'La précision des termes est une condition de l'approfondissement du problème'.[3]

One of the arts of language, grammar and dialectic were by far the most developed and influential in the twelfth century. The two arts shared certain technical terms, and a number of new lines of thought were prompted by the attempt to explain discrepancies between the use of a given term in grammar and its use in dialectic. According to the Roman grammarians names (they included both nouns and adjectives in the class of *nomina*) normally signify both substance and quality, but dialectical tradition restricts the signification of such words as 'white' or 'literate' to quality only. 'A white' is not normally a substance;[4] only 'a white something' is a substance. *Nomen, verbum, substantia, qualitas, relativa* and a number of other terms common to both studies had also, since patristic times, been technical terms of Latin theology. It may be true, as F. Ferré has suggested, that 'the primary duty of the theologian is not to philosophise about his

---

[1] John Stuart Mill, *Autobiography*, ed. J. Stillinger (Oxford, 1971), p. 13. I am grateful to the editor of the *Downside Review* for permission to reprint material from my article 'The Borrowed Meaning: Grammar, Logic and the Problem of Theological Language in Twelfth-Century Schools', 96 (1978), 165–75.

[2] L. Nielsen, 'On the Doctrine of Logic and Language of Gilbert of Porreta and his Followers' *Cahiers*, 17 (1976), 42–3.

[3] J. Jolivet, *Arts du langage et théologie chez Abélard* (Paris, 1969), p. 205.

[4] Priscian, ed. H. Keil, *Grammatici Latini*, II.55.6, and cf. Boethius on Aristotle's *Categories, PL* 64.239.

language but to use it,'[5] but twelfth-century scholars found
it increasingly difficult to find ways of using ordinary or
technical terms in theological discussion at all, without
examining what they were doing in terms of the contemporary philosophy of language. They found themselves in a
position not unlike that of the modern theologian when they
tried to understand what special use of language was required
in order to talk about God.

The central concern of those twelfth-century scholars who
were interested in the theory of language lay in the problem
of meaning or signification. The author of one dialectical
treatise remarks that it is said that every proposition or
question has two kinds of 'meaning' (*duos sensus*), one
grammatical, the other dialectical, but that there is more than
one school of thought on the point among his contemporaries.[6] If we are to use human language to talk about God it
is exactly this question of its meaning or reference which
presents itself most forcibly. Unless we can show that what
we are saying has some meaning in connection with God,
or that it refers to him in some way, we cannot be sure
that we are saying anything about God at all. We may be
talking about an imaginary being.

In his *Dialectica* Abelard discusses the different ways in
which a word may have meaning, the *modi significandi*.[7] He
asks, as Augustine had done in the *De Magistro*, whether
every *nomen* has a meaning, that is, a *res* or thing to which
the name refers, and of which it creates an understanding in
the mind (*intellectum generare*).[8] If the subject was not new,
its treatment in Abelard and his twelfth-century successors
was quite novel in its concern with technical exactitude.
Abelard was taking the first steps towards the formulation
of 'the doctrine of *suppositio terminorum* or the doctrine of
the different ways terms may stand for things'[9] which was to
be the foundation of medieval signification-theory. Abelard
distinguishes between sounds which have a natural meaning

---

[5] F. Ferré, *Language, Logic and God* (New York, 1961), p. 105.
[6] *LM* II^i, p. 184.   [7] Abelard, *Dialectica*, p. 111–12.
[8] Ibid., p. 112.31.
[9] E. W. Warren, Introduction to a translation of the *Isagoge* of Porphyry
(Toronto, 1975), p. 16.

(when we hear a dog bark we know that he is angry) and sounds which have meanings because men have chosen that they shall mean something (*ad placitum significare*),[10] Sounds which derive their meaning artificially from human usage have to be 'imposed' as the names of things. During the course of the century scholars learned to differentiate between that to which a name is given (*cui*), that from which a name is given (*a quo*) and that because of which a name is given (*propter quod*).[11] The basis of these later developments was the assumption that human language is of human devising and that there is no absolute relation between a given word and its meaning. A word, as Humpty Dumpty says, means what its first user chooses that it shall mean. Later it comes to have a generally accepted meaning. That is certainly what Abelard thought,[12] and there is Scriptural warrant for the view in the Genesis account of Adam's naming of the animals.

But if we have only a humanly-devised language, how can we use it to refer to God? What meaning do our words have when we talk about God? This was the nub of the twelfth-century discussion of the application of the theory of signification developed by grammarians and logicians to the problem of theological language. It has always lain at the centre of the problem of theological language, but here we can see it being framed with some precision as a result of new work upon technical terms and technical language in the *artes*. Thierry of Chartres suggests that the names *Pater, Filius,* and *Spiritus* were first given by man to created things (*data sunt primo rebus creatis*). Later they were used in a transferred sense of God by analogy (*postea translata sunt ad deum per similitudinem*). They are not God's own names (*non . . . sint eius nomina*) but they apply to him *translative*.[13] These were questions treated by Pseudo-Dionysius, and by Aquinas' day it was possible to treat the matter of the *divina nomina* in more detail and with due allowance for a number of related issues, as Aquinas himself does in the *De Divinis*

[10] Abelard, *Dialectica,* p. 114.19.
[11] Nielson, op. cit., p. 42; *LM* II^i, p. 227, p. 245.
[12] *Theologia Christiana,* III, 90, p. 230.1154-5.
[13] *Thierry of Chartres,* p. 463.57.

Nominibus. But the influence of Pseudo-Dionysius was only just beginning to make itself felt in the middle of the twelfth century, and for Thierry and Abelard the principal question concerns the 'meaning' of the words we use of God. Abelard, like Thierry, maintains that the words by which we distinguish the Persons of the Trinity have been borrowed from their customary signification (*translata sunt a consuetis significationibus*) and we must therefore consider with care how they may be said to be proper to him.[14]

Gilbert of Poitiers says that God cannot be explained in words (*Deus . . . sermone inexplicabilis*).[15] That does not mean, he concedes, that he cannot be known in some other way. There are three things: *res, intellectus,* and *sermo* ('the thing, the understanding, and the word'). The thing is conceived of in the understanding and signified by the word (*res intellectu concipitur, sermone significatur*).[16] God may, then, be conceived of without words. But just as we cannot explain eternity in words if we restrict ourselves to their proper or usual meaning (*proprie significationis verbis explanare non possumus*)[17] for verbs denote time and there is no time in eternity, so if we choose to employ words, we cannot speak of God except *translative.* Thierry tries to indicate the way in which this transferred sense 'signifies'. 'Nothing', he says, 'can be predicated of God but only a word used in a transferred sense (*translative*), which in some way hints at (*aliquo modo innuitur*) the divine Being which is above all substance.'[18] Words used of God 'imply' or 'hint at' what he is, but they do not have 'meaning' in the way that human words have with reference to created things. They cannot be predicated of the divine substance as they can of created substances. This is a phenomenon equally applicable to all theological statements (*theologicae propositiones*), which all 'hint' in some way at what is above all things' (*innuunt quodam modo id quod est supra omnia*).[19]

---

[14] *Theologia Christiana,* I, 7, p. 74.90 and p. 87 ff.
[15] Gilbert of Poitiers, p. 53.9.   [16] Ibid., p. 67.55.
[17] Ibid., p. 136.28.   [18] *Thierry of Chartres,* p. 195.16.
[19] Ibid., p. 191.83–6.

One way of explaining this problem in technical terms is to say that only the *nomina,* or names, we use for God (just, great, blessed) are predicated of him, not the actuality of God himself, the *res.*[20] When Thierry of Chartres reaches the passage in the fourth book of Boethius' *De Trinitate* where Boethius mentions the ten *praedicamenta* of Aristotle, he pauses over it at unusual length.[21] He is anxious to determine not only how the Aristotelian *Categories* may be applied to God, but also in what ways it may be possible to predicate terms of God, and what facts about God words may be able to establish for us. Several times in the course of his commentaries and lectures on the Boethian *opuscula sacra* he returns to the topic of the way in which we may refer to God's being and nature and attributes 'directly'.[22]

The question of the difference between direct and oblique signification had already been raised by St. Anselm. He had put forward the view that such words as *grammaticus* (a) literate (man), do not signify both the substance, the literate man, and the qualities which make him literate, in the same way (*grammaticus vero non significat hominem et grammaticum et unum*). Such words signify the quality directly and the substance which possesses it obliquely (*grammaticam per se et hominem per aliud*)[23] ('literacy directly and the man who is literate obliquely'). But Anselm did not attempt to extend the principle to cover the ways in which terms may be used of God, and the technical distinction he made does not seem to have entered into the logical tradition of the twelfth-century schools as a direct result of his influence.

Some indication of how far things had gone technically by the end of the twelfth century is to be found in the *Regulae Theologicae* of Alan of Lille.[24] The particular *regulae,* or rules, which Alan puts forward owe a great deal to his study of the *artes.* He gives up a considerable portion of his study

---

[20] Ibid., p. 191.77–8.   [21] Ibid., p. 186–96.
[22] Ibid., p. 463.45–8, cf. Aquinas *De Divinis Nominibus, Lectio I,* 30.
[23] *Anselmi Opera Omnia,* I.157.1–8. Cf. D. P. Henry, *The Logic of St. Anselm,* p. 18 ff.   [24] *PL* 210.

to the question of the way in which the grammarian's parts
of speech and the dialectician's categories may be applied to
God in theological language. In his introductory remarks
Alan borrows a passage which is first to be found in Gilbert
of Poitier's commentary on the *De Hebdomadibus,* where
all the rules and axioms of the individual arts are set side
by side.[25] Alan goes a stage further and compares the axioms
of the liberal arts with the *theologicae maximae* which, he
says, have an 'absolute necessity' and cannot be broken.[26]
These are not to be put before the ignorant,[27] because to
understand them demands deep study.[28] What Alan himself
does in practice is to take axioms which can be identified
as belonging to individual arts, especially to arithmetic,
grammar, and dialectic, and to show their deeper implications for theology — that is, he tried to apply the technical
language and the technically exact methods of the day
directly to the problem of talking about God.

In Rule 10 he looks at predication of terms in connection
with God. When a term is predicated of him, he says, nothing
which may be predicated of him is left outside that predication. If we say 'God is good' it is as if we said 'God is strong'
or 'God is holy'; each implies the other only in the special
case of God. Such predication he calls *copulata* or *conjuncta.*
Terms can be predicated of creatures only *divisim,*[29] particularly, in such a way as to refer to specific attributes one
at a time. From the first it is made clear that language used of
God obeys special rules, but that these rules may be formulated in the conventional technical terms of trammar or
rhetoric or dialectic. In Alan's view we can do more than say
that the tehological language does not obey the ordinary
rules of language; we can make a useful attempt to explain
the adapted rules of grammar and dialectic which theological
language obeys.

'Every name which applies to God applies to him causative-
ly, or by analogy, or adjectivally, or negatively' (*causative;*

[25] Gilbert of Poitiers, pp. 189–90. [26] *PL* 210.621-2.
[27] *PL* 210.622. [28] *PL* 210.628. [29] Rules 22, 23.

similitudinarie, adjective; negative), says Rule 21.[30] Since according to Rule 20 no name can be properly predicated of God,[31] it follows that every name used of him must be transferred from its proper signification (*transumitur a sua propria significatione*) and used in one of these four indirect or 'improper' ways. Names which are predicated of God *per causam,* such as 'righteous, holy, powerful' refer to the divine substance. The others are predicated of him relatively (*relative*), by analogy (Father, Son, brightness), for a reason (God is called angry because he punishes), or negatively (when God is said to withhold grace or harden someone's heart). Alan is perhaps a little too anxious to develop his principle and to find exact technical terms and correspondences at every point, but his general drift is clear enough. Although we must recognize that we can speak of God only by using words 'improperly', we can still identify the rules of the arts of language in our usages when we do so.

Alan recognizes one of the implicit limitations of such adapted theological language. The transference of meaning applies only to the word itself, not to the actuality to which it refers. In the natural world, he says, sometimes both the word and the thing are 'transferred' in an analogy or metaphor, sometimes only the thing, and sometimes only the word. If we speak of a 'white monk' we do not mean that the monk himself is white, but only that he wears a white habit. So it is with God. To say 'God is just' is not to imply that he is just as a man may be just; the ordinary reference of the term, the ordinary 'thing' to which it refers, is not attributed to God with the borrowed term. God's justice is understood to be something quite out of reach of the human notion of justice. This is the crux of the problem of theological language. If we cannot fully know what it is that we are using the borrowed language to refer to, we cannot know that we refer to that something properly or exactly. Alan gives no prominence to the point. He is satisfied that the limitation should be recognized and that it should be clearly understood that what he has to say about the usefulness of the rules of grammar and dialectic applies only to the *nomina* themselves

---

[30] *PL* 210.631. [31] *PL* 210.630.

and not to the actuality or *res* which is God.[32]

Accordingly, he works his way through the parts of speech, considering how each may be used in talking about God. By Rule 30[33] we learn that *nomina essentialia* are either abstract or concrete. Abstract terms, such as 'whiteness', 'blackness', signify properties which do not inhere in specific individuals. Concrete terms, such as 'white' or 'black' signify properties which do inhere in specific individuals. These are less appropriate to God than abstract terms, for abstract terms are 'simpler' and therefore nearer to the supreme simplicity of God himself. By the same general principle, it is clear that substantives are less improperly used of God than adjectives,[34] because adjectives describe the concrete and composite. Positives are more suitable than comparatives or superlatives, because there is no greater or lesser in God. Words for incorporeal things (*spiritus, misericordia*) are more appropriate than words for things which inhere in bodies (whiteness, linearity).[35] Verbs are less appropriate than nouns, because verbs signify time, and there is no time in God.[36] Verbs in the present tense come closer to being fitting than verbs in any other tense, for this reason. Adverbs of place must somehow be understood without the limitation of the idea of place which is implied in 'everywhere' or 'anywhere', and adverbs of time must be similarly understood not to refer to specific periods of time, like 'today' or 'yesterday' or 'tomorrow'.[37] The point need not be laboured. Whenever Alan finds a principle of discrimination within the rules of grammar which allows him to see a reason why one usage may be more suitable than another, he points it out.

Perhaps the most philosophically important point he makes is to emphasize the universality of theological language. It must, he argues, be universal in three respects. Words used of God should be familiar (not neologisms or special terms), in general use (so that everyone may understand them) and comprehensible (not obscure or shrouded

---

[32] *PL* 210.633, Rule 26.
[34] *PL* 210.636, Rule 31.
[36] *PL* 210.639–40, Rules 37, 39, 40.
[33] *PL* 210.635, Rule 30.
[35] *PL* 210.637, Rule 35.
[37] *PL* 210.640, Rules 41–4.

in mystery).[38] The intention is that the theologian should have a stock of ordinary words with which he may, with care and with an eye to their appropriateness in context, speak about God as best he can. But it is clear that the special problem of talking about God in human language could not be expected to yield to these relatively simple contrivances of the grammarians and logicians. Alan himself acknowledges the difficulty of determining what import the *nomina* or names of God have in respect of the *res,* the reality of God, or what they may contribute to our understanding. Words used of God have only a borrowed meaning.

In an attempt to get round this difficulty, some scholars resorted to analogies or *similitudines*. These describe the *res,* the real state of affairs in some aspects of the created world, and suggest a comparison with the divine *res,* the nature or actions of God. They strive to make possible an understanding of the reality of God by some other means than naming him or using words of him directly. This method, too, is unsatisfactory, since analogies are not always obvious. They may even be devised as a means of concealing the truth from some and demonstrating it to others; the parables of the Gospels were designed to do this. As a result the truth may be wrapped up in parables and mysteries (*parabolicis aenigmatibus involuta*), as Peter Abelard points out.[39] Even where the analogy is clear enough, it must be inadequate,[40] because God cannot be compared with created things except in so far as they are pale reflections of him. Looked at from the dialecticians' point of view the analogy has disadvantages at least as great as those of human language. We can come no closer to direct comparison with God than we can to speaking of him directly. Augustine's famous analogy between the Trinity and a river made up of spring, stream, and pool gave a certain illumination, but it would not stand up to hard analysis (as Anselm discovered when he exposed his version of it to public comment in the *De Incarnatione Verbi,* and as Abelard was quick to emphasize in his *Theologia Christiana*).[41]

---

[38] *PL* 210.637, Rule 34.
[39] *Theologia Christiana,* III, 134, p. 245.1632-8.
[40] Ibid., p. 246.1641-2.
[41] *Anselmi Opera Omnia,* II.31-2, 201-5; *Theologia Christiana,* pp. 333-4.

Nevertheless, that power of illumination was valued by those twelfth-century writers who were less concerned with the technical problem of using words or analogies to talk about God, and more interested in evoking a lively faith in their readers. Many of the images and comparisons used by the Fathers or to be found in Scripture itself have a power of awakening imaginative sympathy. They are like the *agentes imagines* of the *Rhetorica ad Herennium*,[42] active working images. Gerhoch of Reichersberg mentions the 'strong woman' who is, metaphorically speaking, the fortitude of faith (*sub metaphora fortis mulieris laudanda est fortitudo fidei*).[43] When we move into the realm of metaphor and simile and *figurativa locutio*[44] in general we meet yet another form of indirect language about God. There is a transferred sense here of a literary or rhetorical kind, which has little to do with logic, but which was a common point of resort for twelfth-century scholars who were baffled by the impossibility of talking about God directly. It was certainly more generally attractive, and probably more influential in the thinking of the majority of contemporary scholars, than the technical contrivances of the grammarians and dialecticians.

The problem of the proper application of the *artes* to the study of the Bible and to theological speculation, which greatly occupied twelfth-century scholars, appears here in the smaller (but absolutely central) problem of their usefulness in helping scholars to penetrate further than ordinary language will allow. Can we speak of God more directly if we do so with greater technical precision, if, that is, we abide by the rules of grammar, dialectic, and rhetoric so that we are quite sure that we are using language exactly? Gregory the Great thought not. *Indignum vehementer existimo ut verba caelestis oraculi restringam sub regulis Donati,*[45] 'I think it most unfitting for me to confine the words of the Heavenly Oracle beneath the rules of Donatus.' In the middle of the twelfth century the Benedictine scholar Hugh, Bishop of Rouen,

[42] *Rhetorica ad Herennium*, III.xxii.37.

[43] Gerhoch of Reichersberg, *Opera Inedita*, ed. P. Damian, O. Van den Eynde, P. A. Rijmersdael (Rome, 1955), 2 vols., Vol. I, 170.17–171.1, *De Laude Fidei.*

[44] Gerhoch of Reichersberg, *Letter to Pope Hadrian about the Novelities of the Day*, ed. N. M. Haring (Toronto, 1974), p. 32.24.

[45] *PL* 75.516.

took the same view. 'Whatever can be said of God according to God ought to be understood not by our own rules but by his.' Our words (*verba nostra*) are of no use in speaking about God if we employ them according to the rules of grammar, rhetoric, or dialectic (*non more grammatico, non rhetorico, non dialectico*).[46] These are words of proper caution. There must above all be reverence in the use of human language about God: *summi et summa cum reverentia nominandi Dei.*[47] But they are also, in a sense, a counsel of despair: *Deus enim semper est id quod est, qui determinari seu describi vel diffiniri non potest, quia incomprehensibilis est*[48] 'For God is always that which he is, and he cannot be determined or described or defined because he is beyond understanding'. The students of the secular arts could not 'apply to God any word by which they can define or show what God is'.[49] Had all their contemporaries taken such advice we should have had no academic theology. The business of the academic theologian is to find means, with the aid of all the human sciences he has at his disposal, of making some headway against this fundamental barrier to the knowledge of God. He may not aspire to break through it, but he makes it his business to discover more exactly where it lies.

Gerhoch of Reichersberg, Hugh of Rouen, and others were trying to hold at arm's length the problem which M. Durrant has identified as that of 'the logical status of God'.[50] Unless we can determine the function of the names we use for God in statements, questions and propositions we cannot reason about him by any formally acceptable procedure. To try to do so is merely to play a 'language-game',[51] where the rules are followed with perfect internal consistency but without any reference outwards to the *res* to which we intend them to refer. If the tricks we must play with technical (and even ordinary) language in order to use it of God are to be anything more than devices, we must find some assurance that in speaking of God *translative* we are making some kind of

[46] *PL* 192.1252.   [47] Rupert of Deutz *De Voluntate Dei, PL* 170.437.
[48] *PL* 192.1252.   [49] *Sententias Parisienses*, p. 5.27.
[50] M. Durrant, *The Logical Status of God* (London, 1973).
[51] J. McQuarrie, *Thinking about God* (London, 1975), p. 6.

statement about what he is. These statements cannot, however, be objectively verifiable in any straightforward way because, as McQuarrie points out, we cannot 'stand back and observe him, as we might do in the case of a natural phenomenon'.[52] Yet in order to speak of God as 'almighty', 'everlasting', 'merciful' we must be able to point to the being of whom such names are predicated.[53] If we construe 'God' as a proper name we must be able to specify its bearer.[54] At best we can 'take the word God as a proper noun'[55] for purposes of argument, rather as Anselm took 'evil' as a *quasi-aliquid*, 'a sort-of something', for purposes of discussion, so that words could be taken to refer to it in a recognizable way, even though he believed that evil in itself was nothing.[56] Cupitt recognizes this imperative need to compromise, to follow the normal rules of language as though they applied to God directly, if any theological thinking at all is to be done. 'To be able to move, a theology needs to include at least one affirmative statement about God: a statement, that is, expressing a proposition whose logical subject is God.'[57]

To attempt anything of the kind requires both flexibility of mind and a thorough grasp of the laws of discourse. These are the conspicuous qualities bred by the academic training of the twelfth century and perhaps of any age. Gerhoch of Reichersberg and Hugh of Rouen preached caution; if their view had been followed out to its logical conclusion theology would not have been 'able to move'. It 'moved' by coming to terms with the impossibility of using language about God and proposing working methods of ignoring that impossibility, if only for purposes of argument.

4. Scientific Theology and the Mathematical Arts

The advances made by a scientific thought in the twentieth century have posed a number of specific new problems for

---

[52] Ibid., p. 10.   [53] Durrant, p. 12.   [54] Loc. cit.
[55] McQuarrie, op. cit., p. 102, but cf. Aquinas, *Summa Theologica*, I, q.13, art. 8, where *deus* is said to be a *nomen naturale*, the name of a 'nature'.
[56] *Anselmi Opera Omnia*, I.248–51, *De Casu Diaboli*.
[57] D. Cupitt, *Christ and the Hiddenness of God* (London, 1971), p. 20.

theologians and some major general difficulties. Nevertheless, the problem of reconciling science and Christian theology is as old as Christianity itself. Among the scholars of the fourth and fifth centuries who made the attempt Gregory of Nyssa perhaps stands out, but he was not alone in perceiving the existence of the difficulty in patristic times. Despite the differences of approach and method which make the science of the twelfth century so foreign to that of our own day in many ways, certain underlying similarities must always exist in the response of the theologian to the challenge of reconciling Christian doctrine with scientific laws. In particular, the use he can make of the scientist's discoveries and the extent to which the scientist's methods are acceptable to him, are matters which exercise the theologian in every age; it is here that his difficulties especially lie in a period of major scientific advance, where the ground-rules of both scientific and theological discipline are undergoing change.

It has been suggested that the thirteenth century saw a signal change in the relation between theology and science.[1] But even before the newly rediscovered works of Aristotle began to give definition and a new direction of development to that relation, a number of twelfth-century scholars made a significant contribution to bringing the change about, by preparing the ground for the reception of the new material. Much of their work had its beginnings even earlier. Gerbert of Aurillac and Abbo of Fleury were as conversant with the theory of number and some of its theological implications at the end of the tenth century, as some of their successors were more than a hundred years later. What was new in the twelfth century was the focusing of more general attention upon the possibilities of applying the teaching of secular authors to the resolution of the theological problems which arise in connection with the origin and running of the natural world. The mathematical subjects of the quadrivium were also beginning to provide some of the common furniture of men's minds, to an extent which has no precedent in the Middle Ages. The

---

[1] On the twentieth-century problem, see T. F. Torrance, *Theology in Reconstruction* (London, 1965), p. 16. W. Pannenberg thinks the difficulty did not become pressing until the thirteenth century: *Theology and the Philosophy of Science*, tr. F. McDonagh (London, 1976), p. 7.

work which was done as a result shows what could be achieved with materials which had long been available, in a climate which encouraged new uses to be made of them.

It is not at all easy to find a definition of 'science' which will embrace the twelfth-century *scientia* and modern science. In the twelfth century *scientia* means 'knowledge', especially the knowledge of an academic discipline. Aquinas asks at the beginning of the *Summa Theologica* whether theology is a science, and among his contemporaries it was sometimes referred to as 'the art of arts and science of sciences'. If we are to speak of some areas of twelfth-century work as 'scientific' in any recognizably modern sense we must look for terms which refer to at least a comparable field of study. The topics which twelfth-century scholars included under *physica* and which concerned the way in which the natural world works, and those which were covered by *mathematica* (the four mathematical arts of the quadrivium) were conceived of by contemporaries as quite different in kind from the subject-matter of the arts of language, the grammar, logic, and rhetoric of the trivium. They touch on matters which are the province of the modern scientist, even if in a manner much more limited in conception. Clearly, there can be no real comparison of method; nor is the scope of the subject-matter of twelfth-century science as wide as that of modern science. But if science may still be said to take as its object of study the working of the natural or physical world, then we have an area of common ground.

But the theologian must approach this common subject-matter with certain presuppositions. He sees the natural world as a created world. The scientist's subject-matter is, for the theologian, a source of knowledge about God the Creator. The created world presents a body of revealed evidence, to be set beside the revelation given in the Bible. Thierry of Chartres writes of the Genesis account of creation that its value lies in the *cognitio dei*, the knowledge of God it gives (*ex facturis suis*),[2] from the things God has made. This knowledge is available not only to the faithful, but to pagans, too. No one, says St. Paul, in Romans 1:19–20, has any excuse for not believing in the Creator when he looks at the evidence

[2] *Thierry of Chartres*, p. 555.9.

to be found in the created world. The power of such evidence to furnish proofs for the existence of God and to reveal something of his nature is a common theme of twelfth-century writers. Clarenbald of Arras says that 'from the creation of the world strong arguments can be drawn so that it may be proved even to pagans and unbelievers that the world had a creator.'[3] The theologian has, then, a further use for science, beyond that which is the principal concern of what we may call the 'scientist proper'. He wants to understand not only how the natural world works, but also what its workings prove about its Maker.

The imperatives of orthodox doctrine govern scientific thinking for such scholars; they lay down a view of the nature of God which determines the direction of speculation. They do so most conspicuously in connection with the problem of how things began. Here we are concerned with the metaphysical foundations of *physica*. For example, if God is the sole first cause and the source of everything which exists as Christians believe, he must have created everything from nothing. Neither matter nor form can be primordial or in any way independent of God in their existence. If God is omnipotent, no power, force or motion can come ultimately from any other source. If God is the highest Good, he cannot be the source of evil (or, in medieval opinion, of darkness or blindness and things of that kind). If he is also the source of everything which exists, evil, darkness, blindness, and so on can have — as Augustine had concluded — no existence.

These are principles of Greek metaphysics which were from the first built into Christian theology. Some of them are utilized by Aquinas in the *Summa Theologica* to prove the existence of God. Aquinas argues from his observations of the operation of these laws in the natural world to the existence of a Being who is not contained within the world, from physics to metaphysics. But *mutatis mutandis* he regards them as both scientific and theological laws. Towards the end of the twelfth century, in the *Regulae Theologicae*, Alan of Little made his highly original if rather less polished attempt to show how the *regulae* of all the arts were related

[3] *Clarenbald of Arras*, p. 229.

to theological laws. He begins with mathematical principles, with the divine unity or *monas,* and goes on to examine the laws which govern the working of the natural world in terms of the absolute imperative exercised over them by the demands of orthodoxy of doctrine.[4] Everything is made to fit together.

In their commentaries on Boethius' theological tractates, Thierry of Chartres, Gilbert of Poitiers, and others brought out a great many points of contact between the teaching of the textbooks of the secular authors on scientific matters, and the theological problems with which Boethius deals. In Chapter II of the *De Trinitate* Boethius divides *speculativa,* speculative or theoretical studies, into three, in a way directly relevant to the work of the scientific theologian. He distinguishes *naturalis* (physics, which is concerned with the natural world, with forms and matter as they inhere in specific bodies); *mathematica,* which deals with the forms matter takes, and which, although it is not directly concerned with the corporeal, nevertheless cannot be entirely separated from it; and *theologia,* which has to do with what is truly abstract, and has nothing to do with either matter or motion. We might take Boethius' *schema* as a starting-point and look first at twelfth-century work upon some problems which arise in connection with *physica,* and secondly at some difficulties of *mathematica,* in connection with theology.

The twelfth century saw the first full-scale systematic attempts in medieval times to reconcile two accounts of creation, that of Genesis and that of the ancient philosophers who tried to explain the beginning of the world in terms of natural causes. There is, perhaps, a loose parallel in recent times in the problem of reconciliation which Darwin posed for Biblical theology in the nineteenth century. It had perhaps an even greater urgency for twelfth-century scholars, since not only was the literal truth of the Genesis account brought into question by these 'scientists', but the very grounds of proof of the existence and nature of God which

---

[4] Nicholas H. Steneck, *Science and Creation in the Middle Ages: Henry of Langenstein (d. 1397) on Genesis* (London, 1976), pp. 27–32. Aquinas *Summa Theologica,* I, Q.2, Art.3, deals with the proofs for the existence of God. Alan of Lille's *Regulae Theologicae* is to be found in *PL* 210.

the created world provided had to be reassessed in terms of scientific teaching. The twelfth century produced no Darwin. The scientific ideas which were being compared with the Genesis account of creation were not new, and no single scholar was responsible for bringing them back into fashion. They came to notice as a result of a growing general interest in the textbooks which contained them, and especially perhaps in the *Timaeus* commentary of Chalcidius. What was new was the attempt to make a detailed comparison of the two accounts. Thierry of Chartres's treatise *On the Work of the Six Days* takes the Scriptural text as its basis and interprets it point by point according to scientific principles.

Thierry's attempt to bring together the scientist's view and the theologian's view of the beginning of the world stands at an important stage in the development of 'Hexameral literature'. Bede, Isidore of Seville, Walafrid Strabo, Rabanus Maurus, had looked at scientific problems when they discussed the six days of creation. In the twelfth century, William of Conches writes about the *Timaeus* and looks at its implications for the theologian; Thierry of Chartres writes about Scripture and introduces the study of scientific problems. Thierry's approach has none of the sophistication of Aquinas' handling of the philosophical and metaphysical issues raised by the doctrine of creation, in the *Summa Theologica*. Thierry's approach is closer to that of Henry of Langenstein, a scholar of the fourteenth century (d. 1397), who saw in Genesis a vehicle for a survey of the whole range of the science of his day. He covers the problem of origins, matter and form, angelology, light and darkness (and also perspective), astronomy and the hierarchy of the heavens, cosmography, meteors, cause and effect in physics, astrology, aspects of the biological sciences, physiology, and man.[5] If we set Henry's achievement beside that of Thierry it is clear

[5] N. M. Häring has looked at some aspects of this exercise in 'The Creation and Creator of the World according to Thierry of Chartres and Clarenbald of Arras', *AHDLMA* xxii (1955), 137 ff. William of Conches's *Glosa super Platonem* is edited by E. Jeauneau (Paris, 1965). On the Hexameral literature in general, see F. Robbins *The Hexaemeral Literature: A Study of the Greek and Latin commentaries on Genesis* (Chicago, 1912), and for a recent study of one fourteenth century author, Steneck, op. cit. Aquinas deals with creation in *Summa Theologica,* I. Q.44-9.

that the advent of additional textbooks and the scholarly labours of two hundred years had made a great difference to the detailed knowledge scholars could bring to bear on the problems of reconciling theology and science. But it had not greatly altered the fundamental problems which were identified by the theologian who approached his task in the light of scientific knowledge.

Thierry begins by seeking to discover in Scripture an existing rational and scientific method. He says that Genesis shows the causes which brought the world into existence and the order of its creation in time (*rationaliter*), according to reason.[6] He himself proposes to 'try to show by physical *reasons* how heaven and earth were made'.[7] His desire is to discover that there is really no discrepancy between the two accounts, that science does not challenge theology, but rather supports it. This is not the keynote of every twelfth-century enquiry, but it represents well enough the general optimism of the day that the root of the problem lies, not in any profound irreconciliability of the scientist's view of the world with that of the theologian, but in the mechanical difficulty of demonstrating that there is no contradiction between them despite their superficial differences.

It must be conceded that some of the explanations he proposes were controversial ones in his own day.[8] But Thierry is not anxious to engage in controversy, and he does not give any indication that he is aware that he is saying anything to which objections might be made. He intends, as far as possible, to give a straightforward reconciliation of the two traditions. There are, he explains, four causes of the world: efficient, formal, final, and material. God the Father is the efficient cause; God's Wisdom, the Word, is the formal cause; God's benevolence, the Holy Spirit, is the final cause. The material cause is matter, or the four elements.[9] Thierry

[6] *Thierry of Chartres,* p. 555.15–17.   [7] Ibid., p. 562.24–5.

[8] Abelard's distinction of the power of the Father, the Wisdom of the Son and the *benignitas* of the Holy Spirit as being in some sense peculiar properties of the Persons of the Trinity was a source of great controversy, and the extension of the distinction to cover the ways in which the Persons act as causes was not uncommon among his contemporaries.

[9] *Thierry of Chartres,* p. 555.18–19.

takes this traditional explanation and applies it point by point to Genesis. When 'Moses' says: *In principio creavit Deus*, he refers to the efficient cause. Whenever we meet 'God said' we are to take it to refer to the work of the Word, the Son, who is the formal cause. Wherever the text says 'And God saw that it was good', it refers to the *benignitas* of God, the final cause.[10] Thierry is careful to keep as close as possible to Scripture throughout, and to exploit every possible point of contact between the two traditions. It might be objected, with some justification, that these are not the thoughts of a speculative thinker, nor indeed of a scientist, but the rather narrower ideas of a man anxious to fit together all that he has been taught into a single system. But that is exactly the character of much of the twelfth-century work of reconciliation between theology and science. What is new and important is the force with which they felt the need to attempt the task, and the inventiveness with which they devised strategies to make everything work together.

A further controversial issue of the day was the question of the origin of matter, which is implied in the *Timaeus* to be primordial, but which Thierry firmly states to have been made by God.[11] Again, he does not pause to consider the arguments for and against this view which were being put forward by his contemporaries. He concentrates instead on working out in detail how the four elements fit into the Creation story. All matter was made in the first moment of time.[12] In the heavens, fire gave light to the air below it, and to water and earth it gave heat (for the philosophers say that fire has two powers; one is brightness and the other heat).[13] Without departing from the first sentence of Genesis with its reference to heaven and earth Thierry is able to elaborate this explanation considerably. It is in the nature of heat to divide water into tiny droplets, which it lifts up into the air by its own force; this is what we see happening in the formation of

[10] Ibid., p. 556.36–49.   [11] Ibid., p. 556.51.
[12] Ibid., p. 557.67–8.   [13] Ibid., p. 557.73–9.

clouds.[14] He touches on a number of such subjects of contemporary scientific curiosity; are the stars made of water, for example? This can be proved to be the case by a strong argument (*certo argumento probari potest*).[15] Neither air nor fire has any depth or solidity, so it is possible to see through them both. But all visible bodies have a certain density, and density is the property of water or earth. Therefore every body which is visible in the firmament of heaven must be made of water or earth. But earth cannot be lifted into the sky by heat or in any other way. Only water can be lifted. We have seen how clouds are formed by the action of heat upon water. In a similar way, we are forced to conclude that stars must be made of water because they are visible bodies in the heavens.[16] Thierry goes on with his explorations at some length. We must leave him here for the moment. But perhaps enough has been said to indicate the force of his determination that no scientific detail shall be found to be at odds with the Biblical account of the creation, and to show how urgent a matter he felt it to explain to his readers the proper place for scientific teaching in the study of theology, and at the same time to show the peculiarly stimulating restrictions the demands of orthodoxy placed on his scientific thinking.

Boethius also has something to say about the relation between *mathematica* and *physica* and at the specific ways in which both fall short of *theologia*. The objects of the natural world, Boethius teaches, are forms inseparable from matter, and they are in motion (*in motu*). (*Naturalis speculativa considerat enim corporum formas cum materia que a corporibus separari non possunt*).[17] Mathematics artificially arrests the motion of bodies by an exercise of the mind and examines the properties of the forms which inhere in matter as though they were separable — even though they cannot in fact be separated from bodies. It is perhaps easiest to grasp how geometry does this. It deals with the properties of the perfect triangle or cube as though it were possible to repre-

---

[14] Ibid., p. 558.88–90.
[16] Ibid., p. 560.53–67.
[15] Ibid., p. 559.39–40.
[17] See *Theological Tractates*, p. 8.

sent such things without drawing on a flat surface or modelling a lump of matter (where only an approximately exact triangle or cube can be fashioned). Gilbert of Poitiers, writing on a passage in Boethius' *De Hebdomadibus,* acknowledges that the triangle of which Boethius speaks cannot be said to be apart from matter (*praeter materiam*) but only in some way artificially distinguished from it (*divisa a materia*).[18] In the physical world forms cannot be divorced from matter; nor can they be perfectly formed in matter. The *verum triangulum* or the *verum circulum*[19] is a mathematical concept. In mathematics, says Gilbert, we treat the concrete as if it were other than it is, that is, abstractly (*inabstracta aliter quam sint, i.e. abstractim*). The mathematician conceives of forms separately from bodies, but only in his mind (*separatim ab eis conceperit*).[20] We have here an intellectual schematization of nature which Boethius designates a mathematical procedure. Medieval thinkers did not, of course, arrive at the general laws by which they believed the universe to be governed by generalizing from collected evidence. But they believed that in mathematics at least they were abstracting general formal characteristics from the varied examples presented by material bodies. Thierry described the process like this: *formas intuetur que sunt circa corpora*[21] ('[The mathematician] perceives the forms which exist in relation to bodies'). It is in this way that the medieval scientist strives to formulate general laws, to discover the universal in the particular.

But even Boethian mathematics (which we should more properly call Pythagorean in recognition of his enormous debt to Nicomachus of Gerasa)[22] did not aspire to the heights of *theologia.* It simplified and generalized from the untidiness of form which is manifest in created things,[23] but it did not treat of the perfect *simplicitas* of God. It merely provided a conceptual bridge between the manifold particular

[18] Gilbert of Poitiers, p. 216.54.
[19] *Thierry of Chartres,* p. 162.68-9.
[20] Gilbert of Poitiers, p. 86.25-8.
[21] *Thierry of Chartres,* p. 70.87.
[22] Boethius' *Arithmetica* is virtually a translation of Nicomachus' *Introduction to Arithmetic.*
[23] *Thierry of Chartres,* p. 160.12-14.

and the divine unity. The twelfth-century geometer defined an equilateral triangle without being perturbed by the fact that if he drew it on an uneven surface its sides would not be exactly equal. In this view, the validity of the scientific law or the mathematical principle is not affected by the specific failures of corporeal things to conform to it. Because the physical world is mutable, these 'generalizations' must be treated as simplifications which ignore the particular variant. In theology there are no variants, and no distortions, because, as Boethius says, the divine is quite separate from matter and motion and quite free from change or chance.[24]

The late twelfth century satirist Nigellus, writing *Contra Curiales et Officiales Clericos,* speaks of the *experimenta physicae.*[25] But it would be absurd to suggest that we might find in twelfth-century science a departure from exercises of speculative metaphysics towards the patient descriptive cataloguing and classification, the methodical testing of hypotheses by experiment, which is the stuff of much modern science. In suggesting that the validity of the law or the mathematical principle is not thought to be affected by specific failures of specific things to conform to it I have made a statement which may just be true in certain circumstances for the modern scientist. (We might accept that a falling object obeys the laws of gravity even if test measurements have been distorted by the fact that a strong wind has slowed up its fall.) It is always true for the medieval mathematician. It is unlikely, in practice, that a modern scientist will want to recast one of Newton's laws because on the day that he tests it there happens to be a strong wind blowing — although he might revise it in the light of less incidental considerations. But his training ought to make him consider whether he should, because he is bound to maintain a particular form of open-mindedness about the laws of his science. He must regard them as hypotheses which are never exhaustively verified. If evidence comes to light which makes them at all doubtful, he must be ready to abandon them. And that evidence can come only from the individual varia-

---

[24] Boethius, *De Trinitate,* I.2.
[25] *The Anglo-Latin Satirical Poets of the Twelfth Century,* ed. T. Wright, *Rolls Series,* 59 (London, 1872), 2 vols. I.164.

tions of behaviour of objects in the physical world. But
Boethius and his twelfth-century readers would have seen no
advantage to be derived from collecting evidence from the
material world or testing the laws of mathematics or science
upon physical objects. Not only would such evidence and
such tests provide no ground for abandoning the laws if they
were found to contradict them; they would provide no final
confirmation of the laws if they were found to accord with
them. That is because corporeal things were regarded as being
of a lower order, intrinsically fallible and mutable and unreliable. It was inconceivable that they could furnish reliable
proofs of things higher and purer and simpler than themselves.
Aquinas sometimes treated them as though they could, but
he did so in the confidence that they would in fact only confirm the rightness of the notions of classical metaphysics.

Almost the only sense in which observations of the natural
world seemed useful to twelfth-century scholars was in providing material for analogies and illustrations. For this
purpose, the particular has a vividness which the abstract and
general lacks. But when Anselm noticed that candles placed
near together gave out what appeared to be a single light,
or Rupert of Deutz observed that tree-roots spread a long
way in all directions from the base of the trunk, or Ailred of
Rievaulx realized that he could imagine a whole town in a
memory no bigger than his own head, each of them made
use of his observations to illustrate a point in theological
argument. None of them investigated the phenomenon
further because he saw it as something of interest in its own
right, as a means of learning something new about the working of the world.

Of its essence a science, like any academic discipline, is
concerned with what is consistent and predictable in its
subject-matter. No science can be built on the belief that
there is no law and no order in things. Anselm identifies three
'orders of things' (*cursus rerum*): those things which come
about solely by the will of God; those things which happen
according to the laws of nature which God has determined;
and those things which happen by the will of a creature.[26] It
is the second which is the proper subject-matter of science,

[26] *Anselmi Opera Omnia,* II.154.4–5, *De Conceptu Virginali,* XI.

and of scientific theology. A miracle is recognizable only if it is understood that it breaks the law of nature. Human will can be seen at work only where it is clear what would have happened by the law of nature if man had not interfered. It fell to the theologians in the twelfth century, as it does now, to determine the application of these laws of nature in theological contexts.

For the twelfth-century scholar they are essentially mathematical laws. Everything which exists, says Boethius, seems to have an underlying numerical principle or *ratio* (*Omnia quaecumque a primaeva rerum nature constructa sunt, numerorum videntur ratione formata*).[27] So universal are these mathematical laws that they appear to apply even to God himself. Or perhpas it would be more accurate to say that they have the force of law in the created world because they are in accord with the divine nature. Clarenbald of Arras explains that if one is multiplied by one only one results. Here he finds an analogy with the generation of the Son (*ad divinam generationem aliquam similitudinem*), for when the Father begets the Son the begetting or 'multiplication' does not result in there being more than one God. Clarenbald is even able to find a Scriptural text to corroborate what he says: 'That is why the Psalmist says, "God spoke once," because he once begot the Son [who is the Word] from himself.'[28] The Pythagorean mathematics of the theory of whole numbers and the patterns they make, lent itself readily not only to the purposes of the scholars who studied the natural world, but also to the needs of the theologian.

Thierry of Chartres works out some of the applications of mathematical laws to theology in the treatise on *The Work of the Six Days* where he tried to reconcile the Genesis account of creation with the scientists' version. 'There are', he says, 'four kinds of principle which lead men to a knowledge of the Creator' (*quatuor genera rationum*): these are the proofs of arithmetic, music, geometry, and astronomy. 'We must . . . make use of these instruments in theology', he continues.[29]

---

[27] Boethius, *Arithmetica,* ed. G. Friedlein (Leipzig, 1869), p. 12.17-19, Book I.i.

[28] *Clarenbald of Arras,* p. 121, para. 38;.Ps. 61:11.

[29] *Thierry of Chartres,* p. 568.83-5.

The first law of mathematics which is indispensable to the theologian is the principle that unity precedes or gives rise to every kind of 'otherness' or 'mutability' or 'plurality'. Boethius' teaching was that just as a geometical point had to be separated from its fellow by a dimension if a line was to be formed, so unity could never become plurality unless the second unity was in some way 'different from' or 'other than' the first. Two (*binarius*) is therefore, as Thierry puts it, 'the beginning of all otherness', the first to be different from one.[30] It is not difficult to see that mutable creatures differ from their Creator, and that his perfect unity gives rise to their multiplicity.[31] Since all numbers proceed from unity in this way we may say that 'unity is omnipotent in the creation of numbers',[32] and since all things 'weight and measure and place and figure and time and notion',[33] have a numerical basis, that means that 'unity is omnipotent in the creation of things'. Unity is therefore the Creator himself. Thierry is making use of an analogy here, but he is doing something more; he is suggesting that the laws of mathematics are the same for God as they are for his universe, that scientific laws are also, in this instance, theological laws.

Thierry moves on to a second mathematical law. 'Now we must say how equality is produced from unity.'[34] Numbers multiplied by themselves (2 × 2; 4 × 4) produce squares and cubes which, like circles and spheres, preserve equality of dimension (*que equalitatem dimensionum custodiunt*). Numbers multiplied by other numbers (2 × 3; 4 × 5) produce figures with sides of different lengths. The same is true of unity. If it is multiplied by something other than itself it produces numbers which are other than itself. If it is multiplied by itself it produces its own equal (1 × 1 = 1); Moreover it does so *ex sua substantia*,[35] from its own substance. The parallels with the begetting of the Son by the Father in the latter case, and with the creation of the world in the former, were clear enough to twelfth-century scholars. The treatise is unfinished. Thierry proposes to go on to look at the

---

[30] Boethius, *Arithmetica*, p. 87, Book II.vi; *Thierry of Chartres*, p. 568.86–91.
[31] *Thierry of Chartres*, p. 568.92–5.   [32] Ibid., p. 570.45–6.
[33] Ibid., p. 570.35–48.   [34] Ibid., p. 570.52.   [35] Ibid., p. 570.54.

conexio equalitatis et unitatis, the way in which unity and equality together have the Spirit proceeding from them, but he does not arrive at the point where he was to state his third mathematical law of theology.[36] He says enough, however, to show how helpful he finds the mathematical laws to his own purposes, and to declare his willingness to accept them as directly applicable to theological problems.

We have been considering mathematical concepts. But twelfth-century scholars were also interested in problems of language, and in particular of technical terminology. Torrance notes that 'the problem of language in its relation to thought has been raised in a new way in the modern world by the mathematicians, who find themselves forced to use ordinary language in mathematical statement . . . From the mathematicians it has entered philosophy'.[37] This had always been a philosophical matter for ancient and medieval thinkers. But now there was a new awareness of the difficulty of framing mathematical statements in an ordinary language only partly suitable for the purpose. An additional limitation was imposed by the fact that twelfth-century scholars were forced to make do with words encumbered by all sorts of extraneous associations, where a modern logician or mathematician would clarify his exact meaning and use a symbol.

The stock of technical terms of mathematics which proved useful consisted for the most part of Boethius' renderings of Nicomachus' Greek terms for magnitude and multitude, continuous and discrete quantity, composite and incomposite numbers, even and odd, unity and plurality, point, line, surface, solid, dimension, proportion, progression.[38] Readers of the *Arithmetica* looked for means of relating these terms and the concepts they gave names to, to the technical knowledge they possessed in other areas, particularly in dialectic. Boethius again gave a lead here. In his commentary on Aristotle's *Categories* he employs many of these terms in the section devoted to quantity. Peter Abelard, who claims that he is shamefully ignorant of arithmetic, remarks that one of his masters used to draw parallels between mathematical and

[36] Ibid., p. 575.79–80.   [37] Torrance, *Theology in Reconstruction*, p. 17.
[38] *PL* 64.201–38.

dialectical principles when he lectured on quantity.[39] Those
who lectured on the *Arithmetica* certainly pointed to such
parallels. They saw the *Arithmetica* as having a direct bearing
on a number of problems of predication, and thus on the
work of dialecticians and even grammarians.

In a manuscript in Durham Cathedral Library which contains William of Champeaux's commentaries on the *Rhetorica
ad Herennium* and on Cicero's *De Inventione*,[40] there is also
a commentary on Boethius' *Arithmetica*. The author seizes
upon a passage in Book I, i, where Boethius lists the mathematical *praedicamenta* or categories: *qualitates, quantitates,
formae, magnitudines, parvitates, aequalitates, habitudines,
actus, dispositiones, loca, tempora*.[41] Boethius never refers to
these as 'categories', but his twelfth-century commentator is
struck both by their tantalizing resemblance to the Aristotelian categories, and by their differences from them. Boethius,
he says, is trying to explain what existence is.[42] Everything
which does not grow or shrink Boethius considers to have
true existence (*vere esse*). Qualities and quantities endure
invariabiliter, growing neither larger nor smaller: 'These are
the genera and species which are in the *Categories*, just as
Porphyry says. Whiteness is invariable, and colour, and other
things like that.' The qualities of the *Arithmetica* are
identified with the qualities of the *Categories*, its 'quantities'
with the quantities of the *Categories*; 'forms' are qualities'
'magnitudes' and 'smallnesses' are quantities; 'equalities' are
relatives; 'conditions' refer to the category of 'having'; 'acts'
to 'doing'; 'dispositions' to 'situation'; 'places' to 'where';
'times' to 'when'. Boethius gives no example for 'passion' and
so he adds: 'and whatever else', and so on:

Hec sunt genera et species que sint in *Predicamenta* sicut Porphyrius
asserit. Albedo invariabilis est et color at alia huiusmodi. Unde statim
subiungit *hec sunt qualitates*, id est genera et species que sunt in *Pre
dicamenta* qualitas, et *quantitates*, id est genera et species que sunt in
Predicamenta quantitas. *Forme* ad qualitatem referuntur. *Magnitudines*
et *parvitates* ad quantitatem. *Equalitates* ad ad aliquid. *Habitudines* ad

---

[39] Abelard, *Dialectica*, p. 59.1-13.
[40] On these commentaries, see K. M. Fredborg, 'The commentaries on Cicero's
De Inventione and *Rhetorica ad Herennium* by William of Champeaux', *Cahiers*,
17 (1976).   [41] Boethius, *Arithmetica*, p. 8.5-8.
[42] Durham Cathedral Library, MS C IV.7, f.51, col.2.

habere. *Actus* ad facere. *Dispositiones* ad situm esse. *Loca* ad ubi. *Tempora* ad quando. Et quia de pati nullum exemplum dederat, subditus *et quicquid adunatum* quodam loco et cetera.[43]

Some forcing of parallels has been necessary to make the Aristotelian categories fit Boethius' list in the *Arithmetica* so neatly. But the commentator has considered it a helpful and illuminating exercise, because it halps to 'place' the study of the *Arithmetica* (which was new and strange to his contemporaries)[44] in relation to a more familiar discipline. The exercise demonstrates how dominant were the technical principles of the arts of language over work in other disciplines. But it shows, too, how close some twelfth-century scholars came to making the attempt to bridge the gap between mathematical statements and the philosophy of language which Torrance identifies as one of the tasks of the modern mathematician. They devised no symbolic logic, but they tried to apply logic to mathematics with the aid of their developing arts of language.

This *rapprochement* between the mathematical arts and the arts of language, between trivium and quadrivium, is of some importance because it reflects a general wish among twelfth-century scholars to find means of reconciling apparently quite disparate disciplines. The meeting some of them tried to effect between science and theology is only a part of a grand exercise of reconciliation on every front which laid the foundation for much later work. It did so most notably by providing a common technical vocabulary, a technically exact terminology with the aid of which different kinds of study could be brought together, compared, and contrasted. Points of contact between disciplines are always minutely identified and carefully labelled. The scholars of the thirteenth century took such procedures much further, but already in the twelfth the ground-plan of their work was being meticulously mapped out.

We have come a long way from Rupert of Deutz's unsophisticated attempts to suggest that the study of the liberal arts may not be inappropriate for the student of Scripture,

[43] Loc. cit.
[44] References to the *Arithmetica* in twelfth-century writings are conspicuously more common than in earlier work.

since the Bible provides such excellent examples of their use in practice. But we have not travelled far in time. Within a generation of Rupert's work on the *De Operibus Spiritus Sancti* all these developments of method and terminology had been set in motion by scholars who were trying to discover more exactly where the limits of the usefulness of the human arts and sciences to the theologian lay. Some scholars preserved Rupert's attitude in their own work. The academic theologians created a new tradition side by side with the old, which never quite superseded it. It is their work which made theology an academic discipline. And it was their achievement to engage the best efforts of academic theologians in an attempt to make the arts work for them. No previous generation had done so with such rigour. As a result of their explorations, questions came to light which are still of the first importance for philosophers and theologians alike.

IV   A Missionary Theology

1. The Academic Challenge

It no longer comes naturally to call a man a heretic. The term has gone out of fashion. This is partly because there is no longer a single Church whose teaching sets the standard of orthodox opinion for all Christians. It is not easy to state in generally acceptable terms exactly where heresy begins. But it is also a result of the fact that we have grown used to the existence of differences. If heresy can still be said to possess its root meaning of making a choice, we have come to feel that a man has a right to choose his religious opinions. It certainly cannot be assumed that every good Christian knows a heretic when he sees one, or that it is his duty to bring other men's views into line with his own.

As a result, the focus of Christian efforts towards unity has shifted. If we cannot agree who is a heretic, we must look to other means of preserving the soundness of Christian doctrine than crusade and inquisition. Instead of trying to suppress those who differ we must search for common ground with them in a shared acceptance of doctrinal fundamentals. It is becoming comparatively rare for the members of one religious sect to try to force others to conform to their views and abandon their own. The tendency of recent attempts at reconciliation has been to look for a means of understanding the historical origins of differences, in an attempt to get behind them and see whether they are really differences at all.

The whole drift of this movement towards reconciliation runs counter to the twelfth-century urge to sharpen and point the differences, to make it quite plain to ordinary people where dissidents from the orthodox view are in error. The search for the basis on which Christian differences may be removed is a sophisticated theological task. But the work of the twelfth-century theologians in clarifying the differences was a necessary preliminary, and it, too, was far from simple. Never since patristic times had heresy and unbelief had so many faces. The task of cataloguing alone was immense, and these scholars did a great deal more than list and distinguish heretical opinions. They found arguments with which to defend the orthodox position, both old arguments borrowed from the Fathers and new ones of their own. They won, temporarily, a battle for unity which was fought again and lost at the Reformation. The unity they preserved was that of a single Church in the Latin West. They were therefore fighting for a principle of unity quite different from that which informs the Church's search for unification today. They were trying to prevent a fragmentation which now has to be repaired.

These activities did not take place only in an academic context. Indeed the academic dimensions of the struggle have received comparatively little attention because the political implications of the existence of heresy pressed themselves so forcibly upon contemporary notice, and it is these which have attracted most attention among modern scholars. Religious dissent constituted a threat to established authority not only in the Church but also in the state. It therefore had a political complexion. Rulers marshalled military as well as spiritual forces against the unbelievers. It requires an exercise of the imagination now to understand the quality of the anxiety which aroused a crusading fervour in orthodox believers and real fear of the political consequences of toleration in their leaders. Perhaps the nearest we can come to it is to compare the popular heretics with modern freedom fighters, urban guerrillas and members of people's liberation movements. The parallel will not hold very far; many such groups have no religious affiliation whatever, and they resort to forms of violence for which the twelfth century has no equivalent. But those groups of heretics who disputed the rights and powers of the priesthood, the validity and value of the sacraments, the need for Church buildings, the Church's right to wield the 'material sword' of temporal power, the right of the clergy to possess private property, were questioning the need for institutions and practices upon which the very structure of society was founded. These were, in a sense, anarchists, and the danger they posed to peace and the established order was real enough. S. Runciman notes how

close the Church in the south of France came to defeat at the
hand of the heretics there.[1] The flouting of the Church's
authority is not now tantamount to the flouting of political
authority vested in the state. In a more secular society, the
heat many twelfth-century Christians felt has gone out of the
confrontation between one group of believers and another.

A good deal of that heat was generated by a sense that the
problem of heresy was growing. The twelfth century saw
not only a vast increase in the number of popular heretics
and in the number of different sects they belonged to, but
also a new awareness of the existence of other faiths than
Christianity. For several centuries Jews had lived among
Christians in Western Europe, in communities which enjoyed
a good deal of prosperity and something closer to respect
than toleration from their Christian neighbours. During these
years the Jewish community performed an indispensable
financial service. But only at the end of the eleventh century,
it seems, did Jews and Christians begin to hold discussions
with one another in any numbers about their respective faiths.
It was not that Christian scholars had previously had no
understanding at all of the difference between Christianity
and Judaism. But now, in formal and informal conversations,
they were drawn into a rather different exercise. They began
to try to convert the Jews. They strove to find means of
making an opponent's view seem untenable to him and their
own convincing and attractive. They began, in other words,
upon a missionary task, and one in which a command of the
academic arts of argument was a distinct advantage. There
was no equivalent contemporary development of discussions
with Moslems, partly no doubt because the difference of
language set up a barrier to technical theological discussion.
That came later. Nevertheless, the existence of the Moslems
was known and recognized far more widely in northern
Europe than it had been before the crusades began. As to the
Greeks, the implications of the schism of 1054 do not seem
to have become clear to the Latins until nearly the end of
the eleventh century, when discussions of doctrinal differnces
began in earnest. These three groups, Jews, Moslems, and

[1] S. Runciman, *The Mediaeval Manichee* (Cambridge, 1955), p. 130.

Greeks, had scholars of their own who were, academically speaking, at least the equal of the Christian scholars of the Latin West. Where the popular heretics posed an academic challenge which was perhaps incidental to the threat they constituted to the established social and political order, these 'unbelievers' threw down a very direct and testing academic challenge, throughout the twelfth and thirteenth centuries, first the Jews, then the Greeks, and finally the Moslems taking the centre of the stage.

The existence of these other faiths and areas of alternative Christian opinion all laid a missionary responsibility upon orthodox Christians — not everywhere equally, and not equally in every decade of the twelfth century, but with this in common, that they were taken to represent a departure from true faith. This underlying unity of their task was from the first very apparent to monastic writers and to academic theologians alike.

A most striking quality of the work of some of the earlier twelfth-century writers who addressed themselves to the problem of heresy is the air of sheer perplexity with which they faced the task. Anselm of Havelberg found it difficult to understand why God should allow heretical sects to come into existence at all, and even more puzzling that they should thrive.[3] But Christian intercourse with Jews, Greeks, Moslems, Cathars, Waldensians, and the adherents of number- less small evanescent sects, in trade, in ordinary social contact, in diplomatic exchanges, on the battlefield, in every depart- ment of life, meant that the existence of unbelievers could not simply be ignored. Their presence made orthodox Christians review their own position. There had always been a duty to spread the Gospel, but now there was a clear need for an apologetic — even a polemical theology. In the eleventh century, when contacts with holders of different religious views had been so much less frequent, the missionary task had not seemed to pressing. Now a larger sense of its scope and purpose matched the sheer urgency of the task. The only

---

[2] See B. Blumenkranz's edition of Gilbert Crispin's *Disputatio Judei et Christiani*, on early dialogues of this kind.

[3] *Dialogus*, ed. G. Salet (Paris, 1965), cf. Bruno of Segni, *De Statu Ecclesiae*, PL 165.1121-36.

practical response to the growing problem of heresy was to try to eliminate it by the pen or by the sword.

The soldiers in this scholarly war for unity were in a quite different position from that in which modern Christians sometimes find themselves. They were not engaged in the defence of the intellectual respectability of their faith in the face of popular scorn. Nor did they meet apathy. Everyone agreed that religion was important. Their energies went into their efforts to show by forces of reason why the orthodox view was right and all other opinions wrong. They did so in a fighting spirit: 'God's cause is at stake; let us be ready!'[4] For academic theologians this was necessarily a battle of the mind rather than of the body.

In their survey of the *Heresies of the High Middle Ages,* W. L. Wakefield and A. P. Evans avoid any detailed consideration of 'the doctrinal deviations that sprang from learned discussions among intellectuals, arising in and usually confined to the schools and universities'.[5] These, they argue, affected few, and their appeal was to the mind, not to the heart. This view of the academic response to heresy might be challenged on several grounds, but perhaps chiefly because it leaves out of account that aspect of the eleventh- and twelfth-century spread of heresy which had the most profound effect upon the intellectual life of the day. It was in the schools that the theological and philosophical challenge of heresy was taken up, and the 'learned discussions' which ensued were of the greatest interest to contemporary scholars. Such arguments are of concern to us here because they significantly altered the direction of development of speculative theology at a time when it was at its most fluid and receptive to influence. The danger to the established order was as real on the academic front as it was on the political and social front in areas where there was a good deal of popular heresy. Scholars were fighting a running battle for orthodoxy of doctrine throughout the twelfth century. Fundamental questions were being asked within the Church and outside it, and a great deal was genuinely at risk. It was not even always clear to those

[4] Hugh of Amiens, *PL* 192.1258.
[5] W. L. Wakefield and A. P. Evans, *Heresies of the High Middle Ages* (Columbia, 1969), p. 3.

whose desire was simply to be orthodox in their beliefs where the right view lay. It is on occasions in the history of the Church when this has happened that the most far-reaching overhauling of doctrine from its foundations has taken place. In this respect the twelfth century may be compared with the early Christian centuries and with the period of the Reformation, and with our own times.

If we are to see the threat as contemporaries saw it, as one great danger as well as a series of distinct challenges from various directions, we must not try to improve too much on that 'looseness in the use of the word heresy'[6] which Wakefield and Evans perceive in twelfth century writers. But in one respect it is helpful to come closer to what the writer of one of the Laon sentences calls *heresis stricte accepta.*[7] It is *mentis elatio,* a proud obstinacy in deliberately adopted erroneous opinion, which (according to John of Salisbury) Gilbert of Poitiers claimed to be the distinguishing mark of the heretic: 'for it is not ignorance of the truth but pride of spirit which makes a heretic'.[8] Heresy is dogged, tight, and narrow in its defence of its unorthodox standpoint. Whether in a given case the principal danger appeared to Church authorities to lie in a threat to the security of law and order in Church and state,[9] or to orthodox doctrine, heresy was dangerous because of the absolute determination of heretics to stick to their opinions. These were not the ignorant and misguided whom Anselm seems to have had in mind when he wrote the *Cur Deus Homo* to persuade the *infideles* to adopt the orthodox view,[10] but men hardened in error. Without that hard edge of challenge the response of the academic theologians would perhaps have been less vigorous, less sustained, and therefore less influential upon the development of academic theology at large.

The earliest of the eleventh- and twelfth-century popular heretics were men of no academic pretensions, a number of

[6] Loc. cit.

[7] O. Lottin, *Psychologie et morale aux xiie et xiiie siècles,* p. 223, para 280.

[8] *Historia Pontificalis,* p. 22.

[9] Wakefield and Evans, p. 3, E. Griffe *Les Debuts de l'aventure cathare en Languedoc 1140–90* (Paris, 1969), p. 16.

[10] *Anselmi Opera Omnia,* II.50–61.

them itinerant weavers.[11] Men such as Clementius of Bucy,
Eudes de l'Étoile, Pons of Perigeux, won followers among
ordinary people by all sorts of means — often by sheer
demagogy — but certainly not by scholarly argument.[12] It
was only when versions of their teaching came to the notice
of scholars that the doctrinal principles involved were
identified and defined. This was not always done, it is to be
supposed, with such accuracy that what the theologians have
to say will help us to determine the views the heretics really
held. The orthodox theologians sought to find arguments
which would meet the objections they *thought* the heretics
were putting forward. When Peter the Venerable wrote his
treatise against the Petrobrusians, a sect he first encountered
in the late 1120s, he was able to identify their doctrines as:
objection to infant baptism, to the paying of respect to the
Cross (which they believed ought rather to be hated because
Christ suffered upon it), to church buildings (for a God who
is everywhere has no need of them), to the efficacy of the
Mass and to prayer for the dead.[13] These are themes which
appear again and again in polemical treatises directed against
sects of popular heretics, and there is no reason to doubt
that, substantially, they were views which many heretics
held. But their importance for the formation of an academic
missionary theology lies in this: the academic rigour which
gave form and definition to polemical theology was injected
into the debates by the apologists for the Church and not by
the heretics themselves.

Scholars identified an old enemy with some relief when
they found that the Cathars held dualist views which re-
sembled those of the Manichees of Augustine's day. They
were able to turn to the Fathers for help in framing their
arguments. Alan of Lille was pleased to find that there was
no need to discover and develop new arguments (*non novis
elaborandum est inventis*), because Augustine, Hilary,
Jerome and other Fathers had provided *rationes authenticae*

---

[11] *The Mediaeval Manichee*, p. 121.   [12] Ibid., pp. 119–21.
[13] Peter the Venerable, *Contra Petrobrusianos Hereticos*, ed. J Fearns, *CCM*
X (Turnholt, 1968).

already.[14] But the novelty and topicality of 'present-day heresy', the *novae abusiones*[15] of the day, are also a consistent theme of the polemical theologians. If these were old issues they needed renewed attack. Hugh of Amiens wrote a treatise 'against the heretics of his own day',[16] and the 'Praepositinus' *Summa*, too, seems to have been written because it was topical.[17] Sometimes an actual encounter with holders of erroneous opinions prompted the writing of a treatise, as appears to have been the case with Hugh's work.[18] But even without such an incentive, there was a sense of urgency about the polemicist's task which gave forcefulness and energy to the work the academic theologians and the monastic apologists did in the field of missionary theology.

The Unbelievers

The principal division the apologists for orthodoxy made was between their own standpoint and the collective views of all 'unbelievers' who differed from them. The difference might be as great as that which separated Christian from Moslem, or a particular as the differences between Greek and Latin Christians on the procession of the Holy Spirit and the use of leavened or unleavened bread in the Eucharist, but all *infideles* had in common the fact that they were not true believers. A considerable vocabulary was already in use in the twelfth century for describing holders of erroneous opinions: *infideles, haeretici, increduli, pagani, gentiles, sectatores, philosophi, impii, schismatici*. The meanings of these terms were not all clearly differentiated as yet, but their very proliferation suggests a widespread awareness of the existence of a growing problem. When Anselm refers to *infideles* in the *Cur Deus Homo*[19] he means those who dispute the doctrine

---

[14] *Contra Hereticos, PL* 210.308. Runciman traces the evidence for continuity between the earliest dualist heresies and their medieval forms, in *The Mediaeval Manichee*. Whatever historical continuity there may have been, the twelfth-century dualists differeed from their predecessors on a number of doctrinal points.

[15] Gerhoch of Reichersberg, *Letter to Pope Hadrian about the Novelties of the Day*, p. 11.   [16] *PL* 192.1255-98.

[17] *The Summa Contra Haereticos ascribed to Praepositinus of Cremona*, ed. J. N. Garvin and J. A. Corbett (Notre Dame, 1958), p. xv.

[18] T. G. Waldman, 'Hugh of Amiens, Archbishop of Rouen', 1130-64, Oxford D.Phil. thesis (1970), pp. 116-17.   [19] *Anselmi Opera Omnia*, II, 50-61.

of the redemption: he gives no other details of their opinions, because he intends to meet the objections of every dissident on this point, whether he is an ordinary Latin Christian who finds it difficult to accept orthodox teaching about this particular doctrine, or an unbeliever who questions the faith more comprehensively. In rather the same all-embracing spirit Bernard writes of the duty of correcting heretics and converting the heathen in the *De Consideratione*. With a sweeping gesture he takes in all kinds of unbeliever: it is a Christian's duty, he says, 'to convert the unbelieving to faith, not to put off those who have been converted, to bring back to the fold those who have fallen away, to direct the perverse into the right path, to recall the troublemakers to the truth, to convince those who have been led astray, by invincible reasoning'.[20] He makes an exception in the case of the Jews (*De Judaeis excusat te tempus: habent terminum suum qui praeveniri non poterit*). The Jews cannot be converted until the appointed time comes. But otherwise, Bernard groups all unbelievers together; the Christian has a missionary responsibility for them all.

Within a generation or two it became increasingly difficult to believe that reasonable explanations will convince all right-minded men. It became obvious that unbelievers may be holders of well-thought-out and established opinions. Such *sectatores* steadily made their differences apparent to twelfth-century apologists; Abelard refers to sects of faith (*fidei sectae*)[21] and he goes to some trouble to discover common ground on which the Christian may meet the Philo-sopher or the Jew. The 'unbeliever' is able to dictate the terms of the discussion throughout. Anselm takes for granted the existence of such common ground of reason — and in the *Cur Deus Homo,* if not always in the *De Processione Spiritus Sancti,* it is he who dictates the terms of the discussion. Once he has listed the *objectiones infidelium* and given a brief response to each, he feels free to devote the greater part of the *Cur Deus Homo* to putting forward his own arguments.

In the light of the new awareness of the extent of the

[20] *Bernardi Opera Omnia* 3, p. 433.
[21] Petrus Abaelardus, *Dialogus inter Philosophum, Christianus et Judaeus,* p. 41.

problem, Peter Abelard assembled a list of patristic texts in an attempt to define heresy. Like Honorius, who made a list of all the heresies he had been able to find mentioned or refuted in the writings of the Fathers and elsewhere,[22] Abelard turns to the Fathers for information. They had left a considerable legacy of literature on the subject. Augustine, he says, considers a heretic to be someone who holds false and novel views (*falsas ac novas opiniones*).[23] The fact that more new heretics had been added to the old lent a peculiar pointedness to this reference to the novelty of heretical opinions. In the middle of the century Gerhoch of Reichersberg said that he intended to write a book against two heresies which are partly old, partly new (*partim antiquas, partim novas*).[24] Towards the end of the century, Alan of Lille speaks of the *novi haeretici,* the new heretics of his own day, in his four books against the heretics.[25] Heresy was not a new problem, but it was felt to have taken on a new and more serious character. Pictures of heretics being refuted by the Church's apologists appear in contemporary manuscripts as a reassurance to the faithful.[26]

In the eleventh century it was not so much popular heresy which troubled scholars as the 'academic' heresy of the *dialectici haeretici,* the 'dialecticians of our own day', to whom Anselm addresses himself in the *De Incarnatione Verbi.*[27] These loud-mouthed advocates of the power of the liberal arts to upset orthodox teaching had already put in an appearance in the person of Berengar and his followers in Lanfranc's day,[28] and Lanfranc had met them on their own ground and shown the unsoundness of their arguments to them in their own terms.[29] These discussions had been concerned chiefly with the application of the rules of grammar and dialectic to the sacraments. Roscelin of Compiègne moved on to even more central doctrinal issues, by questioning the acceptability of the doctrine of the Trinity, on the grounds that it could not be made to accord with the rules of

[22] *PL* 172.233.　　　　　　　　　　[23] *Theologia Christiana,* pp. 202–5; 403–4.
[24] *PL* 194.1162.　　　　　　　　　　　　　　　　　　　[25] *PL* 210.307.
[26] J. G. Alexander, *Norman Illumination at Mont St. Michel,* 966–1100 (Oxford, 1970), pp. 100–2.　　　　　[27] *Anselmi Opera Omnia,* II.9.21.
[28] J. de Montclos, *Lanfranc et Berengar.*
[29] M. T. Gibson, *Lanfranc of Bec,* pp. 85–8.

dialectic; he had accused Anselm of making statements which could only be interpreted, by the laws of the arts of language, as denials of orthodox teaching.

Only in a rather special sense can these *dialectici* be called *haeretici.* They cannot be said to belong to any sect. Their heresy lies in the erroneousness of their opinions rather than in any collective threat they might have posed as a group. Anselm's master Lanfranc[30] speaks at the beginning of the *De Corpore et Sanguine Domini* of the darkness of error in which Berengar and his followers lie, the *tenebrae erroris,* and of the secret disputations they hold (*clandestinae disputationes*), in which they abuse their God-given powers of reasoning.[31] These errors have been arrived at by a distortion of the truth and the threat they pose is to the truth which it was, ironically enough, the traditional function of dialectic to distinguish from falsehood. These errors are dangerous because they are infectious to those with a little training in the arts of grammar and dialectic. They appear to possess a technical solidity which experienced masters like Lanfranc and Anselm were able to show to be quite illusory. But it was not difficult for the *dialectici haeretici* to impress the half-educated with their arguments.

Honorius Augustodunensis added to his book *On Christian Authors* (*De Scriptoribus Ecclesiasticis*) a catalogue of different kinds of heretic. 'It remains' he says, 'to note one by one those who throw up the obscuring cloud of black smoke of heretical dogma.'[32] He includes eight kinds of heresy among the Jews and seventy-five of which the *philosophi* are the 'patriarchs'. A good proportion of these Honorius has learned about through his wide reading. They are not heresies he is likely to have seen being actively held among his contemporaries. But it is clear enough from the conscientious care he has given to compiling his list that during the last years of the eleventh century the emphasis was changing. Where Lanfranc had been concerned principally with errors of reasoning, with the heretical opinions sometimes held by grammarians and dialecticians, already in Anselm's day such an attitude was becoming a little out of

---

[30] Ibid., pp. 91, 95.   [31] *PL* 150.408.   [32] *PL* 172.233.

date. By the turn of the century Honorius writes for a readership far more generally aware of the existence of a wide
range of theological problems raised by holders of heretical
opinions. He therefore makes a list of different kinds of
heretic and gives a brief explanation of the principal beliefs
of each.

If encounters with dialecticians — the spiritual heirs of the
philosophi to whose influence Honorius attributes so much
heretical thinking — first prompted this new awareness, it was
undoubtedly the discussions with the Jews which exerted the
next most signal influence at the end of the eleventh century.
Anselm's old friend and pupil Gilbert Crispin is the author of
a *Disputatio* which purports to be the result of a series of
conversations with a Jew of Mainz, culminating in a formal
debate.[33] Peter Abelard wrote a *Dialogue* in which a Philosopher, a Jew and a Christian meet in argument before a
judge, who is to decide who puts the most convincing case.[34]
These are only two of the better-known examples of debates
with the Jews. Even if the existence of many 'philosophical
societies' of the kind Gilbert describes his other *Disputatio*,
the *Dispute with a Heathen*, seems unlikely,[35] there can be
no doubt that discussion did take place, and that Christian
scholars found the Jews generally well-informed, and learned
in Old Testament Scripture in particular. There is some
evidence to suggest that the Jews mingled freely with well-to-
do Christians, in the towns of northern France at least,[36] and
their curiosity about Christian beliefs led some of them into
discussions. Hermannus Judaeus was himself converted to
Christianity as a result of such social and business contact
with Christians.[37]

At about the same time, or very soon afterwards, Latin
scholars began to take an interest in the difference of
opinion between Greek and Latin Christians over the pro-

---

[33] *Gisleberti Crispini Disputatio Iudaei et Christiani,* ed. cit.
[34] Thomas, ed. cit.
[35] Gilbert Crispin, *Dispute of a Christian with a Heathen,* ed. C. C. J. Webb,
MARS iii (1954), 55–77.
[36] B. Smalley, *The Study of the Bible in the Middle Ages,* pp. 149–56.
[37] *Hermannus quondam Judaeus, Opusculum de Conversione Sua, MGH* 4
(1963).

cession of the Holy Spirit, which had been such an important factor in the schism between East and West in 1054. It did not become clear to Latin scholars for some time that the Greek Christians now constituted a separate church over which the decisions of the Latins on points of doctrine had, in practice, no authority. The theological issues involved seem at first to have attracted so little general attention from scholars that when Urban II looked round the assembled ecclesiastical dignitaries at the Council of Bari in 1098 his eye lit upon only Anselm of Canterbury as a suitable apologist for the Latin position. His choice of Anselm is unlikely to have been so spontaneous as Eadmer's account would suggest,[38] but nevertheless he evidently knew of no very considerable number of scholars on whom he could call. Anselm delivered a speech to the Council, and later wrote the treatise *De Processione Spiritus Sancti* which we must suppose to have been based on what he said there.[39] Anselm concentrates exclusively upon the philosophical and theological difficulties raised by the doctrine. He does not allow himself to be diverted, and he gives the impression that he is working his way through the resolution of the problem, if not for the first time, at least in the absence of any body of existing contemporary literature which would have framed additional questions for him. He has not found it necessary to begin the work as he began the *Cur Deus Homo* by listing a number of *objectiones infidelium*; there is, he emphasizes, only one point of difference to be settled.[40] By the middle of the twelfth century, this matter had become the subject of much more widespread discussion. Anselm of Havelberg conducted a public debate with the Greeks in an attempt to meet them on their own ground and overcome their objections in that way. A number of related questions to do with the doctrine and methods and even the language of the Greeks had by now become commonplace in the schools.[41] The controversy had become general and the Greeks were recognized as holders

---

[38] Eadmer, *The Life of St. Anselm*, ed. R. W. Southern (London, 1961), pp. 112-13.

[39] *Anselmi Opera Omnia*, II.177.   [40] *Anselmi Opera Omnia*, II.178.

[41] See my article 'Anselm of Canterbury and Anselm of Havelberg: The controversy with the Greeks; *Analecta Praemonstratensia*, liii (1977), 158-75.

of doubtful opinions.

The first contacts Christian scholars from the north of Europe made with the Moslems seem to have stirred neither fear nor very much curiosity. William of Malmesbury regards them as little more than one of the pagan sects which have happened to survive until his own day (*usque ad hanc diem*); 'For the Saracens and Turks worship God the Creator, considering Mahomet to be not God but his prophet. The Vindelici worship Fortune . . .' and so on.[42] Even in the twelfth century few scholars had more than a sketchy notion of Moslem beliefs. Otto of Freising seizes upon the crucial point that the Moslems deny that Christ is the Son of God or that he brought salvation to the human race.[43] Alan of Lille includes some arguments against Islam in the fourth book of his *Contra Haereticos,* but he gives comparatively little space to this 'heresy'. Even the translation of the *Koran* into Latin under the direction of Peter the Venerable[44] does not appear to have awakened any sense among the scholars of the mid-twelfth century that Islam posed a serious threat to Christianity.

R. W. Southern has suggested a number of reasons for this, not least the fact that the Moslems engaged in no active campaign of conversion in the north of Europe. The Moslems remained a distant threat,[45] while the leaders of popular heresy pressed their case closer to home and could be seen to be leading Christian people astray. Their sheer multiplicity, the readiness with which they sprang up, their very obviousness to the most casual observer, meant that popular heresies captured attention. But there is perhaps a further reason of greater consequence for the work of polemical theologians. Islamic doctrine posed several major theological questions, but it did not touch on those matters about which the

---

[42] William of Malmesbury, *Gesta Regum,* ed. W. Stubbs, *Rolls Series* 90ª (1887), p. 230.

[43] Otto of Freising, *Chronica,* ed. A. Hofmeister, *Quellen, MGH Script. in usum schol.* (1912), p. 317.

[44] M. T. D'Alverny, 'Deux traductions latines du Coran au moyen age', *AHDLMA* xvi (1948), 67–131. Robert of Ketton carried out the translation, which was finished by 1143.

[45] R. W. Southern, *Western Views of Islam* (Harvard, 1962), p. 39.

Christian West was especially tender-minded in the twelfth century. The Christian theologians of the day were anxious to show in exactly what way it was possible for Christ to be both God and Man. The focus of their interest lay in problems of *persona* and *natura* and *assumptio,* of the way in which Christ can have been free of original sin, of the nature of the sacrifice which was made when he died on the Cross, and the question of whether it was made to God or to Satan. Moslems accepted the Virgin birth of Christ, although they considered him merely a prophet. Their teaching had nothing to contribute to the burning contemporary issues. Neither as a threat to the faith of ordinary people nor as a source of doctrinal confusion did Islam constitute any very pressing problem for the theologians of the twelfth century. Alan of Lille makes them the least of the 'heretics' to whom he addresses himself. For him Cathars and Waldensians come first, and then the Jews.

These, then, were the heretics and unbelievers with whom Latin theologians were faced in their missionary work of writing theological books to put errors right and to convert the holders of mistaken beliefs to a sound faith. Alongside the book-work and teaching of academic theologians, preaching to popular and student audiences and public disputation went on. Some of the polemicists took part in active work in the mission-field, as Alan of Lille did in the South of France; Alan himself was one of the foremost exponents in his day of the art of preaching. The writing of polemical theology was never an exclusively academic exercise because it was designed to have a practical utility for Christians who were not scholars. But it had a markedly academic character, and unless we make allowance for that we shall fail to understand what gave the polemical theology of the twelfth century its intellectual energy.

2. Theological Method against the Unbelievers

St. Bernard castigated the heretic Henry for clinging obstinately to his opinions with a determined disregard for the truth.[1]

---

[1] *PL* 182.435, *Letter* 241.

To his mind what Jews and Moslems and Greek Christians
and dualist heretics had in common was their refusal to see
the force of the truth; he and his fellow apologists for
orthodoxy addressed themselves to this common 'perverse-
ness' in their search for methods of converting, or at least
refuting, unbelievers. It is therefore only to be expected
that the techniques they employed against different sects
should have a good deal in common. Describing a treatise
written by a monk called William against the same heretic
Henry in the mid-1130s, R. I. Moore comments that 'it is a
pity that William is so much less concerned to report Henry's
arguments than his own'.[2] Certainly if we want to learn
about the beliefs of the heretics,[3] it is regrettable that
William tells us so little about Henry's opinions. But if he did
not do full justice to the beliefs of his opponent he wrote
according to the canons of a polemical theology which was
rapidly beginning to lay down ground rules of its own; he is
an exponent of a theological method for use against unbelievers.

This was in any case an age of reconsideration of first
principles, of new and more precise definition of beliefs long
held more or less unquestioned by a great many faithful
people, whose first concern was to hold an orthodox faith,
and to whom it perhaps never occurred to examine their
beliefs in detail. It was less easy now for an educated man to
hold his faith in unthinking simplicity. A number of 'very
difficult questions', as Peter Abelard calls them,[4] were now
current in the schools. How, for example, can there be three
Persons when there is no plurality in God?[5] If the human
language in which theology is conducted is not eternal, but
came into existence with the world,[6] how can it adequately
express the eternal theological truths it purports to describe?[7]

---

[2] William's work is edited by R. Manselli, *Bulletino dell' Instituto Storico
Italiano* (1953), pp. 36–62. The English translation from which the extracts
which follow are taken is to be found in R. I. Moore, *The Birth of Popular
Heresy* (London, 1975), pp. 46 ff.

[3] Moore's bibliography is one of the most recent although selective. For a full
list up to 1966, see H. Grundman, *Bibliographie zur Ketzergeschichte des
Mittelalters*, 1900–66 (Rome, 1967).

[4] *Theologia Christiana*, III, 89, pp. 230 ff.

[5] Ibid., p. 231.1171–2.   [6] Ibid., p. 242.1511.   [7] Ibid., p. 230, para 90.

It would be misleading to suggest that these questions and others like them did not occur to the monastic scholars of earlier generations. But they are questions which cannot be precisely framed without some technical knowledge of the arts of language and the mathematical arts, and they are unlikely to have troubled many in an age when such matters were not the stuff of ordinary discourse in the classroom. In Anselm's day it was not yet clear how extensive the ramifications of questioning like this were likely to become or, to use a current contemporary image, how far the roots of the tree would prove to stretch when they were explored. Anselm was always confident that clear reasoning could only confirm the soundness of orthodox doctrine. Remarkably soon after his death the complex of discussion had grown so vast that the objections to orthodox doctrine which the heretics and unbelievers made often coincided with topics raised for discussion in the schoolroom. Academic theologians were often asking the same or very similar questions to those of the heretics. Heresy was to be found in the Church as well as outside it. The very processes of revision and reconsideration which gave twelfth-century theological thinking its vigour, involved the discovery of arguments about matters in dispute with the heretics and unbelievers, too. A polemical strategy devised to combat heresy outside the Church met a similar challenge within, and it would falsify the position to try to distinguish the methods involved too sharply.

In his *Disputations,* a series of school exercises on theological questions, Simon of Tournai deals with several problems which were also of interest to the dualist heretics. The dualists distinguished the material or bodily creation in which resided all that was evil, from the spiritual which they regarded as the principle of goodness. Simon asks whether all wickedness is transmitted in the flesh and the soul itself clean of sin at its creation. Simon enquires whether there is any force in the following argument:

Everything is good in that it exists.
The Devil exists.
Therefore the Devil is good.[8]

[8] Simon of Tournai, *Disputationes*, ed. J. Warichez, *SSLov.* 12 (1932), Disp. XXXI (iii), p. 93.23–4.

The dualists could have answered Simon's question for him. They would have said that evil, too, has an existence, and that it is possible for the Devil to exist and to be wholly evil. Simon asks whether men will be resurrected with their whole substance intact, including the hair and nails which have been cut off during a lifetime. If that is to be so, he says, there will be much deformity in heaven.[9] This was an objection which the dualists also put forward, against the view that the body was to be resurrected.[10] Simon does not say that he has had heretical opinions in mind when he framed his questions. These are matters at issue in ordinary schoolrooms, academic questions of the new theological discipline, which simply happen to coincide on occasion with topics of concern to unbelievers of one sort or another. The coincidence made the methods appropriate for resolving these difficulties in the classroom appear appropriate for fashioning arguments against the heretics, too.

There was, moreover, a difference in the spirit in which these questions were raised in the schoolroom and among the heretics. Simon's pupils will, he anticipates, be satisfied by his explanations. The heretics felt the problem of evil particularly deeply; they were outraged by the very existence of evil. It was for them, as Dondaine has so felicitously put it, something experienced in the innermost being, 'experimentée jusque'au plus intime de nous-mêmes.'[11] That is not to suggest that orthodox Christians thought evil unimportant, but academically and rationally satisfactory explanations of the reasons why we may regard evil as having no real existence will not convince people who feel the force and the presence of evil in themselves acutely. It would not be true to say that the methods of argument which worked reasonably well in the schoolroom with pupils anxious to have their uncertainities removed, would be equally effective in polemical writing. But the mere fact that it was often necessary to argue a case over similar problems in either con-

---

[9] Ibid., *Disp.* XXVI, p. 82.

[10] *PL* 210.307-78; Alan of Lille gives a sketch of these doctrines in his *Liber Contra Haereses*.

[11] A. Dondaine, *Un traité néo-Manichéen du xiii siècle: Liber de Duobus Principiis* (Rome, 1939), p. 21.

text encouraged scholars to rely upon the twin methods of proof (one or both of which formed the foundation of every academic demonstration in the twelfth century), that is, authority and reason. Peter Abelard explains at the beginning of the *Theologia Christiana* that every discussion of a disputed point turns on written authority or on reason,[12] and the authors of polemical treatises commonly say that they have chosen one method or the other, or a combination of both.

The choice was not their own. In order to convince an opponent it is necessary to find common ground with him in the methods of argument which are used.[13] Appeals to the final authority of Scripture will carry no weight with pagan philosophers. The Jews would accept only the authority of the Old Testament and the Cathars only that of the New, says Aquinas. Of the Moslems he says, 'They do not agree with us in accepting the authority of any Scripture through which they can be convinced, as we can dispute with the Jews through the Old Testament and against the heretics through the new. For these [Moslems] accept neither. Therefore it is necessary to resort to reason, with which everyone is obliged to agree'.[14] Much the same view had been put forward in the first half of the twelfth century by Peter the Venerable, Abbot of Cluny, when he wrote against the Petrobrusian heretics. 'If they are willing to remain Christians they must give way to authority; if they are men at all they must give way to reason'[15] (for man is a rational animal). At the turn of the twelfth century Gilbert Crispin discusses the common ground of authority which Christians share with Jews in their respect for the Old Testament, and the act that in arguing with a heathen he can depend only on reason.[16] Peter Abelard makes the same point in his *Dialogue of a Christian, a Philosopher and a Jew.*[17] Late in the twelfth century, the author of the *Summa* which has been attributed

---

[12] *Theologia Christiana,* III, p. 194, para. 1.1-2.

[13] Perhaps the most influential of the early attempts to do this was Gilbert Crispin's *Disputatio Iudei et Christiani.*

[14] Aquinas, *Summa Contra Gentiles,* I.2.

[15] Peter the Venerable, *Contra Petrobrusianos Hereticos,* p. 3.2-4.

[16] Gilbert Crispin, *Dispute with a Heathen,* ed. cit., p. 60.

[17] Abelard's *Dialogus,* p. 41-3.

to Praepositinus notes that the Cathars could be convinced only by arguments drawn from the New Testament, for they believed that the God of the Old Testament was the Devil.[18] It is with this proviso in mind that Alan of Lille marshals both reason and authorities against the Cathars,[19] and the author of the thirteenth-century *Book on the Two Principles* proposes to do likewise, and to argue from 'the testimonies of the Holy Scriptures with most true arguments'.[20] Aquinas' discussion of the methods appropriate for polemical writing at the beginning of the *Summa against the Heretics* rested, then, upon a well-established tradition.

The use of authority posed a number of difficulties. The problem did not end with the Bible; some 'unbelievers' accepted patristic authority (the Greeks, for example, relied upon the Greek Fathers), and others did not. (Hugh of Amiens even refers to the 'authority' of historical writers.)[21] The heretic Henry was prepared to accept only the New Testament as authoritative. 'If you bring arguments against me from Jerome or Augustine, or any other doctors', he says, 'I will grant them some force, but they are not necessary for salvation.'[22] William the monk answers him by asking him to define more clearly where his objection lies. If he argues that these writings do not confer salvation, then he and Henry are in agreement, for not even the words of the Bible do that directly. But William believes that patristic writings are helpful in teaching us how to attain salvation, and he says that if Henry refuses to listen to them he is cutting himself off from the Church.[23] Bernard, too, presses the heretical 'foxes' against whom he writes in *Sermon* 65 on The Song of Songs to be clear about the teaching of those Scriptures which they do accept. He knows that these 'little foxes that destroy the vines' will not accept the books of the Old Testament, but remind them that, in addition to the Gospel, which they say that they alone truly follow, they also accept what is said by those who knew Christ, 'all the words,

---

[18] J. N. Garvin and J. A. Corbett, *The 'Summa Contra Haereticos' ascribed to Praepositinus of Cremona* (Notre Dame, 1958).

[19] *PL* 210.312,314.   [20] Dondaine, ed. cit., p. 81.4–5.

[21] *PL* 192.1284.   [22] Tr. Moore, p. 46, and Manselli, ed. cit., p. 36.

[23] Tr. Moore, p. 48.

writings and traditions of those who were bodily present with the Saviour.'[24]

The solution did not lie in employing only arguments from reason, because the heretics themselves insisted upon advancing arguments based on authority. The Cathars in particular claimed that they alone knew how to interpret the Gospel correctly. No headway could be made against them unless their interpretations were challenged by detailed analysis of the texts themselves. Egbert of Schönau, writing in the 1160s, thinks that Christian apologists often shirk their duty here. The heretics, he finds, are always ready with passages to quote in support of their views. He has tried in his treatise against the heretics to note the Scriptural authorities they cite in support of their erros and to make it clear where they misinterpret them. He has also provided a list of texts which the Christian may memorize, so that he will be ready; for it is shameful, he says, that the heretics should be so ready and fluent in their arguments, while educated Christians can find nothing to say against them.[25] Hugh of Amiens gives an example of the way to use authority against the heretics, in his *Contra Haereticos*. Jesus was baptized when he was thirty, say the heretics, and therefore that must be the proper age for baptism; infant baptism is to be avoided. Hugh brings both reasoning and authority to bear. The baptism of an ordinary human being cannot be compared with the baptism of Christ, for we are sanctified by baptism, and Christ sanctified baptism itself when he was baptized. In support of his argument that Christ's baptism was quite different from ordinary baptisms, he cites Matthew 3:14-15 and Luke 3:21-2. In the baptism of Christ (as in the Epiphany and in the first miracle at Cana) there was a theophany, a revealing of his Godhead. Indeed, in the baptism, 'the Trinity itself was made manifest'.[26] Others, who are not self-confessed heretics, may also be misled by misunderstanding the Bible. Some say that baptism is not indispensable to salvation, for Abraham's belief in God was counted as righteousness in him.[27] Whether heretics or ordinary Christians who have

---

[24] *Sermones super Cantica Canticorum*, Sermon 65, para. 3-4, ed. J. Leclerq, C. H. Talbot, H. M. Rochais, *Sancti Bernardi Opera*, II, 172.
[25] *PL* 195.13-14.　　　　[26] *PL* 192.1268.　　　　[27] *PL* 192.1269.

fallen into error are involved, the orthodox Christian must
be ready to show them how to use authority correctly. A
great deal more was involved in meeting heretical and
erroneous views based on misunderstandings of authority
than a mere ability to cap authority with authority. Many
new difficulties arose out of routine Bible study where the
techniques of the arts were employed in the interpretation of
Scripture for the first time.[28] Simon of Tournai emphasizes
that the words may make sense according to the rules of
grammar in one way, but carry another sense doctrinally or
spiritually.[29] Understanding the rules of grammar is not
enough. In order to avoid being misled it was necessary to
understand both the grammatical structure of the sentence
and the orthodox doctrine to which it referred.

The author of a discussion of the problems of arguing
against the heretics and unbelievers of the day (which is
edited by M. T. d'Alverny in her important article on the
first translations of the *Koran* into Latin) has given some
thought both to the general purpose which is to be served by
polemical writing, and to the appropriate method of applying
reason in support of the orthodox case. He has, written, he
says, so as to explain to everyone, Christians and unbelievers
alike, exactly what the Christians believe and exactly what
the unbelievers' doctrine comprises.[30] The polemicist's words
should have both specific and universal application. They
should meet the heretic on his own ground and at the same
time put forward a case which every reader will find convincing. It is most important that it be made clear that
Christians are not 'in error and in the blindness of lack of
faith, in which lie those who do not believe in Christ'. His
task is, in a sense, that of a publicist. All that is needed is a
full and clear exposition of the faith; that will demonstrate
its superiority incontrovertibly. It will speak for itself. As
Hugh of Amiens puts it, 'wholesome doctrine, because it is

[28] The classic study of the work on the Bible which was to develop into the
glossa ordinaria in the course of the twelfth century is still B. Smalley, *The Study
of the Bible in the Middle Ages,* but Miss Smalley is not primarily concerned
with the influence of the *artes.*

[29] Simon of Tournai, ed. cit., p. 32.12.

[30] M. T. d'Alverny, 'Deux traductions latines du Coran au moyen age',
AHDLMA xvi (1948), 69–131, p. 93.

brighter than the sun, destroys heresy wherever it is expounded'.[31] It is the sheer reasonableness of the orthodox view which makes it irresistible — much as Anselm felt it to be when he gave a reasonable account of the necessity for the Incarnation in the *Cur Deus Homo*. Petrus Alphonsus claimed to have written his *Dialogus* between a Christian and a Jew with the intention that his readers should 'hear the reason' (*audiant rationem*) by which he proposes to show up the failings of other beliefs and demonstrates that the Christian faith outshines them all.[32] In this grand design reasoning takes its place beside authority as a ground of proof which is quite irresistible.

But the use of reasoning requires care in achieving the right balance, just as the use of authority does (if for different reasons). Some heretics are ignorant men and members of the sect under attack may be so inexpert in argument that it would be a waste of time to try to persuade them by subtle arguments.[33] It is simply foolish to put 'profound words of argument' before men who do not understand them. For such simple men it is necessary to write in 'simple and commonly-understood words'. A more advanced case may be put in terms of 'philosophical definitions' and according to dialectical rules and all the multifarious art of argument (*disputandi multifariam artem*).[34] If heretics able to appreciate such arguments were rarely to be found in rural communities or even among the leaders of popular heresy in the first half of the twelfth century,[35] there were certainly men in the schools who were prepared to give unorthodox arguments serious consideration, and to sue the secular arts for the purpose. The author of the text edited by M. T. d'Alverny complains that some of these *heretici Christiani* 'spend their time in prolix discussion', turning over questions of genera and species and difference, of substance and accident and relation and quality and quantity, of proposition, assumption and conclusion, as they try to apply the principles of dialectic to theological problems.[36] We are

[31] *PL* 192.1257.   [32] *PL* 157.538.   [33] D'Alverny, op. cit., p. 123.
[34] On the Arrians see S. Runciman, *The Mediaeval Manichee*. For this reference, see D'Alverny, op. cit., p. 23.
[35] Runciman, op. cit., p. 121.   [36] D'Alverny, op. cit., p. 123.

dealing here not with simple explanations which will comple-
ment the use of authority, but with an increasingly technical
procedure.

Sometimes the orthodox resorts to mockery. 'Let me show
the absurdity of your argument again', says the monk,
William, to Henry.[37] He sneers at Henry's two 'clumsily-
chosen precepts' and points to the technical impropriety
(*inconvenientia*)[38] which will follow if they are accepted.
The question at issue is this: the Bible says, 'Preach the
Gospel to every creature.' Ought one to preach to man, or to
non-man? Patently it would be absurd to preach to any
creature but man, who is a rational being and understands
human language. We must understand 'creature' here to refer
to man alone. A literal interpretation of the passage would
be absurd. Similarly it is absurd for Henry to argue that the
Gospel says that every man ought to be a preacher. William
has set his own superior knowledge of proper technical
procedures against what he claims to be Henry's uninformed
argumentativeness. But in so doing he reduces the scale of
the question at issue to a smaller compass. He implies that
there is no question to be answered but that of whether
Henry has understood the text properly.

This tendency for close reasoning to diminish the scale of
the debate might have been an acceptable disadvantage had
the heretics been open to conviction by the sheer reasonableness of their opponents' arguments. Anselm had thought it
possible to convince unbelievers by showing them the sheer
beauty of reasonableness.[39] But the heretics of the twelfth
century approached discussions with Christian apologists in a
very different frame of mind. Peter the Venerable says in
despair that even if his arguments do not succeed in converting the Petrobrusians, they will have some value in that they
will benefit believing Christians and confirm them in their
faith.[40] On some points, Hugh of Amiens thinks, it is better

---

[37] Tr. Moore, p. 47, Manselli, ed. cit.
[38] Both Anselm and Peter Abelard speak of *inconvenientia, convenientia* and
decentia in contexts where much more than the general sense of 'appropriateness'
is intended, and where they carry a relatively precise technical dialectical sense.
[39] *Anselmi Opera Omnia*, II.   [40] Fearns, ed. cit., pp. 3-4.

to give up the attempt to convert the heretics.[41] Sometimes, in exasperation, a theologian reminds his readers of the unprofitableness of asking certain questions. 'Stop worrying about how and why children bear original sin', says William to the heretic Henry. 'If you do not understand this, believe it so that you may understand . . . Do not ask how a man fell into a pit unless you know how to get him out of it again. Do not ask by what justice a man falls into a pit of sin when he becomes flesh, when many arguments of the Gospels, the apostles and the saints confirm that he can get out of it again by the regeneration of water and the Holy Spirit.'[42] His advice to Christians is to 'cultivate a simple faith' rather than to engage in fruitless discussions about the divine.[43] In this way they will avoid the sin of intellectual pride (*mentis superbia*),[44] and they will not run the risk of becoming heretical in their own opinions. The appeal of reasonable arguments to the receptive mind of the Christian who wanted to be orthodox, was of another order altogether from their appeal to the heretic who was obstinately convinced that it was he who was being reasonable. Reason could just as well lead to unbelief as to orthodoxy of opinion.

So much for reason and authority. One further method of argument deserves mention here. Augustine developed a style, particularly in the *Confessions* and the homilies, which was adapted by St. Anselm in his devotional writings and by the authors of a number of eleventh- and twelfth-century pastoral and devotional works.[45] It came to full flower in the twelfth century in the language of Bernard's preaching, with its antitheses and parallelisms, its rhymes and near-rhymes, its exclamations and rhetorical questions. Bernard showed how persuasive sheer eloquence could be in preaching. Gerhoch of Reichersberg and Hugh of Amiens and Peter the Venerable[46] write with a less consummate skill, but with an ear for the persuasiveness of balance, and skilful juxtaposition of ideas, and fine rolling periods, in convincing unbelievers and believers alike by overwhelming their objections in a welter

---

[41] *PL* 192.1284. [42] Tr. Moore, pp. 50–1; Manselli ed. cit.
[43] *PL* 192.1255–6. [44] *PL* 192.1263.
[45] On Augustine's style, see J. Finaert, *S. Augustin rhéteur* (Paris, 1939).
[46] See Fearns, ed. cit., p. xiii on the dating of this work.

of words. A pattern of similar syntactical units often helps the argument forward and gives the reader or listener a mnemonic aid: *fide suscipitur; spe firmatur; charitate perficitur,* says Hugh,[47] and: *Vide ergo in baptismate fidem, in confirmatione sacro facto chrismate spem, in mensa Dominica charitatem; fide namque renovatur, spe sublimatur, charitate glorificatur*[48] ('See, then, in baptism faith, in the confirmation of what was done in the anointing, hope; at the Lord's table, love; for by faith is a man renewed, by hope is a man raised up, by love is he glorified'). This argument in favour of the value of the sacraments does not specifically meet any of the heretics' objections, but it meets an emotional and spiritual need for a sense of the personal value the sacraments have for the believer. Elsewhere, repetition drives a point home: *Factus est de Virgine, factus de nostro genere, non sub peccati traduce, sed abolitio culpae, sed largitio veniae, sed effusio gratiae sempiternae*[49] ('He was made of the Virgin, he was made a member of our race, not under the inheritance of sin, but in abolition of guilt, in generous pardon, in pouring out of everlasting grace'). Parallelism is used for emphasis; again the figure of thought is matched by a figure of diction[50] to give the device additional force: *Haeretici perversa proponunt, et contra sacramenta disputando saeviunt.*[51] 'The heretics put forward perverse views, and rage against the sacraments in their arguments'. In a perhaps rather quieter tone, Peter the Venerable writes a similar contrived and rhetorical prose: *Si vero ad Vetus Testamentum accedam, ostendam unius Abrahe fide gentem maximam a deo electam, assumptam, salvatam; unius Moysi fide et precibus eandem sepe a morte ereptam; unius David fide et devotione tribum et genus ipsius aliis tribubus et toti genti prelatam*[52] ('If I turn to the Old Testament I can show a race especially chosen by God; received and saved by the faith of one man, Abraham; often snatched from death by the faith and prayers of one man, Moses; that one race set about others which are its tributaries, and raised above all

---

[47] *PL* 192.1259.   [48] *PL* 192.1260   [49] *PL* 192.1262.
[50] *Rhetorica ad Herennium,* IV.xlv–lvi on figures of thought and figures of diction.
[51] *PL* 192.1266.   [52] Fearns, ed. cit., p. 45, para. 73.

people'). There can be no doubt that these authors intended that their words should gain additional persuasive force from the use of such devices. It was seen as a perfectly proper means of helping along an argument in polemical writing.

One of the most important skills taught by the classical rhetoricians, and revived towards the end of the eleventh century in the textbooks of the art of letter-writing, was that of putting together a sequence of argument in an orderly manner. The polemicists do not attempt to give their treatises the six parts of a classical oration or the five parts of a letter;[53] We should not expect them to do so. But they show a concern with the best method of arranging their subject-matter which, like their choice of style, is ultimately rhetorical in inspiration. While Simon of Tournai's *Disputationes* have been put together in no discernible order and it was to be some time before the subject-matter of theology as a whole could be resolved into a systematic sequence,[54] the authors of polemical treatises found it a matter of some urgency to arrange their material in such a way that a solid case against the heretics could be built up. No single solution seems to have been hit upon by them all. Hugh of Amiens seeks to present an integrated argument. He shows by discussion of the nature of the Trinity and the process of Redemption that there must be a single Church, a single Bride of Christ, 'the bride of one Husband'.[55] In this way Hugh provides himself with a solid foundation upon which to rest what he says next: the heretics assert that the Church and its sacraments are unnecessary for salvation.

By contrast, Ermengardus follows a point-by-point sequence, so that his treatise can be used a work of reference by anyone who has to rebut a given argument. At

[53] For a general survey of the development of the *ars dictaminis* see J. J. Murphy, *Rhetoric in the Middle Ages* (California, 1974).

[54] In the Prologue to the *Summa Theologica* Aquinas refers to the confusion certain students suffer because no single textbook exists which will help them find their way through the tangle of the theological literature of the day. He has written the *Summa Theologica* to supply what they need. As early as the beginning of the twelfth century Honorius Augustodunensis had tried in the *Elucidarium* to provide something of the kind on a much simpler level, but it was not sufficiently detailed for the requirements of twelfth-century schools. See Y. Lefèvre, *L'Elucidarium et les Lucidaires*.

[55] PL 192.1255-9.

each point he states the heretical assertion under discussion, and then lists, for the most part without comment, all that may be said against it. He gives some New Testament authorities, which the heretics ought to be willing to accept, and notes that there are also many he could have included from the Old Testament.[56] Bernard, Abbot of Fontcaude, adopts a rather similar treatment of one point at a time. His treatise is based on an actual public debate, in which the heretics were challenged by 'true Catholics' who answered their *capitula* one by one. Many authorities were produced by both sides.[57] Bernard sets out his case in an orderly manner, giving both *rationes* and *auctoritates*. The almost forensic character of the challenge the apologists for orthodoxy faced, is thrown sharply into relief by such references as this to the holding of actual discussions with opponents. The atmosphere cannot have been entirely unlike that of the court-room, although it was a court-room very different from that in which Cicero expected his advocate to speak. But when Hugh of Amiens cries *Deus in causa est: assistamus*[58] ('God's cause is at stake; let us be ready!'), he seems to see himself espousing the cause not only as a soldier in battle but also as an advocate in a court of law. The rhetorical air of much polemical writing is more than a top-dressing; the business of persuasion is the first task of the missionary theologian, for without persuasion and conviction there can be no conversion.

In the *Summa contra Gentiles* Aquinas goes through all the known errors to which heretics are prone, setting them out in order so that they can be used conveniently for reference — first errors concerning the Trinity, the Son, the Holy Spirit, the procession of the Holy Spirit, then errors concerning the Incarnation, original sin, the appropriateness and necessity of the Redemption, then errors concerning the sacraments, the resurrection of the body, the world after death, the Last Judgement, the world after the Judgement. He includes the ancient errors with which the Fathers had long ago tried to deal, and the errors of all contemporary dissidents from orthodox Latin Christianity. His arrangement reflects the

[56] *PL* 204.1236.   [57] *PL* 204.795.   [58] *PL* 192.1258.

needs of the schoolroom first and foremost. His is, above all, an academic textbook, whose methods owe much to the techniques of academic theology. In earlier treatises we see scholars feeling their way towards a suitable method by trial and error. The live debate is never very far behind, and the academic tradition is married with it yet only very uncertainly.

The pursuit of the truth is the first duty of all theologians, as twelfth-century scholars often emphasize. But the polemicist must pursue the truth not as a seeker, but as one who goes into battle to defend it. His task is to reduce to nothing the claims of a body of falsehoods which have been stated by his opponents. The existence of such falsehoods helps to focus his attempt, but it also tends to channel thought. There can be little room for free speculation where anything of the kind may lead to the proliferation of new falsehoods. It is not surprising to find these polemical treatises cautious in the extreme, conventional and narrow. Anselm's *discipulus* in the *De Casu Diaboli* remarks in comic despair that every time he hopes that he is coming to the end of the question he sees new shoots sprouting out of the roots where they have been cut off.[59] This is exactly what the polemicist is anxious to avoid.

But while a policy of caution, and a determination to ensure that everything he says converges on the point in hand, will take the polemicist so far, it will not quite do to rely entirely on the work of the Fathers in rebutting heresies. Augustine wrote for a very different society from that in which the twelfth-century scholar found himself. Augustine's medieval heir had to contend, in the schools at least, with men who worried over every detail until they were satisfied. He had to construct an academically satisfactory account of the orthodox view. Neither Gilbert of Poitiers nor Peter Abelard, to take two of the most notorious troublemakers, set out to overturn orthodox doctrine. In so far as either of them found himself questioning it, he did so because it seemed to him that close analysis of textual authorities and the application of the methods of the arts gave grounds for

[59] *Anselmi Opera Omnia*, I. 244.11–13.

specific objections. The popular heretics, by contrast, had
not as a rule arrived at their doctrines by hard analysis of the
texts which they cited in their support. Those texts were
marshalled to give solidity and coherence to an existing unorthodox doctrinal position. Apologists for the orthodox
view could try to meet the heretics' objections by methods of
textual analysis; they could argue against the *dialectici
haeretici* of the schools on their own ground. But for neither
purpose was the existing body of patristic literature entirely
adequate. Many of the points involved had been raised only
recently because they were the fruit of recent work within
the schools.

The habit of bearing in mind the need to defend the
orthodox position gave a stimulus to the development of
twelfth-century theological method. It lent a driving energy
to the search for the truth and coloured theological writing
with an emotional vitality of its own. The missionary urge
was so universal that references to the *haeretici* came naturally
to the minds of many scholars while they were writing a great
variety of different works. The pervasiveness of this influence
is important because it shed a new light on the theologian's
purpose, and it helped to form habits of style and methods of
argument throughout the extensive field of academic theological studies. But in itself polemical theology achieved only
a limited development during the twelfth century. It was
nothing like so fertile as the speculative theology of the day,
or as the developments in the systematic study of the Bible
which provided the groundwork for speculation. But unless
it is given its proper place among the major theological
developments of the twelfth century we shall not see why
they took the direction they did.

V The Work of Creation and the Work of Restoration

1. Philosophers, Heretics, and the Work of Creation

Hugh of St. Victor proposed a grand division of theology into the work of creation and the work of restoration (in which God repaired the potential damage to his plan for mankind which the fall of Adam had threatened).[1] His younger contemporary Robert of Melun took up his idea and developed it. The point both scholars were most anxious to make was that the work of restoration or reparation is the principle subject-matter of the Bible, while the work of creation, the question of the origin of things, may be studied more fully in the textbooks of the liberal arts and secular philosophy. 'Just as the writings of some secular authors deal with the work of creation, so Holy Scripture deals with the work of repara-tion,'[2] says Robert, The Bible is chiefly concerned with the Incarnation of Christ, with all that went before it and all that follows from it.[3]

If we compare what the Bible teaches about the *opus restaurationis* with what the secular authors teach about the *opus conditionis,* we shall see that there is a difference in kind between the two treatments.[4] It is, however, possible to draw some parallels. 'The work of creation is that by which it was brought about that what did not exist came into existence and what was without form was given form, and what had been given form was put in its proper place.'[5] By the work of reparation, 'what was lost has been restored, what has been restored is given form, and what has been given form is put in its proper place.'[6] The first *opus* took six days and the second six ages to be completed.[7] But these

[1] Hugh of St. Victor, *De Sacramentis,* I.2, *PL* 176.183.

[2] Robert of Melun, *Sententiae,* ed. R. Martin, *SSLov.* 21 (1947), Book. I. i.xviii, p. 206.21-2, p. 207.25.

[3] Robert of Melun, *Quaestiones [theologice] de Epistolis Pauli,* ed. R. Martin, *SSLov.* 18 (1938), p. 2.9-13.

[4] *Sententiae,* p. 206.23-4.   [5] Ibid., p. 206.27-8.
[6] Ibid., p. 207.1-2.   [7] Ibid., p. 206.29; p. 207.2.

parallels will not take us very far.

It is no accident that the account of creation given in Genesis is so brief. 'It is clear', Robert claims' 'how far the works of reparation excel the works of creation, for the former confer salvation.'[8] The story of the redemption is far more pertinent to the needs of fallen humanity than the story of creation. The student of redemption theology will find all he needs in Scripture to enable him to see how God has restored the world to the state in which he intended it to be — or, perhaps more precisely, to the prospect of its coming to its appointed end. The student of creation theology must work along other lines to fill out the account given in Genesis, and he must understand that he is labouring at a task which cannot be so spiritually rewarding as that of the student of redemption theology.

But in the middle years of the twelfth century there was a great deal of general curiosity about the philosophical and scientific problems raised by the mystery of how the world began. If the investigation of such matters was regarded as less edifying, it was certainly not lacking in interest. Prompted by a comparison of the Genesis account of creation with the views of the ancient *philosophi*, contemporary scholars asked afresh the ancient questions which Plato had tried to answer in the *Timaeus*. Why did God make the world? Did he make it from nothing, or from some preexisting matter? Did the shapes or forms of things exist from eternity, or were they created by God? Did creation take place in stages or all at once? Did God make evil things as well as good? Do negative things like darkness exist or are they merely an absence of something positive? These are not new questions of Christian theology. Most of them were raised by the Fathers. But they are new in the twelfth century in one important respect. For the first time in the Middle Ages answers were being systematically sought in the writings of the 'secular authors', the *ethnicorum scripture* as Robert of Melun calls them. As a result, a set of scientific explanations was put forward. This was the foundation upon which scholars were able to build when more of Aristotle's works

----

[8] Ibid., p. 209.14–15.

became available to the West in the thirteenth century. Without it, the assimilation of ancient science and philosophy could not have gone forward as it did in the later Middle Ages.

The contrast between the new air of scientific enquiry which animated twelfth-century scholars, and the approach to such problems of *conditio* and *creatio* of an earlier generation, becomes clear enough if we look at the work of St. Anselm. He had a natural flair for metaphysics which enabled him to perceive the importance and many of the implications of these questions without the aid of the textbooks which brought them to the attention of early twelfth-century scholars. It is most unlikely that he knew Chalcidius' commentary on the *Timaeus* or Boethius' *opuscula sacra*. The only authority of any substantial use to him in this connection was Augustine. He was therefore thrown back on his own resources in his attempts to find solutions to an extent which the next generation of scholars was not. His reflections are markedly more philosophical and less scientific than theirs. That is to say, if we may usefully make the distinction, they are concerned primarily with metaphysics and only secondarily with explaining the physical mechanisms involved.

On the verge of another age of major advance in scientific thought, Descartes distinguished between the thoughts he had about created things such as the sky, the earth, light and heat, and the idea he had of a Being more perfect than himself (*Discourse on Method,* 4). That idea, he argued, must have been planted in his mind by that Being himself. Everything else he could have invented; his imagination could supply ideas of things equal or inferior to himself. But it was inconceivable to him that he could have invented the concept of something more perfect than himself. The fundamental distinction he perceived here lies between the way in which the created or natural world may be known and the kind of knowledge which may be had of that which transcends experience of the natural world, and which is, literally, 'metaphysical'. In this way Descartes arrives independently at an argument for the existence of the perfect Being who is God, which has, as has often been pointed out, strong affinities with Anselm's ontological argument in the *Proslogion*. And he also distinguishes between what was to become the traditional subject-matter of science and the subject-matter of the theologian, between the objects of the natural world and that which is beyond and above it and canot be known in the same way. It is here that I should like to draw the line between physics and metaphysics for our present purposes, without entering into the question of the different modes of existence involved, or indeed, whether anything beyond the physical world can be said to 'exist'.

Half a millenium earlier, Anselm had asked what was the nature of God. It seemed to him obvious, as it seemed to Descartes, that God must be the highest and most perfect being, the highest nature and the highest good.[9] Descartes says that in order to understand the nature of God he has only to think whether each thing of which he has an idea is a perfection or not. If it is good, it must be present in the most perfect Being. If it is imperfect, it can have nothing to do with the most perfect Being. Descartes assumes, as Anselm does, that lesser perfections derive their existence from the greater perfection, and, indeed, that everything which exists ultimately derives its existence from the highest Being.[10] These are not, of course, assumptions without ancestry. Their roots in the Platonic and Augustianian tradition are clear enough, but Anselm, like Descartes, had tried to demonstrate their truth. He does not merely assert these principles. He devotes several chapters of the *Monologion* to arguments which demonstrate by reasoning from self-evident principles why they must be so, just as Descartes does. We might, for example, ask: 'Did any instrument or existing material help to bring God himself into being?', 'For what is said to exist through something', says Anselm, usually 'appears to derive its existence from matter, or through some other instrument, such as a tool.' But God exists through himself, and not through anything other than himself, and so this question does not apply to him. It is absurd to ask it. We cannot, on the other hand, conclude from the fact that ordinary rules of existence do not apply to God that God does not exist at all. 'It is as false as it is absurd to say that

---

[9] *Anselmi Opera Omnia*, I.18.3. [10] Ibid., I.18.4–7.

nature without which there is no nature is nothing.'[11] We are simply asking the wrong questions about the mode of God's existence if we try to apply to it the principles which would be appropriate in the case of a created thing, if we try to apply physical laws to a reality beyond physics. The distinction between physics and metaphysics lies for Anselm, as it does for Descartes, between God's creation and God himself. The rules of argument and evidence which apply to the one do not necessarily have any bearing on the other, except in a transferred and adapted sense, by analogy.

Indeed Anselm proposes an analogy. God's existence, he says, is like a *lux lucens* (light shining). The relation which the light, its power to give light, and its actual shining, bear to one another, is like that of being itself, the act of being, and actual existence.[12] We understand quite easily how the light shines 'of itself' and 'through itself'. We should try to envisage God's existence in a similar way. Anselm draws a parallel with the natural world, not because he thinks that the laws of physics are directly applicable to God, but merely so as to illuminate the abstract arguments he has been putting forward with a familiar example. Anselm prefers to appeal to distinctions which can be understood only intellectually and not physically. He argues, for example, that it is impossible for God to exist through something other than himself because to be 'through' something is to be posterior to it and to be in some way less than that through which existence is derived.[13] It is this cast of mind which would have made Anselm a natural metaphysician rather than a scientist in any age.

He found it most congenial to proceed in his thinking in exactly the opposite direction to that which Aquinas advises in his *De Ente et Essentia*: 'We ought to receive knowledge of what is simple from what is complex, and arrive at what comes earlier by way of what comes later, so that learning may take place the more fittingly.'[14] As John Stuart Mill points out at the beginning of his *Utilitarianism*, this is the scientist's approach. Aquinas feels it proper to move from

---

[11] Ibid., I.19.2–21.   [12] Ibid., I.20.11–19.   [13] Ibid., I.19.4–5.
[14] Aquinas, *De Ente et Essentia, Proemium* I.

the particular to the general, to reason about the existence of
the highest Being, by considering how created things exist
individually. He does not advocate anything approaching the
experimental method of the modern scientist, but like the
modern scientist he prefers to establish the laws of the
physical world by observation of the physical world, and
only then does he consider whether they may have a metaphysical application or implication. Anselm begins with
metaphysics and moves from there to consider the working
of the physical world, which he tries to treat in equally
'metaphysical' terms.

In Chapter VII of the *Monologion* Anselm asks what we
can understand about the mode of creation and the existence
of created things from what has been established about the
existence of God. 'I think the first thing to be asked is
whether the universe of things which exist through something
else has its existence from any matter.'[15] He has no doubt
that the world is composed of matter, of earth and air and
water and fire. These four elements, he thinks, can be envisaged as existing in some way apart from the forms they
take in specific objects. Bodies are distinct from one another
only in their forms; formless matter constitutes the material
from which they are all made.[16] Anselm does not question
the independent existence of matter, but only its origin. He
cannot believe that anything can exist which does not proceed from the highest Being'. The 'mountain of things', the
'prolific multitude' of created things, was, he says, produced
by God through himself from nothing. 'Nothing is more
obvious'.[17]

But a problem arises about 'nothing'.[18] According to the
rule that everything which proceeds from something is caused
by it, 'If something is made from nothing, that nothing was
the cause of that which was made from it.'[19] Perhaps that
means that nothing was made at all (as when we say that a
silent man is saying nothing). Or it may mean that there was
nothing in existence from which anything could be made. Or
else it may mean that something was indeed made, but that

---

[15] *Anselmi Opera Omnia,* I.20.19–20.   [16] Ibid., I.21.2–5.
[17] Ibid., I.22.8–10.   [18] Ibid., I.22.13.   [19] Ibid., I.23.16–18.

there was nothing from which it was made (as when we say that a man who is sad for no reason is sad for nothing).[20] It is the third sense which is applicable in the case of God's creation of the world from nothing. The world was certainly made, but there was nothing from which it was made until God created the necessary 'something', which is matter. Again, Anselm has referred his arguments to the criterion of what seems evident to the intellect. Although he is now beginning to consider the physical world he continues to reason metaphysically./ He never comes any closer than this to engaging in what we might call scientific speculations.

In Chapters IX and X of the *Monologion* he begins to examine the question of forms or shapes, which seem to Aristotle and to twelfth- and thirteenth-century scholars so integral to the question of the way in which the world was made. They enquired whether such forms might, like matter, have existed for ever, so that the Creator merely brought form and matter together to make the world. Anselm asks another question. Were God's thoughts there before the world was made? In the mind of God ideas are eternal, he argues, and so the *exemplum* or *forma* or *similitudo* or *regula* for each thing must have existed before God gave it physical or material existence. In this sense only, those things which were made from nothing were not made from nothing, because they existed first in the mind of God. A human craftsman 'says to himself' what he will make before he makes it. God did the same.[21] The movement of Anselm's thought about creation from this point turns in the direction of speculation about the implications of this view for the theory of language. We remain in the realm of those metaphysical ideas which may be entertained in the mind alone, because we remain in the world of words and thoughts and ideas.

The theological methods which Alan of Lille devised in the *Regulae Theologicae* and Nicholas of Amiens in the *De Articulis Catholicae Fidei* are unique in the twelfth century.[22] While Thierry of Chartes and Clarenbald of Arras discussed what Boethius himself had said about axioms in the *De*

---

[20] Ibid., I.23.3–21.   [21] Ibid., I.24.13–14.   [22] Ibid., I.24–5.

Hebdomadibus, Alan of Lille and Nicholas of Amiens tried to put the axiomatic method into practice in theology. Alan's immediate source is Boethius' *De Hebdomadibus*; Nicholas, with his theorems, definitions, petitions, and axioms would seem to have drawn directly on Euclid. But Boethius' method, too, was inspired by Euclid and conceived of by Boethius himself as scientific.[23] Alan does not restrict himself, as Hugh of St. Victor would have advised, to problems which fall under the heading of the *opus conditionis,* the problems which might be expected to yield most readily to scientific enquiry. He wanted to demonstrate that his new theological method was appropriate to all branches of theology. If we compare what he has to say about the creation problems with Anselm's account, it becomes clear that most of the fundamental issues involved were as plain to Anselm as they were to most of his twelfth-century successors. The difference lies partly in Alan's willingness to apply the rules which he expects to operate in the physical world to the metaphysical world, and partly in the orderliness, the remorseless attention to proper procedure which Alan displays in the *Regulae* to an extreme degree, but which his contemporaries strove for, too. Anselm has considerable liberty to allow himself free play of thought. But Alan has deliberately confined himself within his chosen methodology. If we set the two side by side it becomes easier to understand the nature of the 'scientific revolution' in theological thinking which had already taken place by the second half of the twelfth century.

In the *De Articulis,* Nicholas arranges his material in five books. The first deals with the single cause of all things, the second with the creation of the world, the third with the Incarnation, the fourth with the sacraments, the fifth with

[22] Both these texts are in *PL* 210. On the problem of the authorship of the *De Articulis Catholicae Fidei,* see C. Balić, 'Les anciens manuscrits de la Bibliothèque métropolitaine de Zagreb', *Studia Medievalia in honorem R. Martin* (Bruges, 1948), 437-74, especially pp. 62-3, and *Textes inédits,* 68-9. Balić is wrong. Nicholas of Amiens is the author of the *De Articulis,* and the sixth book found in some manuscripts has another author. The *De Articulis* contradicts Alan of Lille's views at several points, and it adopts a Euclidean method of demonstration quite distinct from the Boethian axiomatic method of the *Regulae Theologicae,* which is based on that of the *De Hebdomadibus.*

[23] *Theological Tractates,* p. 40.

resurrection of the dead.[24] It is in the first two that he comes closest to Anselm's concerns in the *Monologion*. He lists and defines the technical terms and concepts his reader will need, with an eye to orderliness of procedure which he has certainly learned from the way Boethius sets out his own definitions and axioms at the beginning of the *De Hebdomadibus*. Prominent among them are some of those which Anselm uses. A *causa,* says Nicholas, is that 'through which' something which we say is 'created' derives its existence (*causa est per quam habet aliquid esse, quod dicitur creatum*). A *substantia* is that which is made up of substance, matter and form. *Materia* is something which can be given form (*formae susceptibilis*). *Forma* is that which, by a process of bringing together of properties (*ex concursu proprietatum adveniens*) makes something which is distinct from any other substance.[25] Anselm provides no such series of preliminary definitions; his definitions are given as and when they are needed to clarify a specific point in the argument.

The same methodical approach is evident in Nicholas's explanations of the laws which can be framed with the aid of these terms and a number of others which he defines. For example, since nothing is prior to or greater than itself, nothing can bring itself into being (Law 3) and nothing is its own cause (Law 8).[26] These laws fit the case of God himself, because they show that he must be the cause without a beginning, the eternal and prime cause, and they also show that all created things must have a cause. Law 5 states that substance is composed of matter and form, and Law 6 that the cause of each individual substance is threefold: matter and form and their union (*cuiuslibet substantia est triplex causa, scilicet materia et forma et earum compago*).[27] Several of the laws overlap, and in many cases they are more or less tautologous with what they are said to 'prove'. (The same might be said for the way in which one Euclidean theorem unfolds out of another.) Boethius himself notes that the higher and more sophisticated axioms are derived from the lower and more generally self-evident ones. The method might be seen as a

---

[25] *Ibid.*   [26] *PL* 210.599-60.   [27] *PL* 210.599.
[28] *Anselmi Opera Omnia,* I.19.4-5.

process of explication of what is already implicit in the physical and metaphysical laws which govern the world. But it is unlikely that Anselm would have felt that the advantages of orderliness outweighed the disadvantages of the sheer cumbersomeness of stating all possible laws so as to set in context the few which are needed in his own arguments. When Anselm needs to state a general law in the course of an argument, he does so. We have already met the rule that 'to be through something is to be posterior to it, to be in some ways less than that through which existence is derived.'[28] Anselm does not identify this as a self-evident axiom (the equivalent of Alan's Boethian *communes animi conceptiones*)[29] or explain how he has arrived at it. He does not suggest that it involves a different methodological procedure from other arguments in the same chapter. We should not expect him to do so because his training and the conventions of his day did not lay such emphasis upon the need for a writer to tell his readers exactly what he is doing. Anselm is in fact very clear and explicit about the methods he uses, but he and his contemporaries were not self-conscious about their methods in the same way as Alan. In so far as the scientific revolution of the twelfth century was a revolution of method it made argument technically more exact, but perhaps at the cost of introducing a certain laboriousness into the proceedings.

The change was under way in Anselm's lifetime. In his *Elucidarium* Honorius Augustodunensis[30] attempted to put together all the theological questions which were current in his day and give short, simple answers to them. He travelled extensively in search of material and he seems to have tried to hear the best masters of the day as well as to read everything he could lay hands on.[31] But despite the wealth of his erudition his is not typical of the twelfth-century masters because he deliberately avoided deep questions and made his answers facile so that they would not stimulate further thought. He did, however, perform one very useful service for

---

[28] *Anselmi Opera Omnia,* I.19.4–5. [29] *Theological Tractates,* p. 40.
[30] See Y. Lefèvre, *l'Elucidarium et les Lucidaires, Bibliothèque des écoles* for a modern edition.
[31] *St. Anselm and his Biographer,* pp. 209–17.

our purposes, and that is to provide us with a list of the questions which were most commonly asked about the work of creation at the beginning of the twelfth century. These are the points his pupil raises in the dialogue:

What was the cause (*quae causa*) of the creation of the world?
(The goodness of God, who wanted to show his grace to his creatures).
How was the world made?
(He spoke and all things were made).
Was there any delay in the course of creation?
(Creation took place in the batting of an eyelid or at the speed of light).
Did God create the world piece by piece or in stages (*per partes*)?
(He made everything all at once (*omnia simul et semel facit*),
but he divided all things into parts during six days).
When were the angels made?
(At the point where is was said 'let there be light').[32]

A little later the question of the origin of evil is also raised.[33] Honorius' scheme provides an excellent basis on which to examine the ways in which the academic theologians of the twelfth century went about resolving these questions — on which they had far more to say than he.

It also provides a point of entry for the discussion of a further difficulty of twelfth-century scholars, which had little if any influence upon Anselm's thought — the room the Genesis account of creation allows for the objections of unbelievers, and particularly of the dualist heretics who rested their case ultimately upon their dissatisfaction with the Christian view of the origin of things. They put forward their own 'scientific' explanations of the way the world began because they found the problems posed by the existence of matter and by the enigma of evil inadequately covered by the teaching of Scripture. This gave an additional urgency to the need for twelfth-century academic theologians to find hard scientific and rational proofs which could supplement the Bible account, as Nicholas of Amiens himself acknowledges in the opening letter to his *De Articulis*: *ut qui prophetiae et Evangelio acquiescere contemnunt, humanis saltem rationibus inducantur*[34] ('so that those who disdain to accept what the prophets and evangelists say, may at least be persuaded by human reason')' Peter Lombard, too, was aware of

[32] *PL* 172.1112, Book I, 5, Lefèvre pp. 363-6.
[33] *PL* 172.1133, Book I, 6, Lefèvre p. 405.   [34] *PL* 210.596-7.

the insistence of some schools of heretical opinion against the orthodox doctrines of creation: 'Some heretics thought that the Father was like the author and craftsman, and that he used the Son and the Holy Spirit as an instrument in working on things.'[35] The need to reconcile the scientific account of the secular *auctores* with the teaching of Scripture was not merely a matter of general academic interest, but an issue of some urgency if the opinions of the heretics were to be prevented from gaining ground.

To Honorius' first question, 'why was the world made?', it was necessary to find an answer which did not suggest that God had any need to create it, because that would imply that he was not entirely perfect and sufficient in himself. Here was a point on which Christian and Platonic thought were in no disagreement. Plato explains in the *Timaeus* that the supreme good has no envy at all, and so he wanted all things to be as nearly like himself as possible. He made the world so that there might be good things in it. Peter Abelard notices this coincidence of teaching with some pleasure: 'Plato states that this best and ineffable founder of all things in nature made all things as good as their individual natures allowed, for he was able to do everything, and envy was entirely foreign to him.'[36] The answer which satisfied 'philosophers' and Christians alike, however, did not meet the require-ments of the dualist heretics. Alan of Lille begins his book against the Cathars by marshalling reasons and authorities to prove that God created not only things spiritual and in-visible, but also things material and visible.[37] The dualists put with some force their view that matter is not the creation of a good God because it is mutable. According to Alan they rested their case on the dictum that 'If the cause is immutable, the effect is immutable.'[38] If we are to suppose that God made a world so inferior to himself, we must believe either that his power is limited, or that he showed envy in so doing, because it seems that he could brook no rival to his own perfection.[39] The dualists thus found con-firmation of their opinions in the very rules the Christians

[35] Peter Lombard, *Sententiae* (Rome, 1971), Book II. xiii. 7.2, p. 394.
[36] *Theologia Christiane*, II, para 29, p. 144.   [37] *PL* 210.308-14.
[38] *PL* 210.309.   [39] *PL* 210.310.

borrowed from the pagan philosophers. To the question, 'Why did God create the world?', their response was not to try to reconcile the teaching of secular studies and the Bible, but to say that he did not create the corporeal world at all, but only the spiritual world of which it is a travesty.

A by no means subordinate question, and one of strong human interest, is why man himself was made.[40] Much depends on what is believed to have happened as a result of the fall of Satan. Peter Lombard's *Sentences* try to reconcile various conflicting passages in Scripture and the Fathers, some of which suggest that God always intended to create man, while others imply that man was made only in order to fill up the places in the heavenly city which were left empty by the fallen angels.[41] Anselm allows himself a long disgression on the point in the *Cur Deus Homo,* so as to demonstrate that the perfect number of inhabitants in the Heavenly City must have been designed from the first to include a certain number of men.[42]

But according to the author of the *Ysagoge in Theologiam* the very question is misconceived. We should ask instead why the world itself was made, if it was not for the use of man. 'See, you have the cause of man in God, and the cause of the world in man. He who was made after everything was he for whom everything else was made.'[43] Hugh of St. Victor takes the same view.[44] Man is seen as too important a piece of creation for it to be possible that he was made only as a result of a calamity in heaven. Genesis itself gives the same primacy of place to man. It says that all other creatures were placed in subjection to him.[45] But again the heretics found it impossible to accept a view which was in accordance with orthodox doctrine and which was not out of keeping with the account of given by the secular philosophers. (Plato says

[40] Robert of Melun *Quaestiones de Divina Pagina,* ed. R. Martin, *SSLov.* 13 (1932), 24–5.

[41] Peter Lombard *Sententiae* II.i.5.

[42] *Anselmi Opera Omnia,* II.74–84; on numerically definite reasoning, see D. P. Henry *The Logic of St. Anselm*, pp. 222–9.

[43] *Ysagoge in Theologiam,* p. 66.29.   [44] *De Sacramentis,* I.ii.1.

[45] Gen. 1:29.

that the created world would have been incomplete without
mortal creatures who possessed immortal souls.) Some of the
dualists found it more consistent with their view that the
corporeal is evil, to believe that the fallen angels were sent to
dwell in human bodies as a punishment. 'They say that the
spirit of a man is nothing but a rebel angel.'[46] There was, in
this view, no need to ask the question: 'Why was man
created?' The most excellent piece of creation has become a
transient thing, a being in torment doing penance in the
body, a being of another order altogether.

A topic of some interest to dualists and orthodox Christians
alike was the reason for the creation of noxious things. The
existence of reptiles and insects which sting or bite man and
poison him, seemed to them strong evidence for the view that
material things could not be the creation of a good God.
'There are some creatures which have no use at all, like
serpents, files and spiders, but which do many kinds of
harm.'[47] Honorius had raised the point when he asked, 'Why
did God create flies and gnats and other things which are
harmful to man?' His answer is that they were made to
humble man's pride by stinging him.[48] Alan of Lille gives a
similar reply to the heretics. No creature, he claims, is without any usefulness. Some things were made noxious so that
man should be moved to goodness by suffering (*quaedam
nociva per quae homo excitatur ad bonum per patientiam*).[49]
Like so many of the answers he was able to make to the
heretics, this depends for its force upon an acceptance of the
view that the world was made for man, and also a willingness
to concede that material things have some goodness of their
own. The problem brings out particularly clearly the internal
consistency of the peculiar system of physics and metaphysics upon which the doctrines of the dualists were based,
and the contrast it provides with the system academic
theologians were trying to construct from the secular authors
and from Scripture.

When we ask how the world was made, we enter the area
of most heated controversy for heretics, philosophers, and

---

[46] *PL* 210.314.
[48] *PL* 172.1117, Book I.12, Lefèvre p. 372.
[47] *PL*210.309.
[49] *PL* 210.309.

orthodox Christians alike. The main point at issue was this: did everything which exists derive its existence from a single cause or beginning, or were there several *principia* or *causa*? As it is framed in the twelfth century this looks more like a metaphysical question than a problem for the natural ·scientist, if only because the answer cannot be arrived at by experimentation or measurement, but only by reasoning. But it is not a question which lies beyond the bounds of scientific interest, and as far as twelfth-century scholars were concerned it was the foundation of physics with which they were concerned when they asked it because they were asking about the foundation of the world. Perhaps the most significant difference between the twelfth-century scientist and his modern counterpart lies in the way in which the problem is approached. The medieval thinker asks the question in the terms of classical metaphysics. He is not concerned with the practical mechanics of cause and effect but with something closer to the laws of logical entailment. Nevertheless, the two approaches have in common an interest in the nature of causation.

Peter Lombard explains that philosophers have long disagreed about the number of causes or sources or beginnings of things. Plato thought that there were three *initia*, God himself, the *exemplar* or model according to which he fashioned things, and the matter or *materia* from which he made them. All these were without beginning and uncreated (*ipsa increata sine principia*).[50] God's work was that of a craftsman rather than a creator. Aristotle, on the other hand, claimed that there were two *principia*, matter and form, or *materia* and *species*.[51] But the philosophers also say, according to Abelard, that 'the highest good, which is God, is both the beginning of all things, that is their origin and efficient cause, and also their end, that is their final cause'.[52] There was, in other words, no consensus of opinion among the *philosophi* with which the teaching of Genesis could be directly compared.

But the *philosophi* were willing to grant a status to form

---

[50] *Sententiae*, II.i.i.2, p. 330. [51] *Sententiae*, II.iii.5, p. 331.
[52] *Theologia Christiana*, II, 28 p. 144. 398-9.

and matter as primordial *causa* which orthodox Christians could not countenance, and the Manichees, too, argued (on rather different grounds) that there must be *two principa*: the source of good and the source of evil. The first duty of the apologists for the Christian position was to make out an unassailable case for the view that God himself is the sole first cause, the *principium sine principio*.[53] It was on this principle that Aquinas later rested one of the five proofs for the existence of God.[54] This beginning without a beginning must be the source of its own beginning (*operante summo principio est*).[55] It is the source 'from which and through which and in which are all things but itself' (*principium ex quo et per quod et in quo sunt omnia nisi ipsa*).[56] It also precedes, in time and in importance, all created things (*omnia creata precedit*).[57] The drift of all such arguments is that the ultimate beginning of things is one. Anselm demonstrates in the *Monologion* that such a *summa natura* must either be single (*sola*) or: *plures eiusmodi et aequales*,[58] several of the same kind which are equal. He shows that it is a contradiction in terms for us to argue that the *principium* may be plural.[59] The strength of such arguments lies in the mathematical elegance they possess, and in their fittingness in terms of the metaphysics of the ancient world. It is perfectly possible for a science of physics to be constructed entirely on the questions which suggest themselves about the mechanical operation of the world; indeed, perhaps that is the proper scope of a discipline which tests its laws experimentally. Only speculatively can we press the enquiry any further. Only mathematics underlies the farther reaches of theoretical physics.

Christian tradition introduces a further difficulty. God is the 'beginning' for the Christian not only in that he is one, but also in that he is three. Gilbert of Poitiers says that it is self-evidently true (*per se verum est*) that the Father is in the beginning and also that the Son is in the beginning and also

---

[53] *Thierry of Chartres*, p. 295.92.
[54] *Summa Theologica*, I, Q.2, Art.3, Obj.2.
[55] Gilbert of Poitiers, p. 193.64.
[56] Ibid., p. 89.21-2. [57] Ibid., p. 87.63.
[58] *Anselmi Opera Omnia*, I.17.11. [59] *Anselmi Opera Omnia*, I.16-18.

that the Holy Spirit is in the beginning. It is likewise true that Father, Son, and Holy Spirit are one beginning.[60] In the face of this paradox some scholars tried to distinguish three kinds of cause, as Thierry of Chartres did in his treatise on the six days of creation. The Father is seen as the efficient cause, the Son as the formal cause, the Holy Spirit as the final cause.[61] The Creator acts upon the material cause of the world (the matter he has made) as efficient cause, giving it form as its formal cause, and bestowing love and guidance upon it as its final cause.[62] The Trinity is here seen as a threefold first cause, working as one in the creation of the world. This effectively excludes the Platonic view that matter and form are independent eternal causes in their own right, by incorporating them into the work of the three Persons. It also allows no room to the Manichean argument that there are two independent first causes whose purposes are opposed to one another. In so far as the Persons may be regarded as three causes, they all work in the same direction and for the same purposes. We are entering here upon aspects of the problem of causes which are peculiar to Christian theology. They have nothing to do with physics, or even with metaphysics, strictly speaking. But it was of the first importance to Christian scholars in the twelfth century that they should be accommodated within a single scheme of explanation.

It was also necessary to take account of the exact words of Genesis. Rupert of Deutz asks why the first words of the Bible are 'In the beginning God created . . .' when God was himself the beginning. It would seem more exact to say 'In the beginning the beginning created'.[63] That would be grammatically inelegant, he thinks, because it would be tautologous; *vitium est in superfluitate dictionis*[64] ('there is a grammatical fault in superfluity of words'). We cannot suppose the writers of Scripture to have been guilty of such an impropriety, and if we look closely we shall find that in

---

[60] Gilbert of Poitiers, p. 171.16–19.
[61] *Thierry of Chartres*, p. 556.54–557.1.   [62] Ibid., p. 556.50–5.
[63] *PL* 167.202, *CCCM*, 21, p. 130.
[64] Ibid., and see Isidore, *Etymologiae*, ed. W. M. Lindsay (Oxford, 1911), I.34.1.

this context (*hoc loco*) *principium* is to be taken as the proper name of the Son: *tamquam proprium quoddam Filii vocabulum.*[65] God made the world through, or in, the Son who is the Word. Not only doctrinal imperatives but also the exact form of the account given in Holy Scripture posed additional problems for those theologians who wanted to reconcile their scientific account of the problem of causes with that of orthodox Christian teaching.

Even if it is accepted that one God is the origin of everything which exists, it is perhaps possible to allow some elasticity to the account without departing from strict orthodoxy, if we say that there are three processes in creation: *primo namque creantur, inde formantur, postremo disponuntur*[66] (first things are created, then they are given form, then they are set in place or 'disposed'). To create is to make something from nothing. Only God can do that,[67] and perhaps we may say that in the three Persons he completed the work of creation in various ways. But Robert of Melun, who gives this account of things, does not appear to feel that it altogether disposes of the problem of the origin of matter and form, which he knows that Plato and Aristotle put forward insistently as prime causes in their own right.[68] Genesis says that God made heaven and earth in the beginning, and only afterwards gave individual forms to created things and 'disposed' them. Robert of Melun has found that questions are often raised about where matter was before the world was made. The questioners say that if the elements were first created without form, either they must have been spread out in different places, which is impossible if there was as yet no such thing as 'place', or else they must have been huddled together in some way.[69] In that case it is difficult to understand how the heavy and the light, the moist and the dry, could have remained together undifferentiated. Besides, it is axiomatic that all created things are in motion, because only in God is there perfect stillness; yet motion involves some shifting from place to place and there was as yet no place into which anything could move. The proposers of such

[65] *PL* 167.202, *CCCM* 21, p. 130.
[66] Robert of Melun (1947), p. 210.10–17.   [67] Ibid., p. 210.15–16.
[68] Ibid., p. 210.19–21.   [69] Ibid., p. 216.15–p. 217.15.

objections felt that they had made out a convincing case for the view that matter and form are not created things, but primordial, for both must always have existed.[70]

It might also be argued that if God made things in stages, he must have left his work *imperfectum* at the end of each of the first five days of creation. Robert of Melun argues that daily experience teaches us that God does make things in this way. A seed must be sown and allowed to grow before it reaches perfection at harvest-time. God makes the seed and then allows time to elapse before the seed becomes a fruiting plant. Even a full-grown tree is an imperfect thing until it is covered in ripe fruit.[71] But the fact that the forms of things may be full realized apart from the initial act of creation was still felt by many to weigh heavily in favour of the view that primordial form had some existence in its own right.

Much of the discussion of these points turned on what Robert of Melun saw as the great question of the day: whether everything was created at once, or successively during the six days. 'This is asked by many', he says.[72] Peter Lombard would like to believe both were true. 'All corporeal things were created once and for all in a material sense' (*materialiter*), he claims, but they were *in forma confusionis*, in a confused form, for six days.[73] If God made everything in an instant we are not forced to postulate that matter or form may have had any independent existence, or made any independent contribution to the process. Anselm had pointed out in the *Cur Deus Homo* that if all creatures were made at once, the human race cannot have been created merely to fill the places left vacant in the heavenly city by the fall of the angels, because there were already men in the world when the angels fell.[74] The issue remained controversial because Genesis is contradictory and even science and philsophy have nothing conclusive to say, but most of all because twelfth-century scholars felt it imperative to attempt a reconciliation of the traditions they had inherited, to create a scientifically acceptable theology.

A further development of this question brings us closer to

---

[70] Loc. cit.   [71] Robert of Melun (1947), p. 219.21-p. 223.5-6.
[72] Ibid., p. 214.24-5.   [73] Peter Lombard, *Sententiae*, II.xxi.5, (62).
[74] *Anselmi Opera Omnia*, II.76.27-77.2.

the concerns of the natural scientist. Whether or not all things were made in an instant at the moment of creation, new created things are manifestly coming into existence all the time by processes of natural reproduction — what Anselm calls the *natura propagandi.*[75] Genesis covers this process in part in its description of the way in which all living things began to bring forth their own kind. But Robert of Melun found that the exact scope of nature's work in relation to that of the Creator was not clear to many of his pupils. Nature, he explains, did not come into operation 'before like began to be propagated from and multiplied by like' (*antequam ex similibus similia propagari et multiplicari ceperunt*).[76] Before then creation took place solely by divine will, and only since then has God worked through nature.[77] The essential point is that nature can do no more than carry on the work God set in motion when he created the world. Nature can make no new kinds of things, but only more individuals according to the kinds God first created. This is the process in which the natural scientist is interested.

To this twofold distinction between creation and propagation Simon of Tournai adds another in his *Disputationes*. We must distinguish the creation of new kinds of things which took place at the beginning and the process of making new plants and animals from old, which is nature's task, from God's work in maintaining things in existence. It is as much a metaphysical as a physical question why the world continues to exist, but at one level it can be answered in terms of the conditions which make it possible for natural processes to operate. Twelfth-century scholars did not ask how the life of plants and animals depends upon a supply of water, on climate, on favourable environmental conditions in general, but how 'the Father and the Son are said to work by preserving what has been made, not creating new kinds of things, but new individuals of [the existing] kinds, daily producing ... like from like, for example, men from men and trees from trees'.[78] The divine work of sustaining, in other words, is carried out through the medium of natural propagation. Twelfth-century scholars attributed the fact that created

[75] Ibid., 1.151.8–11.   [76] Robert of Melun (1947), p. 226.19–22.
[77] Ibid., p. 227.2–6.   [78] Simon of Tournai, *Disputationes*, p. 219.8–12.

things continue to exist to working of natural processes in the context of divine sustaining which allows them to operate.

Simon has yet a further development to offer in his commentary on the 'Athanasian' Creed. *Aliud est creatio, aliud generatio, aliud factura*[79] ('Creation is one thing, generation another, making another'). God uses lesser causes as his instruments and makes new forms from matter by the force of nature (*vi nature*), when by the action of heat and moisture he produces an ear of corn from a grain.[80] Man the craftsman imitates this work of nature, when he makes a shoe to fit a foot.[81] Anselm had already emphasized that a human craftsman could do no more than imitate a pattern which already existed in creation.[82] Simon, too, takes the view that this further form of creation is merely imitation, and imitation of nature at that, since man cannot directly imitate the Creator in the making of matter or form, or in the originality of his conceptions.[83]

The stress the *philosophi* had placed upon the role of form and matter in creation had forced twelfth-century scholars to consider two things: firstly how form and matter could have come into being by creation and how they were to demonstrate that they were not primordial; and secondly, what followed from the existence of form and matter if the Genesis account of creation was to be reconciled with that of the scientists of the ancient world. They pressed their investigation as far as they could by reasoning alone, into territory which would now belong more properly to the experimental scientist. Above all, they tried to link the laws of metaphysics with the laws of physics so as to make a single consistent system of them, and in so doing they moved into an area of difficulty which is still a source of perplexity to philosopher and theologian alike. There is still a gulf to be bridged between what experimental science can tell us about the mechanical functioning of the natural world and the answers philosophers have to offer to the questions which lie behind.

[79] 'Simon of Tournai's Commentary on the So-called Athanasian Creed', *AHDLMA* xliii (1976), 174, para. i.

[80] Ibid., p. 174, para. 2.   [81] Ibid., p. 174, para. 3.

[82] *Anselmi Opera Omnia*, I.26.   [83] Simon, *Disputationes*, p. 218.

For the orthodox Christian encounter with the heretics over the origin of things, we must turn to the problem of evil. The central problem is this: if God is the highest good and the source of all things which exist, how is it possible for that which is not good to exist? Alan puts the Cathars' case as follows: *cum Deus sit principium bonorum, aliud est principium malorum.*[84] 'Since God is the beginning (or source) of good things, something else is the beginning (or source) of evil things'. The dualists explain away the paradox by postulating the existence of a second *principium.* In so doing they make two assumptions. No twelfth-century scholar would quarrel with the first. Everything which exists must have a cause. The second assumption is another matter, for it asserts that evil is a 'something' for which a cause must be found. On this point there was considerable disagreement between scholars who felt that it we say evil is *nihil* ('nothing') the problem of evil disappears, and those who maintained that if evil is to be regarded as dangerous then it must in some sense exist.

This was not a new question to medieval scholars. Anselm argues in the *De Conceptu Virginali* that if evil is nothing,[85] sin and unrighteousness must be regarded in the same light.[86] But he knows that some people, when they hear that sin is nothing, ask why God punishes men for sin, since no one ought to be punished for nothing.[87] Anselm answers the difficulty by saying that we must regard unrighteousness as an absence of righteousness where righteousness should be; God punishes man, not for nothing, but for failing to do as he ought. In this way he avoids one of the most obstinately insoluble of the implications of Augustine's teaching that evil is nothing but an absence of good (*indigentia boni*).[88] Augustine's view meets the Manichean objections, but it leaves many questions unanswered. These were the questions with which late eleventh- and twelfth-century scholars were beginning to concern themselves afresh.

Anselm took the view that 'evil is nothing but not-good, or the absence of good where good ought to be or should

---

[84] *PL* 210.308.
[85] *Anselmi Opera Omnia,* II.146.29.
[86] Ibid. II.146-7.
[87] Ibid. II.147.8-10.
[88] *Contra Julian op. imperf.,* V. xliv, *PL* 45.1480.

properly be'.[89] Other contemporaries, who also thought that evil is the *privatio boni*,[90] said that existence is the special property of the divine and immutable Being of God. Only those things which are in keeping with the divine Being can be said to exist (*que ei coherunt*). What is not in harmony with it (*que vero ab ea discordant*) does not exist. That is why evil is said to be nothing.[91] Anselm proposed the device of regarding evil as 'a sort of something' for purposes of argument[92] (*quasi-aliquid*). The difficulty he hopes to circumvent in this way is one of signification. A word cannot have a meaning if there is nothing for it to signify. A similar problem arises here in the case of both nothing and evil.[93] Augustine had looked at exactly this question in the *De Magistro*,[94] and it had been raised by the Carolingian scholar Fredegisus in his *Epistola de Nihilo et Tenebris*. 'The question is', he says, 'whether "nothing" is "something" or not . . . Every noun signifies something, such as "man", "stone", "tree". When these words are said, we understand that the things they signify exist . . . Therefore "nothing" refers to what it signifies; in this way it is proved that it is not possible for it not to be something.'[95] Working from this point of departure Anselm tries to convince his pupil that merely to make use of the word *malum* in argument is not to imply that evil itself is something.[96]

Anselm also argues that sin consists in a turning of the will of a rational creature against the will of God.[97] The same idea is found among the sentences of the contemporary school of Laon. 'You must know that evil is nothing, either in devil or in man, but will.'[98] Rupert of Deutz, too, says that 'will is the genus of evil' (*voluntas mali genus est*);[99] he means that there are many kinds of will, of which evil will is one, and that evil has no independent existence; it is merely a kind of will. The Laon sentence emphasizes that evil does not belong to the very essence of the will, for that would imply that God

[89] *Anselmi Opera Omnia,* I.251.6-7.
[90] O. Lottin, *Psychologie et morale aux xiie et xiiie siècles* p. 348.245.
[91] Ibid., p. 309, para. 449.   [92] *Anselmi Opera Omnia,* I.248-51.
[93] *Anselmi Opera Omnia,* I.248.15.   [94] *De Magistro,* II. 3, *PL* 32.1196.
[95] *PL* 105.751.   [96] *Anselmi Opera Omnia,* I.251.17-18.
[97] *Anselmi Opera Omnia,* II.68.12.   [98] Lottin, op. cit., p. 221, para. 277.
[99] *PL* 170.437.

made wills which are evil, and thus that he is the author of evil. Evil has no part in the substance of the will.[100] Evil thus subsists in something which does exist, but it has no existence of its own. It might be objected that this does not quite account for the genesis of evil disposition found in an evil will. That, we are told, comes not from God, but from man or angel when he misuses his will.[101] 'Only the intention, which comes of itself, is evil.'[102] Thus the source of evil lies in the failure of the angelic or human will to do what it ought, and not in an evil God, as the Manichees teach. 'For they can do evil of themselves, but they cannot do good unless it comes from God', because all that a creature can give rise to of himself is nothing.[103]

Even if this explanation of the origin of evil is found to be satisfactory — and clearly it did not convince the dualist heretics — it still leaves unanswered a question which concerned many contemporary scholars: why does God allow evil?[104] Rupert of Deutz raises the matter in his treatise *On the Will of God*. He asks whether God permits evil willingly or unwillingly. To say that he does so willingly is to imply that he is in some way the author of evil. To say that he does so against his will is to suggest that he is compelled to do so (*coactus*), and that implies that there is a limit upon his power.[105] Anselm devises an answer in terms of the freedom of will of rational creatures. If God had given the good gift of freedom of will to angels and men but made it impossible for them to use it in more than one way, it would have been no freedom at all. No constraint operated upon either God or Satan in the fall of the angels. One of the Laon sentences suggests another answer. Something may be good in relation to God and bad in relation to a created being. This is the case with the will, which is good as God made it, and bad as the creature uses it.[106] (In a not dissimilar way Anselm explains in the *Proslogion* that God is merciful with regard to mankind, but that he himself feels none of the pain of compassion because he is *impassibilis*).[107]

---

[100] Lottin, op. cit., p. 221.2–3. para. 277.   [101] Ibid., p. 221.9–10.
[102] Ibid., p. 221.12–13.   [103] Ibid., p. 198.11, para. 24.
[104] Ibid., p. 302, para. 448.   [105] *PL* 170.439.
[106] Ibid., p. 302, para. 449.   [107] *Anselmi Opera Omnia*, I.106.5–13.

One of the Laon sentences asks how the Holy Spirit is able to work even through wicked men and unbelievers.[108] Evil is able to influence the working of the world, to disturb its order, even if only in a limited way,[109] and again it seems that God allows this to happen. These were the kinds of questions with which the scholars of the late eleventh and early twelfth centuries were concerned; they did not succeed in answering them all, to their own satisfaction or to that of their successors. The attempt to explain the problem of evil without resorting to the Manichean explanation that evil exists independently, drove them to devise a large number of related solutions to related questions.

To the modern theologian and the modern scientist alike these problems of causes and origins and the whole question of the *opus conditionis* are likely to present themselves in a rather different light. As J. Hick has pointed out, 'the whole mediaeval tradition of discussion of evil depends on theologians taking seriously the notion of the fall of the angels'[110] (for which there is only the slenderest Scriptural warrant). He regards the Augustinian scheme of explanation on which twelfth-century scholars based their own reasoning as amounting to no more than 'the impossible doctrine of the self-creation of evil *ex nihilo*'.[111] The association of evil with darkness and blindness is common in medieval writers. 'What is called evil is nothing but the absence of good; just as blindness is the absence of sight and darkness is the absence of light, for blindness and darkness are not substances.'[112] It would be impossible now to find scientific grounds on which blindness, darkness and evil might be said to be alike. To pretend that twelfth-century scholars were the forerunners of modern scientists in these fields would be absurd. It would be difficult to prove their findings here of detailed relevance or even of much general value to modern theologians. But their technical limitations and their emphasis on certain principles (which may now seem misguided) should not be allowed to obscure the boldness of the new perception that it

---

[108] Lottin, op. cit., p. 232, 284.   [109] *Anselmi Opera Omnia,* II.73.8-9.
[110] J. Hick, *God and the Universe of Faiths* (London, 1973), pp. 62-3.
[111] Ibid., p. 65.
[112] Honorius, *Elucidarium,* Book II, 1, *PL* 172.113-14; Lefèvre pp. 405-6.

was urgently necessary to reconcile theology with contemporary science, if theology was to hold its new place among the academic disciplines and command the respect of the best scholars of the day. They asked the scientist's first question, 'What is the world?',[113] and they asked it as men of God, anxious to show the soundness of orthodox doctrine in the face of the tests to which both science and heresy put it.

2. Philosophers, Heretics, and the Work of Restoration

Early twelfth-century masters were, it seems, often asked by their pupils for a rational argument which would show that the Bible's account of the redemption, the *opus restaurationis*,[1] was not out of keeping with the laws of philosophical and scientific thought. Something like this was already being sought by St. Anselm at the end of the eleventh century. He wrote the *Cur Deus Homo* so as to convince even the most obstinate of unbelievers that it was necessary for God to become man, by the sheer consistency and beautiful reasonableness of his arguments.[2] One of Anselm's admirers, Honorius Augustodunensis, reduced Anselm's sequence of thought to a convenient summary in his *Elucidarium,* so as to answer the profound questions involved as simply as possible for his own readers. He thus again provides a convenient starting-point for an examination of the principal difficulties twelfth-century theologians discovered when they tried to reconcile Scripture's description of the events of the 'work of restoration' with what they learned from their study of the secular arts, and at the same time to sustain the orthodox view in the face of a number of heretical opinions of the day.

We begin from the premiss that Adam's sin had deeply disturbed the order of things. Honorius, like Anselm, sees this disturbance as amounting to a dishonouring of God. It was necessary for the wrong to be put right by restoring or making good the honour which had been taken away. One particularly vociferous contemporary school of thought

---

[113] *Liber Hermetis Mercurii Triplicis de VI Rerum principiis,* ed. T. Silverstein, *AHDLMA* xxii (1955), 217.

[1] Hugh of St. Victor, *De Sacramentis Ecclesiae, PL* 176.183.

[2] *Anselmi Opera Omnia,* II. 48.6–9.

argued that the root of the trouble lay in man's capitulation
to Satan. Its exponents said that since the Fall man had
belonged to Satan. If proper order (*rectus ordo*) was to be
restored, Satan had to be compensated in some way, and man
ransomed from his power. Whether the debt was to be paid
to God or to Satan, however, it was necessary that it should
be paid, so that God's original plan could be carried out, and
men might take their places with the angels in the heavenly
cit. It was for this reason that God had not allowed Adam to
perish altogether; it was not possible for his intentions for
man to be frustrated, and the orderliness of his plan must be
preserved.

Honorius asks what kind of satisfaction needed to be
made. The sin of Adam must have been greater than the
whole world, because it had thrown the world into disorder.
Therefore something greater than the world must be found to
pay the debt. None of the patriarchs or prophets could pay,
because they had all been born in sin. A newly created man
would not do, because he would not have been of the race of
Adam, and so he would not be able to pay Adam's debt for
him. For the same reason, an angel would not do (and for the
additional reason that the redeemer of mankind would
rightly have mankind as his servant for ever, and man was
destined to be the equal of the angels in the heavenly city).
Only God himself could carry out the task, but only man
owed the debt. And so it was necessary for God to become
man in order to redeem mankind. This, in its essence, is the
argument Anselm puts forward in the *Cur Deus Homo* in the
hope that it will prove irresistible even to unbelievers,
because it is so utterly reasonable.

This scheme of explanation, with various modifications, is
to be found in a number of twelfth-century writers.[3] Bruno
of Segni, a contemporary of Anselm's, has it,[4] and Abelard
incoporated it into his brief treatment of the reasons for the
redemption in his commentary on Romans;[5] the Abelardian

[3] Peter Abelard summarizes contemporary view in his Commentary on
Romans, 113–18.
[4] See my article 'St. Anselm and Bruno of Segni: the Common Ground',
Journal of Ecclesiastical History, 29 (1978), 129–44.
[5] See Note 3.

Ysagoge in Theologiam gives it, too.[6] But already in the *Ysagoge* we can see academic method taking over from freer speculation. A pair of alternatives is stated to arise from each resolution of a stage in the problem. After the fall of Adam, either reason demands that man must be restored to the hope of glory, or it does not. Since God's plan must be fulfilled, the first alternative must hold. Man could be restored to glory filthy as he was, or he could first be cleansed. Clearly, it is more fitting that he should enter glory in a state of cleanliness. (Anselm illustrates the point with the story of a rich man who has a precious pearl struck from his hand into the mud by his enemy. Surely, Anselm argues, he will wipe it clean before he restores it to its place in his treasury?).[7] Methodically, one of each pair of alternatives is eliminated. The method is already there in Anselm, but without the sometimes constricting formality of the *Ysagoge* version. Even in the ninth century many ideas about 're-demption' were current.[8] But now the academic theologians of the twelfth century strove systematically to rationalize and reduce to a system the Bible's teaching about the work of restoration.

Anselm's argument provides the essence, too, of Nicholas of Amiens' account of the reason for the Redemption in the *De Articulis Catholicae Fidei*, with the difference that the orderliness of the sequence of argument is even more apparent. One by one Nicholas sets out his rules. By the first Rule we learn that fallen and penitent man *ought* to have been visited by divine mercy (*debuit divina misericordia visitari*).[9] Rule Two tells us that since God had planned that man should be blessed, it was proper for him to restore him (*oportuit*).[10] Rule Three states that man *ought* to have wiped out the sin of man by giving satisfaction for it,[11] Rule Four that neither an angel nor a mere man nor any other creature was able to make satisfaction.[12] Rule Five shows that it was fitting (*opportunum*) for God to make satisfaction for man, but that the debt was owed by man (see Rule Three); there-

---

[6] *Ysagoge in Theologiam*, 158. [7] *Anselmi Opera Omnia*, II.85.
[8] Godescalc d'Orbais, *Oeuvres*, ed. D. C. Lambot, *SSLov.* 20 (1945), p. 279.
[9] *PL* 210.609. [10] Loc. cit. [11] *PL* 210.610.
[12] Loc. cit.

fore it was proper that God should become man and make satisfaction on behalf of the creature (*Ergo oportuit Deum esse hominem, qui satisfaceret pro creaturea*).[13] Not all twelfth-century scholars by any means followed Anselm's train of thought so closely, but the correspondence between his argument and that of Nicholas makes the contrast in their methods of setting the argument out the more striking. Alan has reduced the principles involved to a series of rules. The leisurely consideration of the implications of each point he makes, which Anselm allows himself, has given way to a more briskly-paced treatment. Nicholas's argument is forceful because it is compact, and the reader cannot fail to see how one point leads to the next. Anselm's argument has the same compelling quality only for the reader who has time to digest what he says at leisure. The pattern which is on the surface in Nicholas of Amiens and Honorius, is more subtly woven in Anselm. This is a difference of organization which the twelfth-century development of an academic theology had encouraged.

But Anselm's argument, like that of Nicholas, is acceptable only if we regard the notion of *convenientia* as possessing some binding force. A complex of ideas is involved here: obligation, propriety, fittingness, appropriateness, are all invoked by both scholars as carrying a peculiar kind of necessity in the context of redemption theology. There is a special form of logical entailment in this which is not to be found in discussions of the questions of causation we have been looking at in connection with the *opus conditionis*. God cannot be said to be under any compulsion or under any necessity in the ordinary sense, because he is himself the unmoved mover, the uncaused cause, and no force can act upon him.[14] It is the internal logic of the situation of fallen man which makes it necessary for disorder to be restored to order. It must be supposed that God chose freely to do what was necessary within this frame of reference, simply because that was the right and proper thing to do.[15] It was upon man that the obligation rested, not on God; it

---

[13] *PL* 210.611.   [14] *Anselmi Opera Omnia,* I.106, *Proslogion* VIII.
[15] This is the theme of the first book of the *Cur Deus Homo.*

was proper and fitting for man to be restored, and only by extension, by God's willing choice, could it be said to be proper for him to carry out that restoration himself. The rules of dialectic have to be considerably stretched to accommodate arguments of this kind, as Anselm found before the end of the eleventh century.

A number of problems of arguing about 'change' presented difficulties to twelfth-century scholars who attempted to approach redemption theology with the aid of the secular arts and ancient philosophy. Greek metaphysics and Greek logic alike are designed to deal with what is static in the world order, and not with the problems of dynamics and change which preoccupy modern science,[16] and which already in the twelfth century were beginning to cause difficulties to theologians who attempted to make a rational or scientific approach to the problems of redemption theology.

If the argument from fittingness had force for Christians, it did not prove to have equal force for all 'unbelievers' as Anselm had hoped it would Jews, Moslems, and Cathars remained unmoved by the 'beautiful reasonableness' of its internal consistency. Indeed to many adherents of heretical sects the doctrine of the Incarnation was deeply repugnant. The Cathars, says Bonacursus, 'say of Christ that he did not have a living body, that he did not eat or drink or do anything as a man does, but that he merely appeared to do so . . . They do not believe that the body of Christ arose from the dead, nor that it went up to heaven, nor do they believe in the resurrection of the flesh.' They are repelled by the loving awe in which Christians hold that instrument of torture, the Cross.[17] In the *Summa contra Hereticos* ascribed to Praepositinus of Cremona the same reservations are listed, together with examples of Biblical texts used by the heretics to show that orthodox teaching is wrong.[18] (When we are told that Mary was found to be with child by the Holy Spirit,[19] we should take this as evidence that Christ was not

---

[16] This point is developed by T. Torrance, *Space, Time and Incarnation* (London, 1971).

[17] *PL* 204.777, *Contra Catharos.*

[18] 'Praepositinus' *Summa contra Haereticos,* Book I, Ch. III, p. 46.

[19] Matt. 1:18.

flesh but spirit; when Christ asked who were his mother and
his brothers,[20] he wanted to make it plain that he had no
fleshy kindred; when he walked on the water he showed that
he had no bodily weight.)[21] These are, as 'Praepositinus'
demonstrates by adducing more texts (and as Durandus de
Huesca explicitly says), distorted arguments put forward by
men whose deformed reason understands Scripture in a
deformed sense.[22] Durandus explains that there is more at
stake here than fastidiousness at the idea of God's taking a
bodily nature. 'For if the Word of God, born of the Virgin,
did not come into this world, as the heretics say, the
Christian faith is nothing and the words of the Gospel are
empty, and the holy prophets and apostles were deceivers
and told lies.'[23] Unless it could be shown that the redemption
could be carried out in no other way than by God's becoming
truly man, Christian theology made no sense at all. The
doctrine of the Incarnation is central to arguments of the
kind Anselm had put forward in the *Cur Deus Homo* because
it must be seen to be necessary as well as fitting. The internal
consistency of the argument gains its force and its 'beautiful
reasonableness' from an acceptance of the peculiar necessity
'appropriateness' has in theological arguments.

The Jews attacked the doctrine of the Incarnation for
another reason. Gilbert Crispin places a good deal of emphasis
upon their objection that God incarnate would be God
altered, made mutable.[24] This was a difficulty which troubled
many orthodox Christians, too, and it brings us into the area
of redemption theology where the secular arts were most
helpful — that of the sheer mechanics of God's becoming
man. Anselm saw no difficulty here at all. When he says that
he sees the Incarnation in terms of the lifting up of man to
God's level, rather than the demeaning or diminishing of God
to man's level,[25] he simply leaves out of account a number
of the questions which concerned twelfth-century
theologians: what sort of change was brought about by the

---

[20] Matt. 12:46–50.   [21] Matt. 14:24–6.
[22] Durand de Huesca, *Liber Contra Manicheos,* ed. C. Thouzellier, *SSLov.*
32 (1964), Chapter VII.   [23] Ibid., p. 160.26.
[24] *PL* 159.1018.   [25] *Anselmi Opera Omnia,* II.59.27–8.

death of Christ in Christ himself; what change in him is implied by his possession of a capacity for suffering.

Yet these matters turn on a number of preliminary questions which were being asked in Anselm's day. To these Anselm does provide answers. Roscelin of Compiègne had asked why the Son was incarnate and not the Father or the Holy Spirit, and how, if God is one, it was possible for one Person to be incarnate and not the other two. Anselm explains that the true believer accepts that he did not assume manhood in a unity of nature, but in a unity of Person (*non assumpsisse hominem in unitatem naturae sed in unitatem personae*).[26] It was therefore only with the Person of Christ that human nature was united with the divine nature. In any case, Anselm argues, all sorts of inconsistencies would arise if we attempted to show that the Father or the Holy Spirit was incarnate, because such sons of the Virgin would introduce additional 'sonship' into the Trinity; moreover, they would be merely human sons, and Christ is the Son of God; and so there would be inequalities in the Trinity.[27] Nicholas of Amiens still found this a pertinent question towards the end of the twelfth century. But he answers it in a quite different way. He says that the Son alone became incarnate because the Son is the source of form (*auctor est formae*) and God was obliged to restore 'form' to man 'deformed' by sin (*Deus debuit hominem per culpam deformem reformare*).[28] Alan, in other words, has turned to secular studies for help, and he has made use of the common contemporary notion that the Son is the 'formal cause' of created things, and especially responsible for giving form to matter. He borrows philosophical and scientific explanations of the nature of causation from Chalcidius' commentary on Plato's *Timaeus* and from Boethius' theological treatises, and adapts them for use in academic theology. The great first question about the mutability of the immutable God similarly found a more manageable expression in questions about the meaning of 'person' and the meaning of 'nature', which had been handled even in patristic times with the aid

---

[26] Ibid., II.24.9–10, *De Incarnatione Verbi* IX.
[27] Ibid., II.25–6, *De Incarnatione Verbi* X.   [28] *PL* 210.611.

of principles drawn from the secular disciplines and philosophy.

It is this aspect of the 'mechanics' of God's union with man in Christ which became a matter of topical interest in the middle years of the twelfth century. Here, as in so many other areas of the academic theology of the day, Boethius' *opuscula sacra* exerted a crucial influence. Although he strongly disapproved of the trend towards adopting a 'scientific' approach to such matters, Gerhoch of Reichersberg raises questions of the same kind himself, in his polemical letter to Pope Hadrian. When we call Christ a man, for example, are we using the word 'man' in its proper sense?[29] Gerhoch thought that the asking of such questions could be very misleading, but he found that he had no alternative but to try to give an answer in the technical terms of the day. In his *Liber de Gloria et Honore Filii Hominis* he tackles such questions systematically. If anyone argues that Christ wore his manhood like a garment, a mere *habitum*, Gerhoch would like him to consider exactly what he means by 'habit'. There are, he points out, habits of mind, bodily habits or attributes, and the 'habit' a man wears as clothing.[30] We must, in other words, look closely at the words we use. Otherwise we run the risk of becoming like those who are drunk on the wine of the schools, who have drunk scholastic rather than theological wine (*lectores ebrii, scholastico potius quam theologico vino ultra modum potati*).[31] Such men approach mysteries too boldly, and they argue like academics rather than as men of the Church.[32]

Questions about the Person and Nature of Christ were topical in the schools, but they were also an old stamping-ground of the heretics. Gerhoch himself mentions modern scholars who are no better than the Nestorians or the Photinians, because they claim that the human body of Christ was not God made man, but a mere dwelling-place for God (*non hominem Deum, sed habitaculum Dei*).[33] Simon of Tournai smells heresy here, too. To say that Christ assumed a

---

[29] Gerhoch of Reichersberg, *Letter to Pope Hadrian about the Novelties of the Day*, p. 12.
[30] *PL* 194.1149.
[31] *PL* 194.1074.
[32] *PL* 194.1143.
[33] *PL* 194.1139.

particular man, a second person, is to say that the Son of God is different from the Son of Man, 'and that is the Nestorian heresy'.[34] At the other extreme lie the followers of 'Arrius the heretic', whose dogma was that Christ was merely a creature.[35] In the area of dispute which concerns the way in which Christ can have been both man and God, the influence of secular studies and the pressure of heretical opinion revived by contemporary partisans of these ancient arguments, were beginning to work upon one another abrasively by the middle of the twelfth century.

The doctrine of the Incarnation, in the uncompromising form in which it is set out in the creeds, has never been easy to accept because it cannot be formulated without breaking a conceptual barrier between two worlds of discourse. It is possible to read the Gospel narrative, to understand the human aspects of Christ's birth, his childhood, his ministry, his death, to see him as the example of the way in which a human life may be lived perfectly. The doctrine of the Trinity, for all the metaphysical difficulties it presents, is susceptible of discussion in internally consistent terms, if we accept that the rules which govern statements about God are different from those which govern statements about the created world. The difference is not unlike that between the laws of two-dimensional geometry and the laws of three-dimensional geometry. A triangle drawn on a plane surface has angles which add up to 180 °, but if the same triangle is inscribed on the surface of a sphere, its angles will no longer add up to 180 °. If we formulate new laws to meet the difference the extra dimension makes, we can find ways of discussing the axioms which will hold for the geometry of the third and even higher dimensions. But a triangle cannot both lie in a single plane and be inscribed on a sphere. Even if it were possible for it to do so, we should not know what kind of geometry to use. This is the position in which the doctrine of the Incarnation places us, because it makes it necessary to reconcile the 'two-dimensional world' of the rules of human language, and the 'three-dimensional world' of theological

---

[34] Simon of Tournai, *Disputationes,* XVII, p. 58.21–2.
[35] Ibid., p. 61.

language. Here lies perhaps the greatest Christian paradox of all. To understand it we must first review the rules of discourse which may be helpful in discussing it, and secondly, try to understand the mechanics of the union, the way in which it can have been possible for Christ to be both God and man. These are the two areas of exploration which engaged twelfth-century theologians.

Recent controversy may appear to make these matters less urgent. Attention has been drawn to another question altogether: that of the Gospel-writers' intention in portraying Jesus as the Son of God and the Son of Man, and of the ways in which the earliest Christian writers constructed the orthodox doctrine from their teaching. It has been suggested that the line of doctrinal development went astray, and that these questions of patristic and medieval scholars need not be asked at all if we go back to the historical facts. The Incarnation may be regarded (in a special sense of the term) as a 'myth'.[36] But this approach does not avoid the difficulty of discovering appropriate laws of discourse for talking about the Incarnation. If anything, it compounds the problem by bringing yet another form of technical language into the field. Nor does it answer the question, 'How could Christ be both God and man? It merely dismisses it as a question without meaning, and the device of setting aside in modern philosophy a number of ancient philosophical and theological questions as meaningless has not proved to be the cure-all it was confidently expected to be. 'Non-questions' have an obstinate tendency to recur despite attempts to shut them out. The light in which twelfth-century theologians viewed these problems may now seem crude. But the very simplicity with which they posed them makes them basic questions. The methods of resolution they put forward often have a common-sense quality and that is always a good sign in the treatment of difficult and obscure matters.

Peter Abelard describes the Incarnate Christ as *una compacta persona.*[37] He embraces in this expression a number of doctrinal problems which gave him and his contemporaries

---

[36] See *The Myth of God Incarnate,* ed. J. Hick (London, 1977); *The Truth of God Incarnate,* ed. M. Green (London, 1977).

[37] *Theologia Christiana,* p. 285.622 IV, para. 44.

a good deal of trouble, as they tried to find ways of reconciling the three traditions in Incarnation theology. These, the study of the Bible, which had for so long been the staple of systematic theology, the use of technical principles of the liberal arts which were now helping to fashion the new speculative theology, and that of polemical or missionary theology which had a new urgency from the end of the eleventh century, can all be seen to work together in Abelard's own thought. At the end of Book I of the *Theologia Christiana* he mentions Scriptural testimony to the divinity of the Word,[38] and describes the views of some of the philosophers on the same point, particularly those of 'that greatest philosopher of the Latins, Boethius', who 'wrote on, translated or expounded almost all the liberal arts'.[39] He points out that Boethius composed a defence of the orthodox doctrine of the Incarnation against the views of the heretics Eutyches and Nestorius.[40]

The Bible's teaching on the doctrine of the Trinity and on Incarnation has to be assembled from a series of references to Father, Son, and Holy Spirit, and to their relationship to one another. These are not all by any means unambiguous and they do not form a coherent whole even when they are set side by side. Since patristic times the principles of the secular disciplines had been brought to bear in an attempt to supply a more complete vindication of these doctrines. Heresies concerning the Trinity and the Incarnation are among the most ancient. For a number of historical and practical reasons the three traditions had always come together particularly forcefully in this area, throughout the history of Christian thought. The difficulty of deciding in what sense there may be said to be Person and Nature in the Godhead is greatly compounded by the introduction of the further problem of deciding how the divine and the human can have been united in the Person of Christ. The contribution of twelfth-century scholars was to look at the Incarnation afresh in the terms of these three

---

[38] Ibid., p. 128.1770–1, I, para. 130. (Dan. 3:92.)

[39] Ibid., p. 129.1814–130.1817; I, para. 135.

[40] Ibid., p. 130.1822–5; cf. J. McIntyre, *The Shape of Christology* (London, 1966) and W. Pannenberg, *Jesus, God and Man* (London, 1968), pp. 283 ff. on the classical doctrines and their development in patristic times.

traditions of theological investigation, and to take substantially further some of the solutions first proposed in
patristic times. For the first time for many centuries circumstances created an academic ambience in which all three
could work together constructively.

Twelfth-century thinkers recognized that *natura, persona,*
and *humanitas* are words with many meanings. 'this noun
"person" ', says Abelard, 'can be taken in three or four ways,
or perhaps more, that is, in one way by the theologians, in
another way by the grammarians [who speak of the "persons"
of the verb], in another way by the rhetoricians [who speak
of the "person" as a "rational substance"] or the writers of
comedies [who refer to the actors].'[41] Robert of Melun, a
thinker who drew upon Abelard's teaching, distinguishes
between two senses of 'nature'. 'Nature is the customary
course of things, against which God often acts. Nature is also
often said to be the disposition according to which he made
all things. God never does anything against this.'[42] M. D.
Chenu has looked at a number of aspects of the twelfth-
century view of man and nature and R. W. Southern has considered the sense in which we may speak of humanism in the
twelfth century.[43] In a recent study W. Ullman has set aside
the 'basic conception of *humanitas*', the concept of manhood
which is explored by Gilbert of Poitiers (after Boethius), in
favour of an examination of the development of the ways in
which 'man's *humanitas* enters the historic stage and . . . is
composed of many strains and elements.'[44] These are
important developments in their long-term consequences. But
the attractiveness and interest of such explorations has
tended to obscure the importance of the theological and
philosophical problem which underlies the hard thinking of
twelfth-century scholars about the concepts of 'man' and
'nature' and 'person'.

---

[41] *Theologia Christiana,* p. 263.2228–31; III, para. 181.

[42] Robert of Melun, *Quaestiones* [*Theologice*] *de Epistolis Pauli,* p. 148.8.
On Rom. 11:24. On the many meanings of 'nature', see Gilbert of Poitiers, p.
243.13.

[43] M. D. Chenu, *La théologie au douzième siècle* (Paris, 1957), R. W.
Southern, *Mediaeval Humanism* (Oxford, 1970).

[44] W. Ullman, *Mediaeval Foundations of Renaissance Humanism* (London,
1977), p. 65.

The most influential texts in encouraging new thinking about the way in which the study of the Bible and the study of the secular authors could be used in conjunction to meet the threat of heresy, were undoubtedly Boethius' *Contra Eutychen* and the *De Trinitate*. Even in Carolingian times some scholars were able to draw on these works. Godescalc of Orbais gives Boethius' definitions of *natura* and *persona* and quotes him on the union of God and man in Christ.[45] But he does not make as much of the texts as twelfth-century scholars were able to do in the light of their greater knowledge of the technical skills of the arts. It is doubtful whether Anselm of Canterbury had any knowledge of the *opuscula sacra* at all, to help him in his discussion of the Incarnation. But Thierry of Chartres, Gilbert of Poitiers, and Clarenbald of Arras took Boethius as the starting-point for much of their thinking and the Boethian definitions laid the foundations for a great deal of the work of the day on the subject of the Incarnation.

In the *Contra Eutychen* Boethius himself took arms against heretical teaching with the aid of the technical principals of the philosophy of his own time.[46] Before we can discuss the Person or the nature of Christ, he says, we must understand what we mean by 'nature' and what we mean by 'person'. Accordingly, he defines his terms, as he encouraged his twelfth-century readers to do in their turn. He asks what kinds of things are normally said to have a nature; he picks out in particular 'bodies' and 'substances'. Bodies are always, by definition, corporeal, but substances are sometimes corporeal and sometimes incorporeal; when we speak of the 'nature' of God we refer to the divine 'substance' which is incorporeal. Substances in general have a 'nature' which may either act or be acted upon. But the 'nature' of the divine incorporeal substance is only to act. By such means Boethius begins to demonstrate the existence of significant differences between the divine nature and created natures. Aristotle, he concedes, takes a different view. He allows the word 'nature' to be applied only to bodies, and therefore he would say that

---

[45] Godescalc d'Orbais, op. cit., p. 99, p. 318, p. 383.
[46] *Theological Tractates*, p. 77.1–30, *Contra Eutychen* I.

nature is the *motus principium* or source of movement which is inherent in bodies. But for the Christian philosopher it is not possible to accept that the divine nature is no more than this. For theological purposes, we need a further definition of the word 'nature'. We have no difficulty in understanding the statement that silver and gold differ in 'nature'. 'Nature' may thus be defined as the specific difference (*specifica differentia*) which gives each thing its distinctive form.[47] It is in this last sense that Christ is said to have two natures.

What, then, is a person? 'Person' is clearly not the equivalent of 'nature'. A stone may have a nature (as a corporeal substance), but it cannot be said to be a person. Nor is a tree a person, nor an ox. Only men, angels, and God are persons. Persons are rational substances. Persons cannot be accidents (we do not speak of white or black or size as a person), so there seems no doubt that they must be substances. They cannot, however, be universal substances (animal is not a person, man is not a person) but only individual substances (Cicero is a person, Plato is a person). A person is thus the individual substance of a rational nature (*naturae rationabilis individuus substantia*).[48]

So far things seem straightforward enough. But person and nature are not independent concepts. It is impossible to be a person who has no nature; person cannot be predicated apart from nature.[49] Moreover, a number of technical terms of both Greek and Latin are used in discussions of nature and person, and Boethius devotes some space to describing these additional terms of reference. Both technical problems of predication and matters of technical vocabulary have entered into the discussion, and both were of course of central interest to twelfth-century students of the *artes*. This interdependence of the notions of nature and person led Nestorians to affirm that if there were two natures in Christ there must be two Persons.[50] The relation between person and nature remained a stumbling-block for twelfth-century scholars. Boethius did not resolve these questions of definition

---

[47] Ibid., p. 81.57–8.
[49] Ibid., p. 83.10–11.

[48] Ibid., pp. 83–5.
[50] Ibid., pp. 85–91.

for them in the *Contra Eutychen.* Rather he threw them
open for further discussion by giving them a technical cast
and opening up the possibility of applying further technical
principles to their solution.

The first half of the twelfth century saw a preoccupation
with technical language and especially with theological
language with which earlier medieval centuries have nothing
to compare. When Abelard describes Christ as *una compacta
persona,* made up of divinity and humanity, he does so in
the context of a discussion of the reference or signification
of the words which are used in making such a statement.
Abelard is anxious to demonstrate that, despite the almost
impossible difficulties in which any attempt to express such
mysteries in human language embroils the theologian, it
should not be necessary to resort to extraordinary procedures
in order to make things clear. 'It is not necessary to stretch
the figurative expressions of Scripture beyond what is
written' (*Nec Scripturae figurativas locutiones ultra hoc
quod scriptum est necesse est extendi*). It is not right, he
emphasizes, to alter the usual sense of a word (*a consueta
significatione sermone commutare*) without the most
weighty authority, except for the sake of stylistic con-
trivance.[51] As far as possible ordinary language must be made
to serve.

In the *Sententie Parisienses* a discussion along similar lines
examines the question: can Christ be said to be *homo et
deus,* God and man, in the sense of a *res constans ex humana
natura et divina* (a 'thing composed of both human and
divine "nature" ')? The problem here posed concerns both
the thing signified and the words used to signify it. It seems
on the face of it that what is a part is being called a whole.
The human nature which is joined with the divine is being
called the whole if we say that Christ was fully man, and the
divine nature which is joined with the human is being called
a whole if we say that Christ was fully God; and yet the two
natures are not two wholes but one and that which is of a
part is being attributed to a whole (*et hoc quod partis est
attribuitur toti*). 'I do not see how that expression can be

---

[51] *Theologia Christiana,* p. 285.662–71, IV, para. 44.

technically exact' (*Non possum videre quomodo ista locutio propria sit*), says the questioner. 'It seems to me that this is a figurative expression and that there is a transferred sense in the words, and that this is a truth in an improper sense. Christ is God; Christ is man. Man is God (that is, in this sense, that God is united with human nature). Similarly, God is man (man is united with the divine nature). This is a figurative expression like these: Christ was in the tomb; Christ was in hell; Christ is in heaven.'[52] To say that God was at some time in a specific place is no more literally true than to say that God is man. We cannot follow the ramifications of this discussion here, but it shows clearly enough the difficulty in which twelfth-century theologians found themselves when they began to look systematically at both the realities of the Incarnation and the words which had traditionally been used to describe it.

Part of the difficulty lay in the shortage of existing technical terms in Latin, on which Boethius remarks in the *Contra Eutychen*.[53] He suggests that it may be helpful to look at the range of terms which are available in Greek. The theologians of the twelfth century did so, and not only in connection with the Incarnation. During the first half of the century *ousia, hylos, idea,* become increasingly common in academic writing, along with other words transliterated from the Greek. Another device was to form new words on old models, or to make a new technical usage of old words. Gilbert of Poitiers employs *personalitas* ('personhood') for purposes of comparison with *humanitas* ('manhood').[54] Syntax, too, is adapted to new purposes. Already in the ninth century Godescalc of Orbais turned to adverbs in order to describe the mode of God's existence as nature and person; *naturaliter una et personaliter trina* (God is 'naturally one and personally three').[55] Christ, he says, was *naturaliter . . . iuxta divinitatem* and, *. . . naturaliter . . . iuxta humanitatem*, but *personaliter . . . propter unitatem*.[56] Gilbert of Poiters

---

[52] *Sententiae Parisenses,* ed. A. Landgraf, *Écrits théologiques de l'école d'Abelard*, pp. 31–2.
[53] *Theological Tractates*, p. 86.25.
[54] Gilbert of Poitiers, op. cit., p. 152.23–40.
[55] Godescalc, op. cit., p. 25.29–30, cf. p. 24.25.   [56] Ibid., p. 334.12.

develops the same method a little further in his commentaries on Boethius. The presence of new words and new usages of old words, and of new, or more frequently used, extraordinary grammatical devices, are all indications that habits of thought are being stretched. These signs of expansion are plentifully in evidence in the twelfth century and especially in relation to Incarnation theology.

So much for 'nature' and 'person'. But what of 'man'? T. F. Torrance finds it necessary to say, almost apologetically, perhaps, that 'at no point is theology more relevant today then in the issues it raises about our knowledge of man'.[57] Twelfth-century readers did not need to have the relevance of theology to their lives demonstrated to them; they saw that clearly enough. But they had, as recent studies have shown, an interest in human 'knowledge of man' which is not to be found in any earlier medieval century and which gave a new edge to their concern with the sense in which Christ may be said to have become man. Yet the concept of man which had to be found a place in the theology of the Incarnation is of a highly abstract and schematized kind. There is nothing here of the richness of association which came to be evoked by the word 'humane' or by 'humanity' or even by 'manhood'. This is a 'manhood' which is simply an archetypal nature, that which makes a man neither an animal nor God, nor yet a plant or a stone. The question 'What was the manhood Christ assumed?' is conceived of in abstract, almost mathematical, terms. It is important that we should not lose sight of this simplicity of conception in the welter of new ideas about man which were piled upon it in the course of the century and which have been so attractive to modern scholars.

Godescalc speaks of Adam as the *humanitas masculina a deo de nullo homine creata* and of Eve as the *humanitas feminina a deo de homine illo creata* and of Abel as *humanitas a deo creata ab Adam sata de Eva nata* ('The masculine manhood created by God from no man, the feminine manhood created by God from Adam, and the manhood created by God from the seed of Adam and borne by Eve are all one

---

[57] T. Torrance, *Theology in Reconstruction* (London, 1965), p. 99.

manhood'). They are not *tres* but *triplex et una,* threefold and one.[58] Godescalc envisaged manhood as something exemplified in individual members of the human race from the very beginning, but retaining always its archetypal unity. To turn the notion round, *humanitas,* as Thierry of Chartres says, is that which all men have in common (*Et humanitas similiter omnes homines unit*).[59] Humanity is the same thing in all men, just as divinity is the same thing in all three Persons of the Trinity (*Sed una est omnino divinitatis trium personarum et una omnimodo humanitas omnium hominum*).[60] This drawing of parallels between the notion of manhood and the notion of divinity will not, however, quite solve the problems raised by the Incarnation. It was not the deity of the whole Trinity which assumed manhood but only the deity of the Son (*nequaquam adsumpsit humanitatem . . . tota trinitas sed sola tantummodo filii deitas*).[61] If we are to understand the doctrine of the Trinity and make it acceptable to unbelievers, we must show how manhood may be one thing in all mankind and yet proper to each individual man, and how deity may be one thing in all three Persons and yet proper to each Person. Only *subtiliter,* with subtle reasoning, shall we see how deity may be one *naturaliter* but not *personaliter,*[62] and how Christ assumed, not all mankind, but the manhood of an individual man.

If there are many personifications of humanity in individual men, are we to conclude that there are many humanities? Thierry of Chartres says not *Licet enim sint plures homines non sunt tamen plures humanitates*[63] ('Even if there are many men, there are not many humanities'). Socrates cannot be said to be 'humanity',[64] and no man can do more than exemplify this single 'humanity' in his individual person. To put it another way, in the species *homo* are contained many men, but in the species *humanitas* there are no individuals.[65]

The problem is akin to that formulated by Godescalc three

[58] Godescalc, op. cit., p. 82.4–8.
[59] *Thierry of Chartres,* p. 116.17.
[60] Ibid., p. 175.11–12.
[61] Godescalc, op. cit., p. 24.11–14.
[62] Godescalc, op. cit., p. 20.24–p. 21.1.
[63] *Thierry of Chartres,* p. 175.12–13.
[64] *Clarenbald of Arras,* p. 164, para. 58.
[65] Ibid., p. 92, para. 18.

centuries earlier, in the passage about Adam and Eve and
Abel we have already looked at. Humanity, he suggests, may
be threefold, without being three.[66] In that case, we must
decide whether to believe that a single 'idea' or 'form' exists
for all cats or dogs or mountains or men, which gives form
to all the individual manifestations of these things and which
inheres in them directly in some way, or whether to take the
view that each example of a cat or dog or mountain or man
has a separate form, to which is united matter to give it its
individual existence. In the latter case, some means must be
found of explaining how these separate 'forms' are all
recognizably the forms of cats or dogs or mountains or men.
What is it, in other words, that they have in common with
one another? Boethius explains the difficulty by saying that
these separate 'forms' are images (*imagines*) derived from the
single general or pure 'form'. Pure form is independent of
matter (*praeter materiam*), and in God there is only pure
form, for there is no 'matter' in *divinitas*.[67] Evidently not all
his twelfth-century readers found this satisfactory. Thierry of
Chartres complains that some scholars claim that there is no
single general form, but that there are as many humanities as
there are men.[68] He himself emphasizes that forms give unity
to things; they are not responsible for creating distinctions
between individuals. (Individuals are therefore separate
because they are composed of separate portions of matter,
not because of any diversity of forms.) Therefore each man
participates in the one 'form' which is humanity: *in unione
hominum*,[69] in a union of men. Those who argue differently
say that each man has his own humanity (*unumquemque
hominem habere propriam humanitatem*).[70] For this difference of opinion Boethius is not altogether blameless; his
account is highly compressed, and the portion of his
argument which is specifically concerned with 'humanity' is
brief. His main concern in the *De Trinitate* is to show that
the divine Form is unique among forms, and the case of
humanitas merely provides illustration and contrast.

[66] Godescalc, p. 82.8–14.
[67] *Theological Tractates*, p. 10–13, *Thierry of Chartres*, p. 73.70.
[68] *Thierry of Chartres*, p. 166.14.
[69] Ibid., cf. p. 272.22, p. 175.2–3.   [70] Ibid., p. 175.2–3.

But Christ became man. Did he assume the common humanity of all mankind when he became an individual man? If not, it is difficult to see how he can have become the redeemer of the whole human race in his single person. Anselm's explanation that in some sense he 'stood for' mankind simply because he was born of the stock of Adam no longer seemed adequate. Something philosophically more watertight was now required to meet the questions which were raised by academics. The difficulty is this: we do not normally say that something which is white is 'whiteness'; nor can a man be said to be manhood (*homo non est humanitas*).[71] Yet 'if Christ had assumed a single [human] person, as some foolish men think when they argue that there are many humanities (which is impossible) then he would have saved only one man',[72] says Thierry. Unless we can explain how Christ represented all mankind in his single human nature, we cannot say that he redeemed the whole of humanity. In this way the philosophical problem of forms and ideas — the stuff of the debate between the nominalists and the realists — was brought directly to bear on the central problem of Incarnation theology: that of explaining how the redemption was effective for the whole human race.

A mechanical difficulty seemed insuperable, too, and yet it was essential to find a way round it. It is far from easy to understand the orthodox doctrine that in Christ there were two natures and one Person. Boethius throws the apparent absurdity of the idea into relief by suggesting (only to dismiss it) the possibility that the two natures somehow lay side by side, like two stones, in physical juxtaposition.[73] If that were so, no one thing would have been formed out of two, and Christ would not exist as an individual.[74] That way lay the Nestorian heresy, for the Nestorians believed that there were two Persons as well as two natures in Christ. The heresy of Eutyches lay in the opposite direction. He argued that the two natures did not persist after the union between God and man, but that the human nature of Christ disappeared. Christ was thus one Person and one Nature.[75]

---

[71] Ibid., p. 138.82.   [72] Ibid., p. 251.1.
[73] *Theological Tractates*, p. 92, *Contra Eutychen* IV.   [74] Ibid., p. 94.44-5.
[75] Ibid., p. 100.5-7.

In an attempt to steer a course between this Scylla and this Charybdis twelfth-century academic theologians marshalled all the technical principles they knew, and even outside the context of the commentaries on Boethius' *opuscula sacra* Boethius' influence is much in evidence, because he had raised these matters in the technical philosophical terms they needed. The *Ysagoge in Theologiam* is intended as a complete textbook for beginners, but its handling of these matters involves a good deal of technical expertise because it had become impossible to treat them in any other way in the schools. We might begin with this syllogism:

> *Verbum assumpsit hominem.*
> *Sed omnis homo persona.*
> *Ergo assumpsit personam.* [76]

'The Word assumed man. But every man is a person. Therefore he assumed a person'. The author of the *Ysagoge* sets about the task of showing how Christ can have been fully man without assuming an additional person with his manhood. Not every rational substance is a person, he argues, and not every rational substance is an individual. As long as the soul is joined to the body it is a rational substance united with another substance; moreover the soul is not a person in its own right, because it is not sufficient to make it a person for it to be a rational substance; it must also be individual. [77] Boethius' definition of a person as 'the individual substance of a rational nature' is much in evidence here. [78] Once the soul is separated from the body, the author of the *Ysagoge* goes on to argue, it becomes a person, because it becomes an individual, or separate, rational substance. The body itself does not become a person, because although it is now an individual substance it is not rational. Now before the Incarnation the Word was a person, because he was an individual rational substance. The man who was assumed would also have been a person if he had not been assumed, because then he would have been a separate individual. But when he was assumed he ceased to be an individual, and became one person with Christ. 'Just as there is one person

---

[76] *Ysagoge in Theologiam*, p. 162.31–2.   [77] Ibid., p. 163.19–29.
[78] *Theological Tractates*, p. 85, *Contra Eutychen* III.

from body and soul joined together and separated from other substances, so from the man who was assumed and the Word there was one person.'[79] This union of one person and two natures is, of course, immeasurably greater than the union of soul and body in man, we are assured, but the parallel is illuminating. We have here the result of new work upon old principles. The definition Boethius provides has been made to serve like a knife, whose sharp point discovers an angle of entry, a means of making the necessary distinction which will support the orthodox doctrine. The most useful item in Boethius' definition here has been his reference to the individuality of the person. This is only one of many arguments constructed upon Boethius' foundations in the twelfh-century schools. There are others which owe nothing to Boethius at all. But there can be no doubt that Boethius encouraged twelfth-century scholars to approach doctrinal problems philosophically and to look for technically exact solutions. The mystery of the Incarnation was, as far as possible, brought into the light and examined scientifically.

The Nestorian and Eutychean heretics to whom Boethius addressed himself had their following in the medieval schools. But outside the schools the successors of the Manichees were still putting forward another explanation of Christ's Incarnation which had adherents among academics. Alan of Lille explains that the Cathars do not believe that Christ assumed a real physical body. He took, they say, only the shadow of a human body (*umbra humanae naturae*). They cite the authority of Scritpure, saying that this was why he was able to be born without opening the Virgin's womb, and walk dry-footed upon the waters.[80] Gerhoch of Reichersberg describes the scholars who share these opinions as *humaniformi*. The doctrine has the advantage, as Gerhoch concedes, of circumventing the difficulty of explaining how God could become man without being changed, and how he could die.[81] The heresy of the *phantasticus homo* has a long history.[82] Like the discussion of the mystery of the two natures and one

---

[79] *Ysagoge in Theologiam*, p. 163.29–164.7.   [80] *PL* 210.321.

[81] Gerhoch's *Letter to Pope Hadrian*, p. 67, XVI.24.

[82] C. H. Turner, 'The *Liber Ecclesiasticorum Dogmatum* attributed to Gennadius' *Journal of Theological Studies*, 7 (1905), 78–99.

Person, it was not new in twelfth-century schools, but it gave rise to new lines of thought when it was considered for the first time in the light of a new and technically more advanced knowledge of the liberal arts.

Nicholas of Amiens tries to incorporate into the axioms of his *De Articulis Catholicae Fidei* a number of laws which will demonstrate to such heretics that they are in error. Rule 1 of Book V asserts that the resurrection of body and soul will reunite what death has separated; Rule 3 states that man is resurrected in the flesh of the body he had on earth and that this body will be reunited with his own soul; Rule 4 says that resurrection applies to the greater as well as the lesser. Christ, contrary to heretical opinion, was really resurrected from the dead bodily.[83] All these points had been questioned by contemporary heretics, who ridiculed the orthodox teaching, not only on the grounds that it was repugnant to give such dignity to the material body, but also on the practical grounds that if everyone was to be given back his own body in its entirety, he would have enormously long fingernails and a tangle of hair, when the hair and nails which had been cut during his lifetime were restored to him.

In twelfth-century studies of the *opus restaurationis,* as in contemporary work upon the *opus conditionis*, a complex of influences is at work. Upon the foundation laid by the study of the Bible a great structure was going up, as scholars strove to build a solid edifice of academic theology from the mass of materials they had to hand. Into the building went the technical skills they were learning from their study of the liberal arts and ancient philosophy. And into the design went a number of features which, it was hoped, would serve to keep heretical doctrines out.

---

[83] *PL* 210.615.

VI   The Measure Within

We have been looking at broad changes, at movements of
ideas to which a number of individuals made a contribution.
Few of the scholars with whom we have been concerned
reveal very much of the private path of intellectual and
spiritual development they trod. In many cases they left
no personal testimony; often it is impossible to be sure of the
order in which their writings were composed and it is difficult
to reconstruct a line of development in their thought. But the
fire and energy with which they worked upon the new
academic discipline of theology came from something more
than mere intellectual curiosity, strong though that was in
many of them. Theology has an important for the believer
which sets it apart from all other disciplines of the mind. The
tendency for the academic study of theology to shed the
devotional and contemplative concomitants which accompanied exercises in speculative theology within the monastic
tradition, should not be allowed to blind us to the continuing
association of all these elements in the minds of individual
scholars. Peter Abelard and Thierry of Chartres were profoundly religious men, as well as academics. We shall not do
justice to the special quality of the new academic discipline
unless we allow for the way it has worked inwardly upon
both feeling and intellect, not only in the twelfth century,
but in every age when it has engaged able and committed
men in hard thinking.

'I will draw out, as far as may be, the history of my mind!'
This was John Henry Newman's promise near the beginning
of his *Apologia pro Vita Sua*;[1] he went on to give an account
of the process by which he moved from one doctrinal position
to another, and eventually became committed to his present
settled opinions. The features of the conversion experience
which have received most attention are its more sudden and
dramatic aspects, and above all the spiritual and emotional
changes it brings about. As William James says, 'there is little

---

[1] J. H. Newman, *Apologia pro Vita Sua* (London, 1864), Part II, p. 48.

doctrinal theology in such an experience, which starts with
the absolute need of a higher helper, and ends with the sense
that he has helped us.'[2] But for a few individuals the element
of 'doctrinal theology' has been far more important, and in
some cases the struggle with a set of theological or philosophical difficulties which stand in the way of commitment
has been the very vehicle of conversion. William James refers
to this phenomenon in a general way. Some men, he notes,
find that 'their religious faculties may be checked in their
natural tendency to expand, by beliefs about the world that
are inhibitive'.[3] If for 'beliefs about the world' we read
'doctrinal or philosophical positions', it is possible to cite a
number of instances of men who have found this to be their
own experience, and who have left a full account of their
progression from one view to another in an *apologia*. The
intellectual concomitants of the conversion experience have
been somewhat neglected, and yet they appear to display
marked common features in different individuals in very
much the way that other aspects of conversion seem to do.[4]

There is an additional interest in such accounts because
they have some claim to belong to the genre of polemical or
missionary theology. The author conducts an interior
dialogue with himself, or with God, for the benefit of a pro-
spective convert from another faith or against a hypothetical
heretic or unbeliever. The credibility of the arguments which
are advanced, and the weight of the textual authorities which
may be adduced, are tested against the objections of the 'unbeliever within'. Newman describes the method he has chosen
to adopt, like this:

I will state the point at which I began, in what external suggestion or
accident each opinion had its rise, how far and how they were developed
from within, how they grew, were modified, were combined, were in
collision with each other, and were changed; again how I conducted
myself towards them, and how, and how far, and for how long a time,
I thought I could hold them consistently with the ecclesiastical engage-
ments which I had made.[5]

---

[2] William James, *The Varieties of Religous Experience* (The Gifford Lectures,
Edinburgh, 1901–2), Lecture IX (reprinted London, 1960), p. 20.

[3] Ibid., p. 208.

[4] See my article 'A Change of Mind in some Scholars of the Eleventh and Early
Twelfth Centuries', *Studies in Church History* (1978), 27–38.

[5] Newman, op. cit., p. 48.

He brings his reader as close as he can to 'that living intelligence by which I write, and argue, and act',[6] so that he can follow the changes of mind which have taken place and see how they have come about. Something very much like this inward debate seems to have happened in men who have argued their way to commitment with themselves, whether their conversions took them from one Christian persuasion to another (John Donne, John Henry Newman), from another faith to Christianity (the twelfth century Hermannus Judaeus), from paganism to Christianity (Augustine), from unbelief to Christianity (C. S. Lewis), or from apathetic to committed Christian faith (Guibert of Nogent in the late eleventh century). For each of these a third element must be added to the 'two things' which William James identifies 'in the mind of the candidate for conversion: first, the present incompleteness or wrongness, the "sin" which he is eager to escape from; and second, the positive ideal which he longs to encompass';[7] the third element is the problem posed for a man with a trained mind by the desire to find his beliefs reconcilable with the philosophical criteria he adopts. Such men have demanded intellectual respectability in their beliefs. In their writings they have sought to meet the same need in their readers.

A conversion of this kind cannot of its nature be sudden, although the initial or final change of direction and the moment of commitment may come suddenly enough. Often, many years of intellectual endeavour have been involved, as well as a long period of spiritual striving, and the conversion seems to have taken place in two or more distinct stages. Hermannus Judaeus prides himself that he was not converted as easily as unbelievers and Jews often are (*non enim ea facilitate conversus sum*); for him there was no sudden and thoughtless change (*repentina et inopinata mutatio*).[8]

The peculiar quality of the experience does not, however, exclude the more familiar symptoms of conversion. Hermannus himself testifies to the depression and exhaustion

---

[6] Ibid., p. 47.   [7] James, op. cit., p. 212.
[8] *Hermannus Quondam Judaeus Opusculum de Conversone Sua,* ed. G. Niemeyer, *MGH, Quellen, Zur Geistesgeschichte des Mittelalters* iv (Weimar, 1963), p. 69.11–13.

of spirit which, as William James shows, often precedes
'the conversion crisis'.[9] Hermannus longed to be released
from the darkness and oppression of mind in which he
found himself and prayed in tears for help.[10] Augustine
became profoundly wretched when he discovered that his
struggles to realize his worldly ambitiouns were bringing him
only dissatisfaction.[11] Like Augustine, Hermannus exper-
enced moments of vision,[12] and he was moved to joy as his
doubts disappeared.[13]

Those whose conversions have been the result of long
periods of internal debate were not free of the difficulties
which characteristically attend the period before and after
conversion. Hermannus describes his temptations[14] and says
that at the very time when he was making progress in his
thinking the Devil prevailed on him to take a wife.[15] Guibert
of Nogent writes about the particular problem of lust,[16] as
does Augustine.[17] It would not be true to say that these
experiences of conversion were uncommon in most of their
aspects but such men bring to their passionate search an
intellectual rigour which distinguishes them from other con-
verts and which made them, in several cases, leaders of
thought in their own day. As a result of their protracted
inner debate they were peculiarly well-fitted to present a case
for their faith which would meet many of the objections
raised by the educated men of their own times.

They did not all set out on their enquiries in an energetic
spirit. Hermannus Judaeus began, it seems, almost by accident.
He found himself among Christians on business. (A Christian
priest who had run out of money wanted to borrow from him
because the king had detained him longer than he had expected.) Hermannus had asked for no guarantee from him, and so
his own people advised him to keep the priest under observation, to make sure that the debt was paid. During the time they
spent together, they began to talk about their differences of
belief, as it was not uncommon for Jews and Christians to do

---

[9] James, op. cit., pp. 214–15.   [10] Hemannus, p. 107.2–5.
[11] Augustine, *Confessions*, VI.6.   [12] Hermannus, p. 116, para. 18.
[13] Ibid., p. 108.12–17.   [14] Ibid., pp. 69–70.   [15] Ibid., p. 98, para. 10.
[16] Guibert of Nogent, *De Vita Sua,* ed. G. Bourgin (Paris, 1907), I.15.
[17] Augustine, *Confessions*, II.2–3; II.1–2 and 6.

at the beginning of the twelfth century.[18] Only gradually did
Hermannus find that the curiosity thus aroused was becoming a passion. He began to long for a vision like that of
Daniel,[19] and in time he decided to give himself up entirely
for a period to systematic discussions with Christians, in the
hope of resolving his uncertainities.[20] Augustine says that it
was at the age of nineteen that he first began to search
seriously for truth and wisdom.[21] When he read Cicero's
Hortensius his desire for a fuller understanding of the eternal
truth awoke with great emotional force;[22] it was as if he had
had the vision of the island which C. S. Lewis describes in
The Pilgrim's Regress: 'While he strained to grasp it, there
came to him ... a sweetness and a pang so piercing that
instantly he forgot his father's house, and his mother, and the
fear of the Landlord, and the burden of the rules. All the
furniture of his mind was taken away.'[23] Augustine, too, felt
that all his preconceptions and assumptions about the
purpose of his life had lost their charm and seemed empty
dreams.[24] Whether this intellectual hunger of the spirit was
born suddenly or only gradually it was a sufficiently strong
force in each of these men to override well-established habits
of thought and to provide a new commitment at least to a
search for the absolute, if not as yet to any fixed opinions as
to the nature of that which was to be sought.

The intellectual excitement of this search in certain
individuals, and the intellectual rigour which goes with it,
seems to have its origin partly in an inborn quality of mind,
and partly in habits of mind formed in youth. Augustine
speaks of his own thorough training in the schools of his
day.[25] Guibert of Nogent was well-schooled, too; although
his tutor was a man of limited attainments, his mother saw
to it that he had every educational advantage she could
purchase for him.[26] Newman, too, speaks of the care with
which he was 'brought up from a child to take great delight
in reading the Bible' and to have 'perfect knowledge' of the

---

[18] Hermannus, pp. 72–3.   [19] Hermannus, p. 94, para. 8.
[20] Ibid., p. 96, para. 9.   [21] *Confessions*, VI.11.
[22] *Confessions*, III.4.
[23] C. S. Lewis, *The Pilgrim's Regress* (London, 1933). Chapter I (reprinted
Glasgow, 1977), p. 33.
[24] *Confessions*, III.4.   [25] *Confessions*, I.11.   [26] *De Vita Sua*, I.

Catechism.[27] As his mind matured he reached a stage where this training, which had as yet resulted in 'no formal religious convictions' resulted in 'a great change of thought'. At the age of fifteen, he says, 'I fell under the influences of a definite Creed, and received into my intellect impressions of dogma, which,through God's mercy, have never been effaced or obscured'.[28] Newman is not speaking of an experience of conversion here, but merely of the period when a sound religious uprbinging began to work upon his growing mind, when he understood what it was he has been taught to believe. Augustine, too, had received such a training from his mother, and Guibert of Nogent grew up in a comparable milieu, a Christian home – as did the hero of *The Pilgrim's Regress.*

Guibert of Nogent discovered a hunger for knowledge about his faith and he began to read commentaries on the Bible, especially those of Gregory the Great,[29] and as his understanding grew he found new questions in his mind. Such reading is commonly undertaken with thoroughness and enthusiasm because there is a strong appetite for learning. Hermannus was much struck by the Christians' assertion that the Jews were like brute beasts who were content with the mere husks of Scripture (the literal interpretation) while the Christians enjoyed the sweet kernel (its inner meaning).[30] Accordingly, he studied the text closely, seeking out the exact meaning of every word.[31] Almost any book will do, as Newman found, if it happens to meet the need of the moment, and a chance juxtaposition of works may advance the reader's thinking by making it plain to him where conflicts of opinion lie. There is an element of spontaneous exploration in such reading, but it is, as a rule, balanced by the meticulous care with which the reader works, his assiduity in testing everything he reads against his growing understanding. Augustine describes how his ideas were always changing like a tide which ebbed and flowed, but something solid remained unmoved at the centre of his thinking. Among the rocks to which he clung at such times,

[27] Newman, op. cit., Part III, p. 55.   [28] Ibid., p. 58-9.
[29] Guibert, I.17.   [30] Hermannus, p. 74.6.
[31] Ibid., p. 76.9-14.

the Bible held an important place.[32] Books of all kinds, but
in particular the Bible itself, had an effect upon the process
of intellectual development of all the thinkers with whom we
are concerned. In general it was a stabilizing effect. The
written word not only had an authority — especially for early
and medieval Christians — but it also had the advantage of
being accessible whenever reassurance was needed, or whenever a further difficulty suggested itself. Arguments with
opponents, and conversations with more experienced
Christians were of their nature more ephemeral.

Reading and discussion work together in the mind, as they
clearly did in Newman's case, to bring about a slow and continuous change. Hermannus Judaeus describes how he often
chewed over what he had learned in the stomach of his mind
(*in ventrem memorie sepius mecum ruminanda transmisi*).[33]
Augustine's experience was more distressing to him. Again
and again in the *Confessions* he describes a mind in turmoil,
racing with effort as it tries to find a means of reconciling
contradictory opinions and to discover a standpoint which
will meet the requirements he has set himself — which will
give him, in short, an intellectual as well as a spiritual
satisfaction.

But as the meaning of Christian teaching grew clearer to
these men as they matured, their grasp of philosophical and
theological ideas in general grew stronger, too, and for each
of them there followed a period of comparison, as they
weighed one set of arguments against another. Here the most
significant factor is the influence of contemporary educational processes and the intellectual fashions of the day. The
thinker's task has, in each case, been to keep these in balance
with the 'eternal truths' which he believes himself to be
looking for and to find a way through which will be both
intellectually acceptable to him and in some sense orthodox.
It is of the essence of the process that the conversion leads,
not to the evolution of some new set of beliefs, but to an
acceptance of an established creed.

---

[32] *Confessions,* VII.7.   [33] Hermannus, p. 74.15–16.

Conclusion

The *Summa Sententiarum* is a collection of theological material put together in the middle of the twelfth century, which was for a long time ascribed to Hugh of St. Victor. D. E. Luscombe has called it 'a summary of sentences, a review and critique of opinions' which 'takes us inside a theological school'.[1] The question of its authorship has exercised modern scholars considerably; both Abelardian and Victorine influences have been noticed in it and some attempt has been made to put the surviving versions in an order of development. Its interest for our purposes lies in exactly this composite and eclectic character. It represents, in all probability, a fair sample of the theological work of the schools of northern France at the end of the first half of the twelfth century. In it is to be found all that we might expect to find in a nascent academic discipline. It brings together all the traditions we have seen at work. Scriptural and patristic texts are juxtaposed with arguments based on reason. Proofs of both kinds are set against one another, and in the rational arguments in particular traces of scholastic method are already very evident. 'This can be opposed in this way'; 'some are in the habit of opposing thus'; 'another difficult opposition can be made here'; 'such a question is commonly put'.[2] The over-all order and structure is already marked by the concern for logical or hierarchical unfolding of one topic out of another which Aquinas perfected in the *Summa Theologica*. The first question is: 'What is faith?' — as it was for both Abelard and Hugh of St. Victor. Then, with some digressions, we move on to Trinity and Incarnation, then to creation, and then to the sacraments. The reader is expected to understand the basic terms of the *artes,* and to find no difficulty with the assertion, for example, that no 'accidents' may be attributed to the Trinity.[3]

The *Summa* is more than a curiosity, but it is certainly not

---

[1] D. E. Luscombe, *The School of Peter Abelard,* p. 198. See also pp. 198–213 for a full discussion of the problems raised by this work, and for the literature.

[2] *PL* 176.60–7.   [3] *PL* 176.55.

a major work. It is an almost homely product of the ordinary work of the schools. Its very ordinariness, the run-of-the-mill quality which makes it impossible to attribute it securely to any known master, underlines the significance of the development of schools where theology could be studied almost routinely as an academic discipline. The temperature is a good deal higher in Abelard's *Theologia Christiana*. To quote Luscombe again, 'the challenge contained in such enquiries when cultivated by an intelligence of Abelard's power is an unusually demanding one in any academic society'.[4] Abelard himself says that he has deliberately addressed himself to the most difficult questions of the dialecticians (*pravissimae et difficillimae dialecticorum quaestiones*).[5] But even when less able men were at work, the stimulus to attempt to solve theological problems was present — not least because of the unique and pressing difficulties which arise from the reduction of theology to a system suitable for study in the schoolroom. Alongside the great men who pioneered the development of thology into an academic discipline, worked competent schoolmasters, and pupils of varied ability, who were able to make a contribution and to gain something from the work precisely because there was now a place for those of moderate ability within the ambience of the schools. That is not to suggest that the forming of an academic discipline is a recipe for mediocrity, but only that it provides a framework within which work can be done at different levels, and where, even in the absence of a thinker of outstanding capacity, worthwhile work can go on.

John Henry Newman was particularly interested in the role which ought to be played in a university by both religion and theology. He saw the Church as the natural protector of the teaching of sound and reliable knowledge, and he argues an impassioned case for the claims of theology to be 'a science, and an important one', fit to stand beside any other academic discipline, and indeed inseparable from the secular sciences if they are to be properly understood. Theology is a special case. To the atheist it is not a science at all. To the believer it is of unparalleled importance. If there is any

---

[4] Luscombe, op. cit., p. 308.   [5] *Theologia Christiana*, III.89, p. 230.

substance in theology at all, in other words: 'Granting theology is a real science', Newman claims, 'we cannot exclude it and still call ourselves philosophers'. And 'if there be religious Truth at all, we cannot shut our eyes to it, without prejudice to truth of every kind, physical, metaphysical, historical and moral; for it bears upon all truth'. Newman asked fundamental questions about the relation of theology to the academic subjects of his own day, to 'Astronomy, Optics, Hydrostatics, Galvanism, Pneumatics, Statics, Dynamics, Pure Mathematics, Geology, Botany, Physiology, Anatomy, and so forth', to grammar and rhetoric and all the secular disciplines he knew[6] – much as twelfth-century scholars had enquired about its bearing on the liberal arts.

The cause has been taken up more recently by T. F. Torrance. He has looked for points of contact between theological, scientific, and philosophical thought in the twelfth century, and he has emphasized the 'scientific passion' they have come to share for rigour and discipline, and the laying down of proper methods and appropriate technical language. Of them all, he says, theology must aspire to be the most 'rigorously scientific because of the total claims of its object'.[7] He, too, takes it for granted that if theology is to be an academic subject at all, then it must, for the believer, have a unique importance. There are many respects in which the exact forms such 'dialogue with the other sciences and with philosophy'[8] takes are peculiar to each century. Newman saw special difficulties here too. But in their recognition of the nature of the problems involved and in their concern with making the scientific and philosophical principles of their own⟩ day meet the theologian's needs, twelfth-century scholars faced some of the same difficulties as their more modern counterparts. As we have seen, they, too, found it necessary to discover a means by which they could 'refer their thoughts properly beyond themselves to God'.[9] They, too, were involved in 'epistemological and methodical questions'[10] of an order which still engages the energies of

---

[6] J. H. Newman, *Discourses on the Scope and Nature of University Education* (Dublin, 1852), *Discourse* III.

[7] T. F. Torrance, *Theological Science* (Oxford, 1969), p. 56.

[8] Ibid., p. xiii.   [9] Ibid., p. x.   [10] Ibid., p. xii.

modern linguistic philosophers. It was the desire to make
their treatment of their subject-matter 'clear and orderly'[11]
which inspired Hugh of St. Victor to propose his two-fold
division of all theology, and which gave rise to similar
attempts among his contemporaries (Abelard divides
theology into faith, charity and sacrament). The precise sense
in which theology may be reckoned one of the sciences of
human reason is a point at issue still. It is a perennial
question, of course; Augustine was troubled by it, too. But
in the twelfth century it began to take on a recognizably
modern character within an academic context.

Theology was already recognized as a 'human science',
even thought it is concerned with the divine. It is the *humana
scientia qua deus ab homine intelligitur,*[12] the human science
in which God is known by man. There is an acknowledge-
ment in this definition of Alan of Lille's that if we are to
know God we must study the human mind, since its short-
comings and limitations impede full knowledge of God and
restrict the way in which God is knowable to us. To quote
T. F. Torrance on the twelfth-century problem once more:
in 'scientific theology' we 'probe into the problematic
condition of the human mind before God and seek to bring
knowledge of him into clear focus, so that the truth of God
may shine through to it unhindered by its opacity'.[13] This
involved, in the twelfth century as now, the acquisition of
'clear and orderly forms',[14] a formal and rational procedure
such as had been brought to its highest pitch of development
by the secular arts. It is precisely because academic theology
developed as one of the human sciences that the lesser human
sciences are appropriate to it and it may gain something by
adopting their method and order.

It would not be true to say that the movement of theology
and the arts into close technical juxtaposition gave them
equality of standing in the later years of the twelfth century.
Alan of Lille himself says in a sermon addressed to members
of the clergy who linger too long in the study of the arts
and do not move on to theology, that the arts are mere hand-

[11] Ibid., p. ix.
[13] *Theological Science*, p. ix.
[12] *Textes inédits*, p. 227.
[14] Loc. cit.

maids of theology, servants of heavenly philosophy (*celestis philosophia*) and that it behoves a man to leave them behind as soon as he has mastered them.[15] Theology is like a tree which bears leaves, flowers, and fruit, but wordly philosophy (*terrestris philosophia*) is like a wood full of bare trees, many in their variety, but giving no protection against the frost.[16] His objection, however, is to the study of the arts as an end in itself, not to their use in theological speculation — and indeed they had become so entrenched in the academic discipline of theology by the end of the century that it would have been impossible to root them out altogether.

This had come partly as the result of such grand assessments of their place and of their value as that which Hugh of St. Victor has given us. But it was also the result of a vast, slow, methodical introduction of technical terms and principles point by point into every corner of 'theological science'. Although Newman knew little of medieval theology, he hits upon the very 'prospect' which faced twelfth-century scholars: 'The prospect opens upon us of a countless multitude of propositions, which in their first elements are close upon devotional truth — of groups of propositions, and those groups divergent, independent, ever springing into life with an inexhaustible fecundity.' What is more, they do so, as in the twelfth century', according to the ever-germinating forms of heresy, of which they are the antagonists'. Academic training fosters the natural tendency of the intellect to be, as Newman puts it, 'ever active, inquisitive, penetrating', and encourages it to go about its task with technical exactitude, as 'it examines doctrine and doctrine . . . compares, contrasts and forms them into a science', in this case, the science of theology.[17] It was by this process of steady infiltration that secular studies established their hold and helped scholars work with technical exactitude.

So theology became an academic discipline. The fibres of the subject are still impregnated with the notions twelfth-century scholars introduced or reintroduced from the ancient world. The heavy superstructure of later medieval scholasticism has largely disappeared. The work of the

---

[15] *Textes inédits,* p. 275.   [16] Ibid., p. 277.
[17] J. H. Newman, *A Grammar of Assent* (London, 1870), pp. 146–8.

twelfth-century persists because its most important aspect was the asking of the fundamental questions which must be answered if theology is to find a place among the subjects which can be studied in the schoolroom.

Appendix: Some of the Scholars
Mentioned in the Text

Adam of Balsam (Adam of the Petit Pont), followed Peter Abelard as a teacher of dialectic at Paris.

Alan of Lille (d. 1202), known as the *doctor univeralis*; studied under Gilbert of Poitiers; taught at Paris and Montpellier; died at Citeaux, in his eighties; theologian, preacher, and poet.

Anselm of Canterbury (1033–1109), Prior of Bec from 1063; Abbot of Bec from 1078; Archbishop of Canterbury, 1093–1109; theologian and philosopher.

Anselm of Laon (d. 1117), a pupil of St. Anselm at Bec, later ran the school at Laon with his brother Ralph of Laon.

Bernard of Chartres (d. 1130), is said to have lectured on Chalcidius' commentary on the *Timaeus*; John of Salisbury gives the impression that he was one of the best-known and most influential masters of the early twelfth century.

Clarenbald of Arras, pupil of Gilbert of Poitiers.

Gilbert Crispin, a pupil of St. Anselm's at Bec; author of the most widely-read of the dialogues between Jews and Christians; Abbot of Westminster from 1085.

Gilbert of Poitiers (1076–1154), lectured on Boethius' *Theological Tractates*; a controversial figure whose views were condemned at the Synod of Rheims of 1148; Bishop of Poitiers 1142–54.

Guibert de Nogent, monastic scholar; author of an autobiography, the *De Vita Sua*, in which he describes how St. Anselm helped him with spiritual guidance while he was a monk at Fly.

Hermannus Judaeus, author of a book about his own conversion to Christianity. He was won to the Christian faith partly through the efforts of Rupert of Deutz.

Honorius Augustodenensis, a mysterious figure who travelled widely, at the turn of the century, collecting material for his writings from all over northern Europe; his theology of the Redemption bears the marks of St. Anselm's influence.

Hugh of St. Victor (*c*. 1096–1141), studied under William of Champeaux; taught in the school of the house of St. Victor at Paris; author of theological and mystical writings, and a series of elementary textbooks on the *artes*; encyclopaedist.

John of Salisbury (*c*. 1115–80), heard the lectures of Peter Abelard, William of Conches, Gilbert of Poitiers and others. Left the schools for the Papal Court and a career in ecclesiastical administration; author of a treatise on government and political theory, memoirs of life at the Papal Court, a book about the schools of his youth, letters.

Peter Abelard (1079–42), pupil of Roscelin of Compiègne, William of

Champeaux, Anselm of Laon. Condemned for his theological views at the Council of Soissons of 1121 and the Council of Sens of 1141; theologian and dialectian.

Peter Lombard (*c.* 1100–60), author and compiler of the *Sentences* which became a standard theological textbook throughout the Middle Ages; taught at Paris from *c.* 1139, and was among those who condemned Gilbert of Poitiers in 1148.

Peter the Venerable, Abbot of Cluny; received Peter Abelard into retirement there for the two years after the Council of Sens; author of an important collection of letters and of a treatise against the Petrobrusian heretics.

Richard of St. Victor, successor of Hugh of St. Victor; author of a book on the Trinity and mystical writings.

Robert of Melun (d. 1167), inherited Abelard's mantle as teacher of theology at Paris; author of commentaries and *Sentences*.

Roscelin of Compiègne (d. *c.* 1125), one of the first scholars to use dialectic to challenge orthodox teaching; he attacked St. Anselm's teaching on the Trinity and later confronted Abelard.

Rupert of Deutz (*c.* 1070–*c.* 1129), taught at Liège and Siegburg; Abbot of Deutz near Cologne from about 1120; a Benedictine contemporary of Hugh of St. Victor; influenced by St. Anselm; instrumental in the conversion of Hermannus Judaeus; author of a massive work of Scriptural commentary, *On the Trinity and its Works*.

Simon of Tournai, theologian of the mid-twelfth century; author of a collection of *Sentences* and another of *Disputations*.

Stephen Langton, later to be Archbishop of Canterbury under King John; a theologian of note in the later twelfth century and author of sermons.

Thierry of Chartres, younger brother of Bernard of Chartres; taught at Chartres *c.* 1121, then at Paris; became Archdeacon of Dreux; succeeded Gilbert of Poitiers as Archdeacon and Chancellor of Chartres, 1141; present at the Synod of Rheims, 1148.

Walter of St. Victor (d. after 1180), became Prior of St. Victor; author of a treatise against Peter Abelard, Peter Lombard, Peter of Poitiers, Gilbert of Poitiers, whom he called the 'four labyrinths'.

William of Champeaux (*c.* 1070–1121), retired to St. Victor to teach, to escape Abelard's persecution in the schools.

William of Conches (*c.* 1080–*c.* 1154), a pupil of Bernard of Chartres.

INDEX

Abbo of Fleury vi
Adam of Balsam 22, 228
Adelard of Bath 21
Ailred of Rievaulx 130
Alan of Lille v, 5, 38, 48, 112, 113, 122, 143, 146, 150, 151, 156, 173, 174, 178, 180, 213, 225, 228
Anglo-Saxon scholars viii
Anselm of Canterbury vi, vii, 2, 8, 30, 58, 69, 87, 93, 103, 112, 130, 145, 149, 161, 170, 171, 172, 173, 175, 176, 179, 182, 185, 186, 188, 189, 190, 192, 193, 194, 195, 196, 198, 228
Anselm of Havelberg, 30, 149
Anselm of Laon 9, 21, 228
Aquinas vii, 12, 13, 29, 38, 39, 40, 42, 54, 63, 99, 102, 121, 122, 124, 155, 164, 171, 182
Arabic 21
Aristotle 22, 23, 25, 91, 112, 120, 133, 134, 135, 184
art of preaching 5
Augustine 1, 3, 28, 29, 33, 34, 36, 55, 70, 93, 109, 143, 146, 156, 161, 165, 169, 170, 189, 218, 219

Bacon, Francis 4, 5, 6
Bede vii, 1, 2, 124
Bec 8
Berengar of Tours vi, 2, 27
Bernard of Chartres v, 19, 57, 228
Bernard of Clairvaux 31, 42, 44, 45, 58, 79, 80-90, 102, 145, 151, 156, 161
Bible, 3, 21, 28, 38, 40, 42, 44, 46, 49, 57-90, 105, 117, 121, 123, 157, 167, 183, 192, 202
Boethius 10, 21, 22, 24, 31, 32, 33, 47, 50, 54, 55, 66, 73, 91, 93, 95, 96, 99, 105, 112, 123, 127, 128, 131, 133, 134, 169, 173, 174, 175, 176, 204, 207, 211, 213
Bruno of Asti, Bishop of Segni 9
Bunyan, John 51

Carolingian scholars vii, 20, 28, 204

Cassiodorus 20, 26, 27, 93
Cathars 140, 155, 196
Chalcidius 21, 24, 25, 169
Chartres 8, 10, 13
Cicero 4, 5, 22, 25, 52, 62, 69, 70
Clarenbald of Arras 31, 55, 56, 122, 131, 173, 228

Descartes 46, 169, 170
Donatus 10, 21
Durandus de Huesca 197

Eadmer 149
Euclid 24, 95, 174, 175

Fathers 21
Fécamp 8

Garlandus Compotista 22
Gerbert of Aurillac vi, 2
Gerhoch of Reichersberg 117, 118, 161, 199
Gilbert Crispin 155, 197, 228
Gilbert of Poitiers 11, 12, 31, 46, 47, 48, 49, 51, 52, 57, 58, 59, 60, 78, 97, 98, 111, 113, 123, 148, 165, 203, 228
Godescalc d'Orbais 204, 208
Greek 21, 205
Greeks 140, 144, 149, 151, 156
Gregory the Great 47, 117, 221
Gregory of Nyssa 120
Guibert of Nogent 12, 217, 218, 219, 220, 228

Henry of Langenstein 124
heretics 137-166, 200, 213
Hermann of Carinthia 21
Hermannus Judaeus 148, 217, 218, 221, 228
Hilary of Poitiers 50
Honorius Augustodunensis 32, 147, 148, 176, 177, 178, 193, 228
Hugh of Amiens, Bishop of Rouen, 117, 118, 156, 157, 160, 161
Hugh of St. Victor 15-16, 25, 26, 34, 39, 40, 60, 61, 62, 63, 78, 93, 95, 96, 166, 174, 179, 222, 225, 226, 228

Isidore of Seville 20, 26, 27, 124

Jerome 43, 143, 156
Jews 140, 148, 152, 155, 196, 197
John of Salisbury 5, 7, 11, 49, 57, 58, 228

Koran 150, 158

Lanfranc of Bec vi, 2, 8, 27, 147
Laon 8, 9, 13, 39, 142, 189, 191

Macrobius 5, 24
Mill, John Stuart 1, 4, 107, 171
Moslems 140, 150, 152, 155, 196

Newman, John Henry vii, viii, 12, 19, 20, 21, 215, 216, 217, 219, 221, 223, 224
Newton, Isaac vii, 129
Nicholas of Amiens 173, 174, 175, 177, 194, 195, 214
Nichomachus of Gerasa 25, 133
Notker of St. Gall 2

Otloh of St. Emeram vi, 12
Otto of Freising 150

Paris 8, 10, 13
Peter Abelard v, 9, 13, 22, 26, 31, 32, 33, 35, 39, 44, 45, 49, 54, 55, 57, 58, 59, 78, 79, 80-90, 152, 155, 165, 178, 181, 201, 202, 206, 222, 223, 225, 228
Peter of Blois 5
Peter Comestor 63
Peter Lombard 30, 38, 41, 42, 45, 177, 179, 181, 228
Peter of Poitiers 47, 63
Peter the Venerable 150, 155, 160, 161, 228
Petrus Alphonsus 101, 102, 159
Plato 5, 23, 35, 170, 178, 181, 183, 184, 198

Porphyry 73, 74
Praepositinus 156
Priscian 10, 21, 22
Pseudo-Dionysius 36, 37, 110, 111
Pythagoras 25

Quintilian 4, 5, 6

Rabanus Maurus 124
Ralph of Laon 9
Remigius of Auxerre 2
Richard of St. Victor 52, 229
Robert of Melun 167, 184, 185, 203, 229
Roscelin of Compiègne vi, 2, 13, 82, 198, 229
Rouen 8
Rousseau, Jean-Jacques 4
Rupert of Deutz 11, 29, 38, 40, 41, 43, 61, 62, 63, 64, 57-79, 105, 130, 183, 189, 190, 229
Russell, Bertrand vii

Shakespeare, William 5
Simon of Tournai 80, 153, 154, 163, 186, 187, 229
Socrates 25
Stephen Langton 63, 229

Tertullian 33
theologia 29
Thierry of Chartres 31, 37, 49, 50, 51, 52, 97, 100, 110, 111, 112, 121, 123, 124, 125, 126, 131, 132, 173, 208, 209, 229

Urban II, Pope 149
utilitas 4

Walafrid Strabo 124
Walter of St. Victor 229
William of Champeaux 134
William of Conches 35, 99, 124, 229
William of St. Thierry 58, 104

X